SpeedPro Series

HOW TO MODIFY YOUR

RETRO OR CLASSIC CAR

FOR HIGH PERFORMANCE

Daniel Stapleton

How to modify and upgrade a retro or classic saloon or sports car for modern road or motorsports use
• Instruments • Engine • Gearbox • Overdrive • Wheels • Tyres • Supercharging and turbocharging
• Suspension • Oil cooling and systems • Clutch • Cooling • Brakes • Back axle and Drivetrain
• Exhaust • Dyno tuning • Carburation • Preparation for motorsports

T0386277

Other great books from Veloce –

Speedpro Series
- 4-Cylinder Engine Short Block High-Performance Manual – New Updated & Revised Edition (Hammill)
- Alfa Romeo DOHC High-performance Manual (Kartalamakis)
- Alfa Romeo V6 Engine High-performance Manual (Kartalamakis)
- BMC 998cc A-series Engine, How to Power Tune (Hammill)
- 1275cc A-series High-performance Manual (Hammill)
- Camshafts – How to Choose & Time Them For Maximum Power (Hammill)
- Competition Car Datalogging Manual, The (Templeman)
- Cylinder Heads, How to Build, Modify & Power Tune – Updated & Revised Edition (Burgess & Gollan)
- Distributor-type Ignition Systems, How to Build & Power Tune – New 3rd Edition (Hammill)
- Fast Road Car, How to Plan and Build – Revised & Updated Colour New Edition (Stapleton)
- Ford SOHC 'Pinto' & Sierra Cosworth DOHC Engines, How to Power Tune – Updated & Enlarged Edition (Hammill)
- Ford V8, How to Power Tune Small Block Engines (Hammill)
- Harley-Davidson Evolution Engines, How to Build & Power Tune (Hammill)
- Holley Carburetors, How to Build & Power Tune – Revised & Updated Edition (Hammill)
- Honda Civic Type R High-Performance Manual, The (Cowland & Clifford)
- Jaguar XK Engines, How to Power Tune – Revised & Updated Colour Edition (Hammill)
- Land Rover Discovery, Defender & Range Rover – How to Modify Coil Sprung Models for High Performance & Off-Road Action (Hosier)
- MG Midget & Austin-Healey Sprite, How to Power Tune – New 3rd Edition (Stapleton)
- MGB 4-cylinder Engine, How to Power Tune (Burgess)
- MGB V8 Power, How to Give Your – Third Colour Edition (Williams)
- MGB, MGC & MGB V8, How to Improve – New 2nd Edition (Williams)
- Mini Engines, How to Power Tune On a Small Budget – Colour Edition (Hammill)
- Motorcycle-engined Racing Car, How to Build (Pashley)
- Motorsport, Getting Started in (Collins)
- Nissan GT-R High-performance Manual, The (Gorodji)
- Nitrous Oxide High-performance Manual, The (Langfield)
- Race & Trackday Driving Techniques (Hornsey)
- Retro or classic car for high performance, How to modify your (Stapleton)
- Rover V8 Engines, How to Power Tune (Hammill)
- Secrets of Speed – Today's techniques for 4-stroke engine blueprinting & tuning (Swager)
- Sportscar & Kitcar Suspension & Brakes, How to Build & Modify – Revised 3rd Edition (Hammill)
- SU Carburettor High-performance Manual (Hammill)
- Successful Low-Cost Rally Car, How to Build a (Young)
- Suzuki 4x4, How to Modify For Serious Off-road Action (Richardson)
- Tiger Avon Sportscar, How to Build Your Own – Updated & Revised 2nd Edition (Dudley)
- TR2, 3 & TR4, How to Improve (Williams)
- TR5, 250 & TR6, How to Improve (Williams)
- TR7 & TR8, How to Improve (Williams)
- V8 Engine, How to Build a Short Block For High Performance (Hammill)
- Volkswagen Beetle Suspension, Brakes & Chassis, How to Modify For High Performance (Hale)
- Volkswagen Bus Suspension, Brakes & Chassis for High Performance, How to Modify – Updated & Enlarged New Edition (Hale)
- Weber DCOE, & Dellorto DHLA Carburetors, How to Build & Power Tune – 3rd Edition (Hammill)

RAC handbooks
- Caring for your car – How to maintain & service your car (Fry)
- Caring for your car's bodywork and interior (Sahota)
- Caring for your scooter – How to maintain & service your 49cc to 125cc twist & go scooter (Fry)
- Efficient Driver's Handbook, The (Moss)
- Electric Cars – The Future is Now! (Linde)
- How your car works (Linde)

Enthusiast's Restoration Manual Series
- Citroën 2CV, How to Restore (Porter)
- Classic Large Frame Vespa Scooters, How to Restore (Paxton)
- Classic Car Bodywork, How to Restore (Thaddeus)
- Classic British Car Electrical Systems (Astley)
- Classic Car Electrics (Thaddeus)
- Classic Cars, How to Paint (Thaddeus)
- Ducati Bevel Twins 1971 to 1986 (Falloon)
- Jaguar E-type (Crespin)
- Reliant Regal, How to Restore (Payne)
- Triumph TR2, 3, 3A, 4 & 4A, How to Restore (Williams)
- Triumph TR5/250 & 6, How to Restore (Williams)
- Triumph TR7/8, How to Restore (Williams)
- Volkswagen Beetle, How to Restore (Tyler)
- VW Bay Window Bus (Paxton)
- Yamaha FS1-E, How to Restore (Watts)

Expert Guides
- Land Rover Series I-III – Your expert guide to common problems & how to fix them (Thurman)
- MG Midget & A-H Sprite – Your expert guide to common problems & how to fix them (Horler)

Essential Buyer's Guide Series
- Alfa GT (Booker)
- Alfa Romeo Spider Giulia (Booker & Talbott)
- Austin Seven (Barker)
- Big Healeys (Trummel)
- BMW E21 3 Series (1975-1983) (Reverente, Cook)
- BMW GS (Henshaw)
- BSA Bantam (Henshaw)
- BSA 500 & 650 Twins (Henshaw)
- Citroën 2CV (Paxton)
- Citroën ID & DS (Heilig)
- Cobra Replicas (Ayre)
- Corvette C2 Sting Ray 1963-1967 (Falconer)
- Ducati Bevel Twins (Falloon)
- Fiat 500 & 600 (Bobbitt)
- Ford Capri (Paxton)
- Harley-Davidson Big Twins (Henshaw)
- Hinckley Triumph triples & fours 750, 900, 955, 1000, 1050, 1200 – 1991-2009 (Henshaw)
- Honda CBR600 Hurricane (Henshaw)
- Honda CBR FireBlade (Henshaw)
- Honda SOHC fours 1969-1984 (Henshaw)
- Jaguar E-type 3.8 & 4.2-litre (Crespin)
- Jaguar E-type V12 5.3-litre (Crespin)
- Jaguar XJ 1995-2003 (Crespin)
- Jaguar XK8 & XKR (1996-2005) (Thorley)
- Jaguar/Daimler XJ6, XJ12 & Sovereign (Crespin)
- Jaguar/Daimler XJ40 (Crespin)
- Jaguar Mark 1 & 2 (All models including Daimler 2.5-litre V8) 1955 to 1969 (Thorley)
- Jaguar XJ-S (Crespin)
- Jaguar XK 120, 140 & 150 (Thorley)
- Land Rover Series I, II & IIA (Thurman)
- Mazda MX-5 Miata (MkI 1989-97 & MkII 98-2001) (Crook)
- Mercedes-Benz 280SL-560DSL Roadsters (Bass)
- Mercedes-Benz 'Pagoda' 230SL, 250SL & 280SL Roadsters & Coupés (Bass)
- MGA 1955-1962 (Sear, Crosier)
- MGB & MGB GT (Williams)
- MG Midget & A-H Sprite (Horler)
- MG TD, TF & TF1500 (Jones)
- Mini (Paxton)
- Morris Minor & 1000 (Newell)
- New Mini (Collins)
- Norton Commando (Henshaw)
- Peugeot 205 GTI (Blackburn)
- Porsche 911 (930) Turbo series (Streather)
- Porsche 911 (964) (Streather)
- Porsche 911 (993) (Streather)
- Porsche 911 (996) (Streather)
- Porsche 911 Carrera 3.2 series 1984 to 1989 (Streather)
- Porsche 911SC – Coupé, Targa, Cabriolet & RS Model years 1978-1983 (Streather)
- Porsche 924 – All models 1976 to 1988 (Hodgkins)
- Porsche 928 (Hemmings)
- Porsche 986 Boxster series (Streather)
- Porsche 987 Boxster and Cayman series (Streather)
- Rolls-Royce Silver Shadow & Bentley T-Series (Bobbitt)
- Subaru Impreza (Hobbs)
- Triumph Bonneville (Henshaw)
- Triumph Herald & Vitesse (Davies, Mace)
- Triumph Spitfire & GT6 (Baugues)
- Triumph Stag (Mort & Fox)
- Triumph TR6 (Williams)
- Triumph TR7 & TR8 (Williams)
- Vespa Scooters – Classic 2-stroke models 1960-2008 (Paxton)
- VW Beetle (Cservenka & Copping)
- VW Bus (Cservenka & Copping)
- VW Golf GTI (Cservenka & Copping)

Those Were The Days ... Series
- Alpine Trials & Rallies 1910-1973 (Pfundner)
- American 'Independent' Automakers – AMC to Willys 1945 to 1960 (Mort)
- American Station Wagons – The Golden Era 1950-1975 (Mort)
- American Trucks of the 1950s (Mort)
- American Trucks of the 1960s (Mort)
- American Woodies 1928-1953 (Mort)
- Anglo-American Cars from the 1930s to the 1970s (Mort)
- Austerity Motoring (Bobbitt)
- Austins, The last real (Peck)
- Brighton National Speed Trials (Gardiner)
- British and European Trucks of the 1970s (Peck)
- British Drag Racing – The early years (Pettitt)
- British Lorries of the 1950s (Bobbitt)
- British Lorries of the 1960s (Bobbitt)
- British Touring Car Racing (Collins)
- British Police Cars (Walker)
- British Woodies (Peck)
- Café Racer Phenomenon, The (Walker)
- Drag Bike Racing in Britain – From the mid '60s to the mid '80s (Lee)
- Dune Buggy Phenomenon, The (Hale)
- Dune Buggy Phenomenon Volume 2, The (Hale)
- Endurance Racing at Silverstone in the 1970s & 1980s (Parker)
- Hot Rod & Stock Car Racing in Britain in the 1980s (Neil)
- Last Real Austins 1946-1959, The (Peck)
- MG's Abingdon Factory (Moylan)
- Motor Racing at Brands Hatch in the Seventies (Parker)
- Motor Racing at Brands Hatch in the Eighties (Parker)
- Motor Racing at Crystal Palace (Collins)
- Motor Racing at Goodwood in the Sixties (Gardiner)
- Motor Racing at Nassau in the 1950s & 1960s (O'Neil)
- Motor Racing at Oulton Park in the 1960s (McFadyen)
- Motor Racing at Oulton Park in the 1970s (McFadyen)
- Motor Racing at Thruxton in the 1970s (Grant-Braham)
- Motor Racing at Thruxton in the 1980s (Grant-Braham)
- Superprix – The Story of Birmingham Motor Race (Page & Collins)
- Three Wheelers (Bobbitt)

Truckmakers
- DAF Trucks since 1949 (Peck)

Auto-Graphics Series
- Fiat-based Abarths (Sparrow)
- Jaguar MKI & II Saloons (Sparrow)
- Lambretta Li Series Scooters (Sparrow)

Rally Giants Series
- Audi Quattro (Robson)
- Austin Healey 100-6 & 3000 (Robson)
- Fiat 131 Abarth (Robson)
- Ford Escort MkI (Robson)
- Ford Escort RS Cosworth & World Rally Car (Robson)
- Ford Escort RS1800 (Robson)
- Lancia Delta 4WD/Integrale (Robson)
- Lancia Stratos (Robson)
- Mini Cooper/Mini Cooper S (Robson)
- Peugeot 205 T16 (Robson)
- Saab 96 & V4 (Robson)
- Subaru Impreza (Robson)
- Toyota Celica GT4 (Robson)

WSC Giants
- Audi R8 (Wagstaff)
- Ferrari 312P & 312PB (Collins & McDonough)
- Gulf-Mirage 1967 to 1982 (McDonough)
- Matra Sports Cars – MS620, 630, 650, 660 & 670 – 1966 to 1974 (McDonough)

Biographies
- Amédée Gordini ... a true racing legend (Smith)
- André Lefebvre, and the cars he created at Voisin and Citroën (Beck)
- Cliff Allison, The Official Biography of – From the Fells to Ferrari (Gauld)
- Edward Turner – The Man Behind the Motorcycles (Clew)
- Jack Sears, The Official Biography of – Gentleman Jack (Gauld)
- Jim Redman – 6 Times World Motorcycle Champion: The Autobiography (Redman)
- John Chatham – 'Mr Big Healey' – The Official Biography (Burr)
- The Lee Noble Story (Wilkins)
- Pat Moss Carlsson Story, The – Harnessing Horsepower (Turner)
- Tony Robinson – The biography of a race mechanic (Wagstaff)
- Virgil Exner – Visioneer: The Official Biography of Virgil M Exner Designer Extraordinaire (Grist)

Toys & models
- Britains Farm Model Balers & Combines 1967-2007, Pocket Guide to (Pullen)
- Britains Farm Model & Toy Tractors 1998-2008, Pocket Guide to (Pullen)
- Britains Toy Models Catalogues 1970-1979 (Pullen)
- British Toy Boats 1920 onwards – A pictorial tribute (Gillham)
- Diecast Toy Cars of the 1950s & 1960s (Ralston)
- Ford In Miniature (Olson)
- GM In Miniature (Olson)
- Plastic Toy Cars of the 1950s & 1960s (Ralston)
- Tinplate Toy Cars of the 1950s & 1960s (Ralston)

General
- 1½-litre GP Racing 1961-1965 (Whitelock)
- AC Two-litre Saloons & Buckland Sportscars (Archibald)
- Alfa Romeo 155/156/147 Competition Touring Cars (Collins)
- Alfa Romeo Giulia Coupé GT & GTA (Tipler)
- Alfa Romeo Montreal – The dream car that came true (Taylor)
- Alfa Romeo Montreal – The Essential Companion (Taylor)
- Alfa Tipo 33 (McDonough & Collins)
- Alpine & Renault – The Development of the Revolutionary Turbo F1 Car 1968 to 1979 (Smith)
- Alpine & Renault – The Sports Prototypes 1963 to 1969 (Smith)
- Alpine & Renault – The Sports Prototypes 1973 to 1978 (Smith)
- Anatomy of the Works Minis (Moylan)
- Armstrong-Siddeley (Smith)
- Art Deco and British Car Design (Down)
- Autodrome (Collins & Ireland)
- Autodrome 2 (Collins & Ireland)
- Automotive A-Z, Lane's Dictionary of Automotive Terms (Lane)
- Automotive Mascots (Kay & Springate)
- Bahamas Speed Weeks, The (O'Neil)
- Bentley Continental, Corniche and Azure (Bennett)
- Bentley MkVI, Rolls-Royce Silver Wraith, Dawn & Cloud/Bentley R & S-Series (Nutland)
- Bluebird CN7 (Stevens)
- BMC Competitions Department Secrets (Turner, Chambers & Browning)
- BMW 5-Series (Cranswick)
- BMW Z-Cars (Taylor)
- BMW Boxer Twins 1970-1995 Bible, The (Falloon)
- BMW Custom Motorcycles – Choppers, Cruisers, Bobbers, Trikes & Quads (Cloesen)
- BMW – The Power of M (Vivian)
- Bonjour – Is this Italy? (Turner)
- British 250cc Racing Motorcycles (Pereira)
- British at Indianapolis, The (Wagstaff)
- British Cars, The Complete Catalogue of, 1895-1975 (Culshaw & Horrobin)
- BRM – A Mechanic's Tale (Salmon)
- BRM V16 (Ludvigsen)
- BSA Bantam Bible, The (Henshaw)
- Bugatti Type 40 (Price)
- Bugatti 46/50 Updated Edition (Price & Arbey)
- Bugatti T44 & T49 (Price & Arbey)
- Bugatti 57 2nd Edition (Price)
- Caravan, Improve & Modify Your (Porter)
- Caravans, The Illustrated History 1919-1959 (Jenkinson)
- Caravans, The Illustrated History From 1960 (Jenkinson)
- Carrera Panamericana, La (Tipler)
- Chrysler 300 – America's Most Powerful Car 2nd Edition (Ackerson)
- Chrysler PT Cruiser (Ackerson)
- Citroën DS (Bobbitt)
- Classic British Car Electrical Systems (Astley)
- Cobra – The Real Thing! (Legate)
- Concept Cars, How to illustrate and design (Dewey)
- Cortina – Ford's Bestseller (Robson)
- Coventry Climax Racing Engines (Hammill)
- Daily Mirror 1970 World Cup Rally 40, The (Robson)
- Daimler SP250 New Edition (Long)
- Datsun Fairlady Roadster to 280ZX – The Z-Car Story (Long)
- Dino – The V6 Ferrari (Long)
- Dodge Challenger & Plymouth Barracuda (Grist)
- Dodge Charger – Enduring Thunder (Ackerson)
- Dodge Dynamite! (Grist)
- Draw & Paint Cars – How to (Gardiner)
- Drive on the Wild Side, A – 20 Extreme Driving Adventures From Around the World (Weaver)
- Ducati 750 Bible, The (Falloon)
- Ducati 750 SS 'round-case' 1974, The Book of the (Falloon)
- Ducati 860, 900 and Mille Bible, The (Falloon)
- Ducati Monster Bible, The (Falloon)
- Dune Buggy, Building A – The Essential Manual (Shakespeare)
- Dune Buggy Files (Hale)
- Dune Buggy Handbook (Hale)
- East German Motor Vehicles in Pictures (Suhr/Weinreich)
- Fast Ladies – Female Racing Drivers 1888 to 1970 (Bouzanquet)
- Fate of the Sleeping Beauties, The (op de Weegh/Hottendorff/ op de Weegh)
- Ferrari 288 GTO, The Book of the (Sackey)
- Fiat & Abarth 124 Spider & Coupé (Tipler)
- Fiat & Abarth 500 & 600 – 2nd Edition (Bobbitt)
- Fiats, Great Small (Ward)
- Fine Art of the Motorcycle Engine, The (Peirce)
- Ford Cleveland 335-Series V8 engine 1970 to 1982 – The Essential Source Book (Hammill)
- Ford F100/F150 Pick-up 1948-1996 (Ackerson)
- Ford F150 Pick-up 1997-2005 (Ackerson)
- Ford GT – Then, and Now (Streather)
- Ford GT40 (Legate)
- Ford Model Y (Roberts)
- Ford Thunderbird From 1954, The Book of the (Long)
- Formula 5000 Motor Racing, Back then ... and back now (Lawson)
- Forza Minardi! (Vigar)
- Funky Mopeds (Skelton)
- GT – The World's Best GT Cars 1953-73 (Dawson)
- Hillclimbing & Sprinting – The Essential Manual (Short & Wilkinson)
- Honda NSX (Long)
- Intermeccanica – The Story of the Prancing Bull (McCredie & Reisner)
- Italian Custom Motorcycles (Cloesen)
- Jaguar, The Rise of (Price)
- Jaguar XJ 220 – The Inside Story (Moreton)
- Jaguar XJ-S, The Book of the (Long)
- Jeep CJ (Ackerson)
- Jeep Wrangler (Ackerson)
- Karmann-Ghia Coupé & Convertible (Bobbitt)
- Kawasaki Triples Bible, The (Walker)
- Kris Meeke – Intercontinental Rally Challenge Champion (McBride)
- Lamborghini Miura Bible, The (Sackey)
- Lamborghini Urraco, The Book of the (Landsem)
- Lambretta Bible, The (Davies)
- Lancia 037 (Collins)
- Lancia Delta HF Integrale (Blaettel & Wagner)
- Land Rover Series III Reborn (Porter)
- Land Rover, The Half-ton Military (Cook)
- Laverda Twins & Triples Bible 1968-1986 (Falloon)
- Lea-Francis Story, The (Price)
- Le Mans Panoramic (Ireland)
- Lexus Story, The (Long)
- little book of microcars, the (Quellin)
- little book of smart, the – New Edition (Jackson)
- little book of trikes, the (Quellin)
- Lola – The Illustrated History (1957-1977) (Starkey)
- Lola – All the Sports Racing & Single-seater Racing Cars 1978-1997 (Starkey)
- Lola T70 – The Racing History & Individual Chassis Record – 4th Edition (Starkey)
- Lotus 49 (Oliver)
- Marketingmobiles, The Wonderful Wacky World of (Hale)
- Mazda MX-5/Miata 1.6 Enthusiast's Workshop Manual (Grainger & Shoemark)
- Mazda MX-5/Miata 1.8 Enthusiast's Workshop Manual (Grainger & Shoemark)
- Mazda MX-5 Miata: The Book of the World's Favourite Sportscar (Long)
- Mazda MX-5 Miata Roadster (Long)
- Maximum Mini (Booij)
- Meet the English (Bowie)
- Mercedes-Benz SL – W113-series 1963-1971 (Long)
- Mercedes-Benz SL & SLC – 107-series 1971-1989 (Long)
- MGA (Price Williams)
- MGB & MGB GT– Expert Guide (Auto-doc Series) (Williams)
- MGB Electrical Systems Updated & Revised Edition (Astley)
- Micro Caravans (Jenkinson)
- Micro Trucks (Mort)
- Microcars at Large! (Quellin)
- Mini Cooper – The Real Thing! (Tipler)
- Mini Minor to Asia Minor (West)
- Mitsubishi Lancer Evo, The Road Car & WRC Story (Long)
- Montlhéry, The Story of the Paris Autodrome (Boddy)
- Morgan Maverick (Lawrence)
- Morris Minor, 60 Years on the Road (Newell)
- Moto Guzzi Sport & Le Mans Bible, The (Falloon)
- Motor Movies – The Posters! (Veysey)
- Motor Racing – Reflections of a Lost Era (Carter)
- Motor Racing – The Pursuit of Victory 1930-1962 (Carter)
- Motor Racing – The Pursuit of Victory 1963-1972 (Wyatt/Sears)
- Motorcycle Apprentice (Cakebread)
- Motorcycle GP Racing in the 1960s (Pereira)
- Motorcycle Road & Racing Chassis Designs (Noakes)
- Motorhomes, The Illustrated History (Jenkinson)
- Motorsport In colour, 1950s (Wainwright)
- MV Agusta Fours, The book of the classic (Falloon)
- Nissan 300ZX & 350Z – The Z-Car Story (Long)
- Nissan GT-R Supercar: Born to race (Gorodji)
- Northeast American Sports Car Races 1950-1959 (O'Neil)
- Nothing Runs – Misadventures in the Classic, Collectable & Exotic Car Biz (Slutsky)
- Off-Road Giants! (Volume 1) – Heroes of 1960s Motorcycle Sport (Westlake)
- Off-Road Giants! (Volume 2) – Heroes of 1960s Motorcycle Sport (Westlake)
- Pass the Theory and Practical Driving Tests (Gibson & Hoole)
- Peking to Paris 2007 (Young)
- Pontiac Firebird (Cranswick)
- Porsche Boxster (Long)
- Porsche 356 (2nd Edition) (Long)
- Porsche 908 (Födisch, Neßhöver, Roßbach, Schwarz & Roßbach)
- Porsche 911 Carrera – The Last of the Evolution (Corlett)
- Porsche 911R, RS & RSR, 4th Edition (Starkey)
- Porsche 911, The Book of the (Long)
- Porsche 911SC 'Super Carrera' – The Essential Companion (Streather)
- Porsche 914 & 914-6: The Definitive History of the Road & Competition Cars (Long)
- Porsche 924 (Long)
- Porsche 928 (Long)
- Porsche 944 (Long)
- Porsche 964, 993 & 996 Data Plate Code Breaker (Streather)
- Porsche 993 'King Of Porsche' – The Essential Companion (Streather)
- Porsche 996 'Supreme Porsche' – The Essential Companion (Streather)
- Porsche Racing Cars – 1953 to 1975 (Long)
- Porsche Racing Cars – 1976 to 2005 (Long)
- Porsche – The Rally Story (Meredith)
- Porsche: Three Generations of Genius (Meredith)
- Preston Tucker & Others (Linde)
- RAC Rally Action! (Gardiner)
- Rallye Sport Fords: The Inside Story (Moreton)
- Roads with a View – England's greatest views and how to find them by road (Corfield)
- Roads With a View – Wales' greatest views and how to find them by road (Corfield)
- Rolls-Royce Silver Shadow/Bentley T Series Corniche & Camargue – Revised & Enlarged Edition (Bobbitt)
- Rolls-Royce Silver Spirit, Silver Spur & Bentley Mulsanne 2nd Edition (Bobbitt)
- Runways & Racers (O'Neil)
- Russian Motor Vehicles – Soviet Limousines 1930-2003 (Kelly)
- Russian Motor Vehicles – The Czarist Period 1784 to 1917 (Kelly)
- RX-7 – Mazda's Rotary Engine Sportscar (Updated & Revised New Edition) (Long)
- Scooters & Microcars, The A-Z of Popular (Dan)
- Scooter Lifestyle (Grainger)
- Singer Story: Cars, Commercial Vehicles, Bicycles & Motorcycle (Atkinson)
- Sleeping Beauties USA – abandoned classic cars & trucks (Marek)
- SM – Citroën's Maserati-engined Supercar (Long & Claverol)
- Speedway – Auto racing's ghost tracks (Collins & Ireland)
- Sprite Caravans, The Story of (Jenkinson)
- Standard Motor Company, The Book of the
- Subaru Impreza: The Road Car And WRC Story (Long)
- Supercar, How to Build your own (Thompson)
- Tales from the Toolbox (Oliver)
- Taxi! The Story of the 'London' Taxicab (Bobbitt)
- Toleman Story, The (Hilton)
- Toyota Celica & Supra, The Book of Toyota's Sports Coupés (Long)
- Toyota MR2 Coupés & Spyders (Long)
- Triumph Bonneville Bible (59-83) (Henshaw)
- Triumph Bonneville!, Save the – The inside story of the Meriden Workers' Co-op (Rosamond)
- Triumph Motorcycles & the Meriden Factory (Hancox)
- Triumph Speed Twin & Thunderbird Bible (Woolridge)
- Triumph Tiger Cub Bible (Estall)
- Triumph Trophy Bible (Woolridge)
- Triumph TR6 (Kimberley)
- TWR Story, The – Group A (Hughes & Scott)
- Unraced (Collins)
- Velocette Motorcycles – MSS to Thruxton – New Third Edition (Burris)
- Volkswagen Bus Book, The (Bobbitt)
- Volkswagen Bus or Van to Camper, How to Convert (Porter)
- Volkswagens of the World (Glen)
- VW Beetle Cabriolet – The full story of the convertible Beetle (Bobbitt)
- VW Beetle – The Car of the 20th Century (Copping)
- VW Bus – 40 Years of Splitties, Bays & Wedges (Copping)
- VW Bus Book, The (Bobbitt)
- VW Golf: Five Generations of Fun (Copping & Cservenka)
- VW – The Air-cooled Era (Copping)
- VW T5 Camper Conversion Manual (Porter)
- VW Campers (Copping)
- Which Oil? – Choosing the right oils & greases for your antique, vintage, veteran, classic or collector car (Michell)
- Works Minis, The Last (Purves & Brenchley)
- Works Rally Mechanic (Moylan)

From Veloce Publishing's new imprints:

Battle Cry!
- Soviet General & field rank officer uniforms: 1955 to 1991 (Streather)
- Red & Soviet military & paramilitary services: female uniforms 1941-1991 (Streather)

www.veloce.co.uk

First published in March 2012 by Veloce Publishing Limited, Veloce House, Parkway Farm Business Park, Middle Farm Way, Poundbury, Dorchester, Dorset, DT1 3AR, England.
Fax 01305 250479/e-mail info@veloce.co.uk/web www.veloce.co.uk or www.velocebooks.com.

ISBN: 978-1-845842-89-5 UPC: 6-36847-04289-9

Readers with ideas for automotive books, or books on other transport or related hobby subjects, are invited to write to the editorial director of Veloce Publishing at the above address.
British Library Cataloguing in Publication Data – A catalogue record for this book is available from the British Library.
Typesetting, design and page make-up all by Veloce Publishing Ltd on Apple Mac. Printed in India by Imprint Digital

SpeedPro Series

HOW TO MODIFY YOUR
RETRO OR CLASSIC CAR
FOR HIGH PERFORMANCE

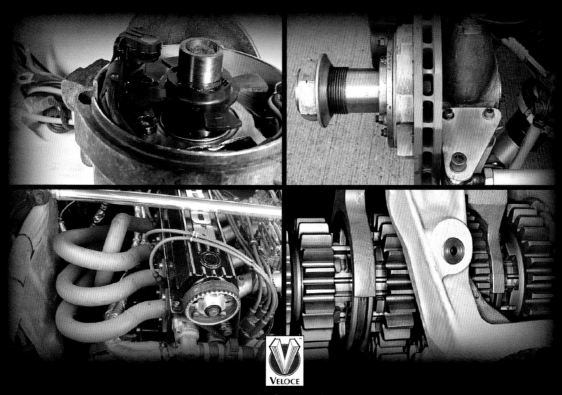

VELOCE

Daniel Stapleton

How to modify and upgrade a retro or classic saloon or sports car for modern road or motorsport use
• Instruments • Engine • Gearbox • Overdrive • Wheels • Tyres • Supercharging and turbocharging
• Suspension • Oil cooling and systems • Clutch • Cooling • Brakes • Back axle and drivetrain
• Exhaust • Dyno tuning • Carburation • Preparation for motorsport

SPEEDPRO SERIES

978-1-845840-05-1

978-1-845840-06-8

978-1-845840-19-8

978-1-845840-21-1

978-1-845840-23-5

978-1-845840-45-7

978-1-845840-73-0

978-1-845841-23-2

978-1-845841-42-3

978-1-845841-62-1

978-1-845841-86-7

978-1-845841-87-4

978-1-845842-07-9

978-1-845842-08-6

978-1-845842-62-8

978-1-845842-66-6

978-1-845842-89-5

978-1-845842-97-0

978-1-845843-15-1

978-1-845843-55-7

978-1-845844-14-1

978-1-845844-33-2

978-1-845844-33-2

978-1-874105-70-1

978-1-901295-26-9

978-1-903706-17-6

978-1-903706-59-6

978-1-903706-68-8

978-1-903706-70-1

978-1-903706-72-5

978-1-903706-75-6

978-1-903706-76-3

978-1-903706-77-0

978-1-903706-78-7

978-1-903706-80-0

978-1-903706-94-7

978-1-903706-99-2

978-1-904788-78-2

978-1-904788-84-3

978-1-904788-89-8

978-1-904788-91-1

978-1-904788-93-5

Contents

Using this book & essential information

USING THIS BOOK

This book assumes that you, or your contractor, will have a workshop manual specific to your car for complete detail on dismantling, reassembly, adjustment procedure, clearances, torque figures, etc.

You'll find it helpful to read the whole book before you start work or give instructions to your contractor. This is because a modification or change in specification in one area may require changes in other areas. Get the complete picture so that you can finalize specification and component requirements as far as possible before any work begins.

For those requiring more information on specific aspects of modification for high-performance, Veloce's SpeedPro series of books is a good place to start (see page 4).

ESSENTIAL INFORMATION

This book contains information on practical procedures, and is intended only for those with the qualifications, experience, tools and facilities to carry out the work in safety, and with appropriately high levels of skill. Whenever working on a car or component, remember that your personal safety must **ALWAYS** be your **FIRST** consideration. **The publisher, author, editors and retailer of this book cannot accept any responsibility for personal injury or mechanical damage which results from using this book, even if caused by errors or omissions in the information given. If this disclaimer is unacceptable to you, please return the pristine book to your retailer who will refund the purchase price.**

In the text of this book **Warning!** means that a procedure could cause personal injury, and **Caution!** indicates that there's danger of mechanical damage if appropriate care is not taken. However, be aware that we cannot foresee every possibility of danger in every circumstance.

Please note that changing component specification by modification is likely to void warranties, and will also absolve manufacturers of any responsibility in the event of component failure and the consequences of such failure.

Increasing the engine's power will place additional stress on engine components and on the car's complete driveline: this may reduce service life and increase the frequency of breakdown. An increase in engine power, and therefore the vehicle's performance, will mean that your vehicle's braking and suspension systems will need to be kept in perfect condition, and uprated as appropriate. It's also usually necessary to inform the vehicle's insurers of any changes to its specification.

The importance of cleaning a component thoroughly before working on it cannot be overstressed. Always keep your working area and tools as clean as possible. When using specialist cleaning fluid or other chemicals, be sure to follow – completely – the manufacturer's instructions, and, if you're using flammable liquids to clean parts, take every precaution necessary to protect your body and to avoid all risk of fire.

Introduction & general principles

The term 'performance' means different things to different people, but for the purposes of this book performance has four aspects:

- Acceleration
- Deceleration (braking)
- Straight line top speed
- Cornering speed

Each aspect of performance can be defined in a way that is useful when modifying the car. The definition can help you decide what tuning options to pursue:

Acceleration = engine torque to vehicle weight ratio. Increasing torque, or reducing weight (or both), assuming a reasonable level of grip, will improve the acceleration of the vehicle.
Deceleration (braking) = braking torque (from brakes) to vehicle weight ratio, assuming a reasonable level of grip. Increasing either braking torque or reducing weight (or both) will improve the deceleration – will shorten stopping distances.

Straight line top speed = ratio of engine horsepower (brake horse power) to the coefficient of drag of the vehicle. Strictly speaking, rolling friction and other factors should also be taken into consideration, but can largely be ignored because at speeds over 100mph, the drag is the limiting factor. Improving horsepower or reducing drag (or both) will increase the straight line top speed. Depending on the vehicle itself, and the desired top speed, it can be more beneficial to reduce drag than increase horsepower. This is especially the case with the older classics.
Cornering speed = grip to weight ratio. Increasing grip, or reducing weight (or both), will increase cornering speeds, but, to a large extent, it's also important how the grip is used – a function of suspension.

Looking at each of the four aspects of performance, and what it takes to improve or raise performance, it can be seen that:

- Reducing vehicle weight improves three aspects of performance
- Increasing grip increases one aspect of performance, but can have a benefit on two others within certain parameters
- Increasing engine power and torque improves two aspects of performance
- Reducing coefficient of drag improves one aspect of performance

Of course, this is only a guide, and there are always exceptions, particularly where an existing aspect of performance is well below what might be considered average. For example, if a car has particularly narrow wheels and tyres, the limiting factor in its acceleration, deceleration, and cornering performance might be its lack of grip. Therefore, although considerably wider wheels and tyres might well increase the weight of the vehicle – thereby reducing its torque to weight ratio – this disadvantage would be outweighed by the benefits yielded by the improvements in grip. So, although the four aspects of performance have their limitations, within reason they will point you in the right direction.

PLANNING

When you're planning modifications to your vehicle, you need to decide what aspects of performance are most important to you, and how much you have to spend (your budget). It's useful to consider the phrase 'chasing a little horsepower with a lot of money.'

The first improvements you make will come quite cheaply, but at some point further improvements become expensive. In racing, where the cars in any given class conform to a certain set of regulations, it's worth the extra expense if the difference is between winning and finishing. On the road this may not be the case, because that money might well be better spent on buying a car with better performance rather than modifying the car you already have.

On the question of how much it's all going to cost, it is only really in the area of acceleration and straight line top speed that you can easily put a price on the benefit gained. For instance, you could say that an engine modification that produced a gain of 5bhp (for example, fitting a K&N performance air filter) and costing approximately £50 (a

bargain), worked out at £10 per bhp. In practice, it's less easy to say how much quicker the car will car with that 5bhp.

Bear in mind, though, that sometimes tuning is not so straightforward, and that extra 5bhp might have a hidden cost in that it takes your total engine output over the design limit of the clutch. What this means is that you might need to buy an uprated clutch before, or when, it breaks. Additionally, at some point you might even have an engine that's so powerful it breaks driveshafts or halfshafts, and so on.

However, it's not just power that makes acceleration and straight line top speed, but weight savings and aerodynamic improvements as well. These can also greatly improve the cornering speed of the car which, in my opinion, will produce the greatest satisfaction. With a weight saving you can cost every kg saved. For instance, a switch to AP Racing alloy brake calipers might yield a saving of around 3-4kg (dependent on original caliper size) at a cost of around £220. This works out at around £64 per kg. If you compare this to other weight savings you'll see

whether or not it's money well spent. However, there are the hidden factors – in this example a hidden benefit – the brake calipers are unsprung weight (see Chapter 12 – Suspension), and an unsprung weight saving produces a higher than normal increase in handling and ride benefits compared to other weight savings. Furthermore, the new calipers might also increase braking torque (shorter stopping distances).

Having worked out costs per unit of bhp and weight, you may want to compare one type of improvement against another. To this end you can consider that 5kg equates to about one unit of power (specifically torque). Finally, never lose sight of the fact that any weight saving yields benefits in three aspects of performance, and when that weight saving is in unsprung weight or anything that rotates at speed, the gain is even more beneficial. So, the smart money is always on weight saving.

You might have heard the phrase 'period-correct,' particularly in the context of classic motorsport. What this means is that while a particular modification might not have been made to a specific car, make or model, it was the case that, in that era or period, it had been done before. For example, putting a supercharger on a classic car would nearly always be period-correct, since a supercharger was used in a racing car back in 1924. If your particular car was never supercharged when in production, fitting one now might not fit the strict period-correct criteria for motorsport, but would be eligible for what I'll call a sympathetic modification, more so with some designs of superchargers than others.

ACKNOWLEDGEMENTS

Michael Ainsworth of Monroe Europe (UK) Ltd, Alloy Wheels International, Keith Anderson of Gunson, Autocar Electrical Ltd, David Anton of APT, Peter Baldwin, Norman Barker of AP Racing, Geoff Barnes of AP Lockheed, BARS, James Bailey of Goodyear Dunlop Tyres

Modified interior of a 1969 Austin-Healey Sprite.

The Avenger Tiger was a factory special, though this one, having been modified, is now more special than most.

UK Ltd, Joe Bennett of AP Racing, Steve Bradshaw, Brembo, Andrew D Burns of Kent Cams, Burton Power, Krystyna Chustecka of FFD Ricardo Ltd, Nigel Corry of Jamex, George Daniels of Autocar Electrical Ltd, Rae Davies, David Elderfield of Rally Design, Brian Ellis, Stuart Evans, Stephen Fell of Trans Auto Sport (UK), Goodyear, Rod Grainger, Jim Gurieff of Whiteline Automotive, Pete Hargrave of Yokohama PT Ltd, Holley, Peter Huxley of Fuel System Enterprises, Alan Jones of Jetex Exhausts Ltd, Peter Jones of Jondel Race Engines, Kenlowe Ltd, Andy King of ZF Great Britain Ltd, John Kirby, Mark Lawrence, Gill Leeds of Concept Multimedia, Jim Losee of Edelbrock, Richard Marshall, Kev Moore Dave Musson of Speedograph Richfield Ltd, MWS Ltd, NGK, Andy Noble of Caterham Cars, Rob Potter of Think Automotive Ltd, Michael Quaife of RT Quaife Engineering Ltd, Bob Ritzman of B&M Racing and Performance Products, Alan Rock of Stack, Jon Savage of Cambridge Motorsport, Ellwood Von Seibold of Spax, Serck Marston, Nigel Thorne, TWM Induction, Vick Autosports, David Vizard, Ron Webb of GGB (Engineering Services) Ltd, Katja Weber of Eibach, Andy West of Concept Multimedia, Phil Woodcock of AP Lockheed, Suzanne Zelic of Eibach.

DEDICATION

To Frank 'Spritenut' Clarici of Toms River, New Jersey, USA, who died in April 2011 and is sadly missed. While Frank was known across the globe for his friendship, knowledge and generosity in the Sprite and Midget classic car scene, he also tastefully performance-modified a classic Austin A40 which he owned for many years. He was a true enthusiast and a friend to many.

Chapter 1

Engine

On initial consideration, modifications to an engine will change only two aspects of performance – more power will increase straight line top speed, and more torque will increase the rate of acceleration. However, where separate improvements have been made to the handling of the car, increases in power and torque may now sometimes be utilised to increase cornering speeds and acceleration out of corners.

Going beyond the aforementioned performance gains, it can be the case that engine modifications will yield a reduction in weight – reducing weight and increasing power represent the ultimate in value for money, in that all four aspects of performance are improved to some extent. One such modification would be replacing a standard cast iron cylinder head with a high-performance aluminium alloy part. Although this type of modification is often one of the most expensive, it's worth saving for. At the other end of the spectrum would be a modification that dramatically increases power and torque, but puts considerable weight

into the car, and where you least want it – at the front end, high up. Modifications that fall into this category include supercharging or turbocharging a previously normally-aspirated engine.

Because the diverse scenarios outlined here can, and do, arise, you need to carefully consider and plan the work you intend doing to your engine. Before that, though, you need a basic understanding of the principles of how the engine works in order to know whether a tuning modification will produce power or torque (or both), and whether it will be at a useful point in the rev range. The term 'engine' usually refers to the four-stroke (Otto) internal combustion engine, though diesel engines (compression ignition) can also be tuned, as can rotary (Wankel) engines. For all these engine types the basic principle does not change, only the method employed to get the extra power.

In the most basic terms, an engine sucks in air, fuel is added (petrol, diesel or alcohol), and the resulting mixture is then burned. The waste products of

this burning (combustion), are pumped out as exhaust gases. The actual power produced by an engine is a function of the force with which the burnt and expanding mixture of fuel and air acts upon the piston (or rotor(s) for rotary engines) which then moves down (or around), eventually turning the wheels on the road.

To get more power from the types of engine we're considering, a greater force needs to be produced, and that generally means larger quantities of fuel and air being burnt, or more frequent (per minute) burning of fuel and air, or both. Both options require more fuel and air for the combustion process. Here, though, the tuner is presented with a choice – a larger engine, or more efficient use of the existing one. Apart from fitting a larger engine, an existing engine can have its capacity increased, via processes known as boring and stroking (more of this later). Making more efficient use of an existing engine is more involved, and requires some further basic explanation.

As the engine sucks air and fuel

into its combustion chambers, the mixture is prevented from escaping before it is burned by a system of valves. Usually, there'll be one or two valves to let in the air/fuel mixture, and the same number (usually) to prevent it getting out. These, respectively, are the inlet and exhaust (outlet) valves. The opening and closing of the valves is controlled by one or more camshafts driven from the crankshaft by a toothed belt, chain, or gears. The camshaft (or camshafts) acts either directly or indirectly (via pushrods and rockers) to open and close the valves. To get more fuel/air mixture into the engine, in order to produce more power, several things need to be considered: first, the size and shape of the route(s) through the cylinder head (the ports) to the valves and then to the combustion chamber; second, the shape of the combustion chamber, including the area around the valves; third, the size and to a lesser extent the shape, of the valves; fourth, the speed, extent and length of time of valve opening. These factors are all controlled by the camshaft, and are otherwise known as 'duration' and 'lift' (speed of opening does not have a specific name).

In deciding what to change, always remember the difference between torque and horsepower. Increases in torque improve acceleration, whereas increases in horsepower will improve top speed. Some engine modifications will increase horsepower more than torque (or may even reduce torque at certain points in the rev range). Other engine tuning modifications will increase both torque and horsepower. Therefore, you need to know which aspect of performance is most important to you, and then make your choices accordingly. The apparent dilemma can be expressed like this: Horsepower sells engines, but torque wins races. The maxim stands good in a road context because torque makes acceleration and on-road drivability. An engine with lots of horsepower but little torque, sometimes described as being 'peaky,'

would be tiresome to drive on the road, other than on very long fast straights.

As well as a basic grasp of engine tuning theory, it's necessary to understand the units of measurement used with respect to engine power, and

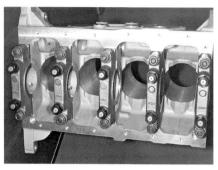

This alloy engine block is a replacement for the standard cast iron item, and represents a very useful weight saving – but it will be expensive.

how to convert from one unit of measure to another. In the early days of motoring, the car was known as the horseless carriage and its power was compared to that of the horse. The term 'horsepower' was coined, and has largely stuck ever since. However, there are American, British (or imperial), and metric units of power, as well as the commonly used units of power measurement. Metric 'horsepower' is referred to as Pferdestarke (the German word for horsepower), and is usually abbreviated to PS. A single unit of horsepower (SAE) is equal to 1.0139PS, 745.70W or 0.7457kW.

As far as torque is concerned, to convert from Nm to lb/in, multiply by 8.851, and for lb/in to Nm, multiply by 0.113 (remembering to convert inches to feet to get the final answer when going from Nm to lb/ft).

The Vegan Tune alloy twin-cam head for the Ford Kent engine fitted in a Caterham 7. (Courtesy Vegan Tune Ltd)

Having your cake and eating it – a bigger engine, tuned, and with forced induction using a Weiand 6-71 supercharger. (Courtesy Steve Bradshaw)

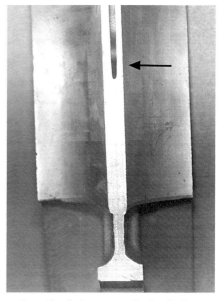

A section between a pair of cylinders shows us that what you might assume is a thick block actually gets very thin at its top, near the water jacket.

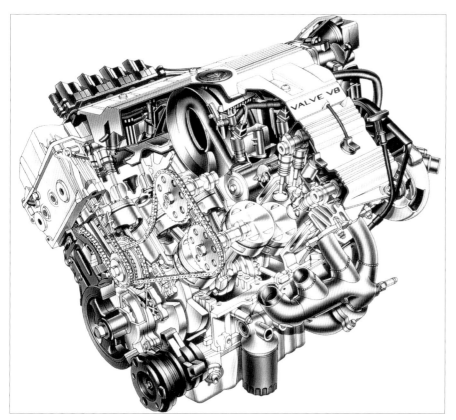

This cutaway drawing of the Cadillac Northstar V8 engine reveals all of the working components of an engine. (Courtesy Cadillac)

Time to start to plan what is to be done to the engine. The following list suggests the order of priority for making the key decisions:
1. Is torque or horsepower to be the dominant gain?
2. Amount of gain sought
3. Rev limit of engine (if tuning will raise above standard)
4. Amount of money available

BORING & STROKING

As mentioned earlier in the chapter, one way to increase the volumetric size (cubic capacity) of an engine is by boring and stroking. The bore of the engine is the diameter of the cylinder and corresponding pistons. The stroke is the distance up and down the cylinder that the piston travels on each stroke (not the physical length of the cylinder). Boring involves increasing the diameter of the engine block's cylinders, stroking is increasing the length of the crank's throw, either by special machining or using a different crank.

As with units of power, there is more than one common measure of

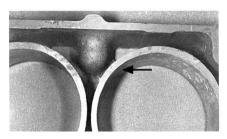

This section of a cylinder wall reveals a small crack – the result of boring to the point where the wall strength is compromised.

Looking up the bore from the crankcase – the use of a long throw crank can necessitate removal of metal on anything that might get in the way of the longer throw.

engine size, better known as capacity. Usually this will be given in cubic centimetres (cc) or litres (1000cc per litre), calculated as follows:

$$V = \pi r^2 h$$

V = volume, r = radius of the cylinder, and h = the stroke

In the United States of America, or when considering the size of an American engine, it's usual to measure using cubic inches (cu). For instance, the English AC 428 convertible had an American engine of seven litres. If you convert this (7.013 to be exact) to inches you get 428. By comparison, the little known Buick 215 cubic inch engine sounds small, but when it became Rover's engine it was a massive, in the United Kingdom at that time, 3523 litres.

The extent to which you can bore the cylinders, sometimes known as 'overboring,' depends on the engine block casting, the thickness of the cylinder walls, and piston availability. So, for example, although a 1300cc engine can be bored out to 1400cc, it could never be bored out to 2000cc. However, any increase in capacity is useful and, if an engine is worn and needs a rebore, it's worth considering boring to a near maximum size rather than simply having it bored to the next oversize. Overboring can be a very cost-effective way to get more power out of an engine (especially a tired one), though once bored out to maximum no further rebore will be possible, and the engine block becomes scrap unless it's possible to fit new cylinder sleeves (not possible on most engines).

'Stroking' an engine refers to lengthening the crankshaft stroke, thus increasing the 'swept volume' of the cylinders by using more of their length. Sometimes, an engine can be stroked by replacing the crank with one from a larger capacity engine from the same manufacturer or 'family,' though it might be as easy to use the whole engine if it's available. In other instances, small increases in stroke can be achieved by having a machine shop grind the crank. The largest changes in stroke will come from having a special crankshaft made; quite expensive, and not always possible.

When boring and stroking are combined, anything from a modest to a large increase in engine capacity can be achieved, producing a useful increase in power over the standard engine (in rough proportion to the size of the increase in capacity). Of course, it might be simpler and cheaper to use a bigger engine in the first place.

The efficiency of boring and stroking are subject to limitations imposed by the cylinder head(s). Any head can be improved, more of which later, to improve the speed and/or volume of the fuel/air mixture flowing through it. However, at some point an absolute maximum of gas flow will be reached. This absolute maximum will vary from head-to-head, but it's worth checking with an engine specialist familiar with your engine before building a super-size bored and stroked engine. The reason for this caution is that the engine may fail to realise its full potential in relation to its capacity because of the limitations of the head(s).

CRANKSHAFT MODIFICATIONS

There are a variety of modifications that can be made to the crankshaft. However, the first thing to have done to any crank is crack testing. **Caution!** Only if the crank is sound is it worth proceeding with other work. If the crank has cracks, it's scrap.

When a crank breaks it can wreck the rest of the engine, so always get it crack tested. This one failed due to over-revving from a missed gear change.

The two most common operations performed to cranks are balancing and hardening; these are performed by specialist machine shops to both strengthen the crank and increase its resistance to fatigue. The cost is low in comparison to many other machining operations, and is money well spent. Other work done to the crank is to reduce fatigue and improve the oil supply to the crank bearings, but these are much less necessary for road use unless very high rpm usage is envisaged (in comparison to the standard rpm for the engine type). Finally, if the crank breaks, it's likely to destroy the rest of the engine, including the block and head, so its importance shouldn't be overlooked.

Here you can see how, for the same engine, this four-bolt main bearing cap differs from the standard two-bolt item.

CRANKSHAFT MAIN BEARING CAPS

If you plan to use your engine above 6500rpm, it's worth strengthening the crankshaft main bearing caps. The traditional process involved machining the top of the bearing cap to accept a piece of steel bar (machined to fit flush to it), with both components then bolted to the block with longer-than-standard bolts. This steel bar is known as a bearing strap. An alternative approach would be to replace the main bearing caps with stronger items made from steel (many standard caps were made from cast iron). A further alternative was to fit steel main bearing caps of a different design, such that they are wider than standard and fasten to the block with four bolts rather than two (this, of course, requires the block to be drilled and tapped for two additional bolts). The advantage of this four-bolt steel main cap is that not only is the bearing area strengthened, but the rigidity of the block is improved. The only disadvantage to using either a strap or a four-bolt main bearing cap is the increase in weight, but it's a worthwhile penalty for safer high engine rpm.

COMPRESSION RATIO INCREASES

Compression ratio (CR) relates the amount of space occupied by the air/fuel mixture drawn into the engine (piston at bottom of cylinder) to that when the mixture is compressed by the piston at the top of the cylinder. For example, a compression ratio of 9.5:1 means that the air/fuel mixture occupies 9.5 units of space when drawn into the cylinder, and is then compressed to 1 unit of space when the piston is at the top of its stroke. The higher the compression ratio, the more the mixture is 'squeezed.'

An increase in CR is something to be considered as part of the overall tuning process. A change in camshaft may dictate an increase in CR, whereas a change to forced induction, such as supercharging, may dictate no change, or perhaps even a reduction in CR. Increases in CR should be carefully considered because a petrol (or alcohol) engine that has too high a CR will require a higher fuel octane rating if it is to run without self destructing. Changes in CR can be made in several ways.

One way to increase the CR is by skimming the cylinder head or engine block, the latter to a lesser extent, in order to reduce the space the fuel/air mixture will be compressed into in relation to the swept volume (bore x stroke) of the engine. Another way is to use high compression pistons which have a reduced dish in the piston crown (top), flat, or even domed crowns. The CR can be reduced by changing the pistons for items with a dish at the crown (top), or larger dish in the crown, or an increased combustion chamber size created by enlarging the chamber.

Caution! Never use a CR that causes 'pinking'/'pinging' with the ignition timing set within the correct parameters. To do so would lead to rapid engine damage, usually piston failure (a hole in the crown or total destruction).

CYLINDER HEAD MODIFICATIONS
Changes to the combustion chamber

The combustion chamber in the cylinder head is where it all happens. Once the fuel/air mixture has travelled through the inlet ports and an open valve, the valve is closed and the mixture is compressed by the rising piston. On all engines, the top of the piston, the crown, also forms part of the combustion chamber. Next, the compressed fuel/air mixture is ignited by a spark delivered by the sparkplug(s). To a large extent, it is how the flame front created by the spark travels through the combustion chamber that dictates the amount of power produced. The combustion needs to be smooth and rapid. Furthermore, because it's happening in a very small period of time, the distance the flame travels needs to be as short as possible. Once ignited, the fuel air mixture rapidly expands (explodes), and the resulting force pushes outward in all directions, but, of course, the only component yielding to the force is the piston, which is forced down the cylinder.

Usually, modifications to the combustion chamber centre around ensuring that the valves are not shrouded – that is, so close to the chamber walls that the incoming fuel/air mixture is obstructed, and, likewise, the exhaust gas on its way out. For some engines this isn't a problem, or only becomes one when larger valves than standard are fitted.

Not all cylinder head work equates to the removal of vast amounts of metal, as can be seen by the subtle, but very useful work done to this Renault 5 Turbo head.

There's also a benefit in precisely equalising the volume of each combustion chamber. Very occasionally it's desirable to alter the shape of the combustion chamber more radically (by welding, for example), but such work is not cheap. Most head work can be do-it-yourself (DIY), but only if you have a good reference work particular to the

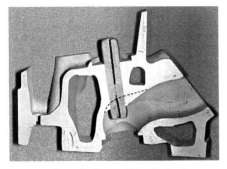

A section of a Rover V8 cylinder head reveals that the port is smaller in section around the valve guide (which is protruding); the faint pencil line indicates where the engine tuner would remove metal to improve gas flow.

On some engines the combustion chamber is in the piston crown, and the valves and cylinder head form a flat surface.

The marks (shiny area) by the bottom left-hand valve (exhaust) were caused by part of a broken valve contacting the cylinder head, leading to an expensive engine failure.

head you're modifying, a good, proven example to copy, and generally know what you're doing. It's far better to know what you're looking for and then purchase accordingly.

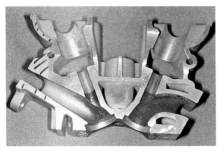

This cylinder head section illustrates how the valves form part of the combustion chamber. The centrepunch marking was used to test for porosity of the casting.

One cylinder head that benefits from porting more so than an increase in valve size is the Ford BD series head, a chamber of which is shown here.

Typical port opening into a combustion chamber.

Changes to valve sizes, including unleaded conversions

I think it'll be helpful when considering increasing valve sizes to think about what the valves are actually doing. Basically, the inlet valve opens the combustion chamber to the outside

Hemispherical cylinder head combustion chamber from the six-cylinder Aston Martin DB5/6 – the XK Jaguar cylinder head is similar.

atmosphere, and lets in the air and fuel mixture. A bigger inlet valve will let in more fuel/air, and a bigger exhaust valve will let out more exhaust gas (all things being equal). Given our basic principles that more fuel/air will provide greater combustion, and, therefore, a greater push to drive the piston down the cylinder, and so on, bigger valves (in association with enlarged ports) will allow the engine to produce more power. It's also worth considering larger valves and seats when converting the cylinder head for use with unleaded fuel, as the extra cost would be minimal compared to the costs of a like-for-like valve size conversion to unleaded.

Porting

Because the size and shape of the ports

In this cut-away engine you can see how the inlet valves sit at a shallow angle in the combustion chamber, in relation to the piston.

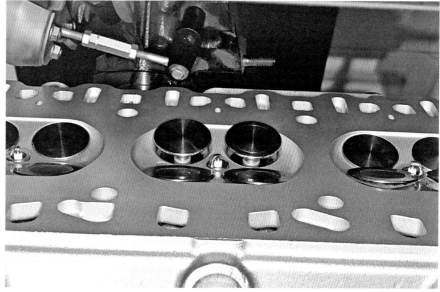

Four-valve per combustion chamber heads are generally considered superior to two-valve per combustion chamber heads, but for high-performance classics the difference is not so great.

A closer look at the valves, on this engine which are vertical in the combustion chamber, in relation to the piston. The valves are operated by an overhead camshaft via cam followers or 'buckets.'

For the Rover A-series engine the standard cast iron cylinder head can be replaced by a high-performance aluminium one like this from Jack Knight Ltd.

This Weslake-designed six-port head is a direct performance replacement for the four-port item on the Ford V6 Cologne engine; just one route to realizing more power from the engine.

control, to a large extent, the volume and speed of the fuel/air mixture and the exhaust gasses to and from the combustion chambers, they have an important effect on performance tuning. Although you might think increasing the port size would instantly produce more power, this is not always the case, because the speed of the gas can drop dramatically and reduce the total volume of gas flow. However, just as ports can be too large they can also be too small, and an expert engine tuner will know what's best for your particular engine. The shape of the port is important because sharp turns can be detrimental to gas flow and, again, an expert engine tuner will know how to re-shape the port to get the best result. Because porting is not only specialised but specific to particular engines, detailed coverage is beyond the scope of this book.

CYLINDER HEAD SWAPS

For some engines, rather than spend a lot of money on modifying the cylinder head, there's the alternative of buying an off-the-shelf performance head. Quite often this cylinder head will have twice as many valves as the standard head. Or it may be a twin overhead cam design replacing a single non-overhead unit. The high-performance head will most likely use a superior combustion chamber design with optimized porting, and so on. Many popular engines, including the Rover A Series, Rover B Series, Ford Pinto, and Ford Kent, to name but a few, have alternative cylinder heads available for them. In some instances a high-performance head is cast in aluminium alloy rather than cast iron, and so is also lighter than the standard head.

CAMSHAFT CHANGES

A replacement camshaft is one way of increasing engine performance, but there are certain drawbacks and limitations. A basic introduction to how the camshaft functions in an engine is necessary before considering the tuning options.

The camshaft controls the opening and closing of the valves. The size and profile of the lobes on the camshaft control how quickly the valve opens, how far it opens, how long it stays open for, and how quickly it closes. Although the valve springs actually close the valve, they cannot close it any quicker than the cam will allow.

If you consider a single revolution of the engine's crankshaft will consist of 360 degrees, it's possible to express other engine 'events' in degrees, such as valve opening times and cam duration. In addition, there is a time during the cycle of the engine that both inlet and exhaust valves are open simultaneously, this is known as 'valve overlap.' The relation between the cam lobes controlling the inlet valves and those controlling the exhaust valves is also a factor in the overall specification of the camshaft. To quickly summarise,

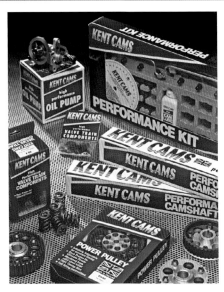

When changing the camshaft you will also need to change the cam followers, and possibly the valve springs, all of which makes buying a complete kit, such as those shown here, the best way to achieve value for money. (Courtesy Kent Cams)

Getting the cam timing exactly right cannot be easily achieved on some engines without an adjustable timing pulley, such as the items from Kent Cams shown here. (Courtesy Kent Cams)

the camshaft(s) will control: speed of valve opening and closing, how far the valve opens (valve lift (off the valve

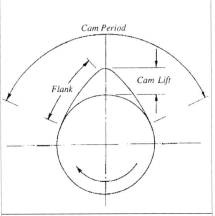

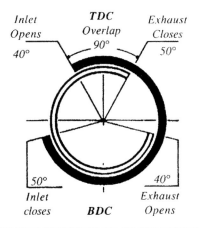

The top drawing shows what cam lift and duration (period) are; the lower one is an illustration of valve timing showing period of overlap.

seat)), how long the valve stays open, and when the inlet valves are open in relation to the exhaust valves. It's also possible to vary the timing of the opening and closing of the valves in relation to the movement of the pistons, and this is know as cam timing. In practice cam timing is not so much changed to gain power, but rather 'timed' to occur at precisely the right moment to ensure no power is lost. With most after-market performance cams it's possible to get the cam timing exactly right only if adjustable cam timing pulley(s) are used, although, if no suitable pulley is available, it's possible to use offset Woodruff keys.

High-lift rockers come in many forms; these are Titan roller-tip items.

As far as cam selection goes, on the face of it, the ideal way to get more power out of an engine is to fit a cam that will open the valves very quickly, a long way, and for a long time. However, returning to the 360-degree cycle, it's apparent that the inlet valve can only usefully remain open when the piston is going down and the cylinder drawing in the fuel/air mixture. This is 180 degrees. The remaining 180 degrees is required for the piston to go up the cylinder and compress the fuel air mixture. For the next 360 degrees the inlet valve must remain closed while the combustion gases push the piston down the cylinder, and remain closed when the piston comes up the cylinder to push out the exhaust via the exhaust valve. At this point there appears to be a problem, because the inlet valve is open for 180 degrees, but cannot remain open for more than a quarter of the time the piston is moving. The problem is solved by rotating the camshaft(s) at half the engine speed, and this is achieved by the camshaft pulley/sprocket being

twice the diameter of the crankshaft pulley/sprocket.

VALVE GEAR MODIFICATIONS
Rocker gear

For those engines where the valves are opened via rockers (or pushrods and rockers), there are useful changes that can be made to gain power or increase component life, or both. Such rockers will either be of a higher ratio than the standard item (high-lift rockers) and thereby increase lift at the valve independent of any camshaft change, or be of different construction and contact pad size to prevent premature failure in a performance application. High-performance rockers are usually quite expensive, but they can represent good value for money in relation to the increase in power they produce.

Pushrods

It's possible for pushrods to bend, though complete failure is rare. A bent pushrod reduces the total lift provided at the valve, and can damage the camshaft lobe if it's resisting movement because it's making contact at some point where it ought not to (pushrod tube or wall on some engines). High-lift rockers and higher than standard engine rpm both place an increased load on standard pushrods. The solution is to use a high-performance pushrod which will, most likely, be of thicker, but tubular rather than solid, design. If you find there is no off-the-shelf pushrod for your engine, it's possible to have a bespoke set made, since the tubular design is such that any one of a multitude of end pieces can be made.

PISTONS

Piston are central to the amount of power produced in the engine because they do more than one job; they provide suction to draw in the fuel/air mixture, compress it, are acted against during combustion, and then push out the exhaust gases. Pistons are subject to high loadings and temperatures in the

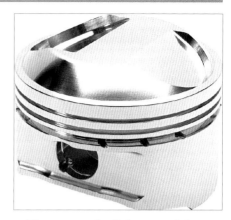

Pistons come in all shapes and sizes, and this one illustrates a domed crown with valve reliefs. (Courtesy Cambridge Motorsport)

This piston is dished, and features valve reliefs. (Courtesy Cambridge Motorsport)

process. A change in piston may be required for a variety of reasons. The most common is that the standard piston is not strong enough to withstand the loadings imposed by a tuned engine, and would most likely fail, particularly at high rpm. The difference, other than cost, is that standard pistons are made by casting the molten metal, while performance pistons are forged by a stamping process with semi-molten metal; the forged pistons are stronger.

High-performance pistons will be lighter than standard pistons, though, in some instances, it's possible to lighten the standard ones. Piston weight is important because the greater the weight the more energy will be absorbed in accelerating and decelerating the piston on each stroke, with three out of every four (in a four-cylinder engine) producing no power. Changes in engine compression may require a change in piston, as will changes in bore diameter. When choosing pistons, balance cost against desirability. Finally, if you are supercharging or turbocharging what was previously a normally-aspirated engine, you'll probably need completely different pistons from the standard ones – follow the advice of the super/turbocharger manufacturer.

CONRODS

Connecting rods (conrods) connect the pistons to the crankshaft (on the crankshaft throw). The small end of the conrod is fitted to the piston by a large pin – more like a thick-walled section of tube than a pin – while the large or big end of the conrod is joined to the crankshaft by means of a section known as the cap, which bolts to the main conrod body. For any engine where power and, particularly, rpm, have been increased, some consideration needs to be given to the conrod. The conrod and the conrod bolts are, like the piston, subject to enormous loadings, and can fail. A rod can bend or break in tension, while, if the rod bolts work loose or break, complete failure of the rod ensues. Upgrades to the conrods need not be expensive, and the rods can be

crack tested before being balanced and then surface treated (lead shot-blasted or polished – alternative ways of relieving stresses that could contribute to failure). At the very least, replacement of the standard rod bolts, with race quality items such as those from ARP, is recommended.

ENGINE SWAPS

Possibly one of the oldest approaches to performance tuning is the engine swap, often using a larger engine from a different model within a manufacturer's range. Manufacturers sometimes swapped engines to create high-performance versions of a basic model, such as the Lotus twin-cam-engined Escort and Lotus Cortina, and Jeff Uren put an Essex V6 engine from a Ford Zodiac into a MkII Ford Cortina to create the Savage Cortina. So, with some thought you can have your own period-correct engine swap.

When it comes to engine swaps, a front-engined, rear-wheel-drive car has

A decent rocker or cam cover, such as the pair shown here for a Ford Essex V6 from Burton Power, makes even a standard engine look businesslike. (Courtesy Burton Power)

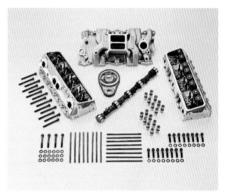

Some companies provide a complete engine tuning kit, including head(s), cam(s), and manifold(s). This offering is from Holley.

the greatest potential. Front-engined, front-wheel-drive cars are often limited to using a larger engine from the same manufacturer, and even then things may not be easy because of the way the gearbox is usually bolted directly to the bottom of the engine (the engine crankcase).

In some cases, however, the engine swap is not all it might seem because it's actually based on the original engine or engine block. An example of this type of conversion is the Vegan Tune VTA engine. This engine is based on Ford's Kent engine block. The most obvious difference lies with the alloy twin-cam cylinder head. The engine can be built

A nice touch (if you can afford it) is a decent set of steel rods, such as these Farndon items. (Courtesy Cambridge Motorsport)

This V8 fits neatly into Bhau Thakgr's Sierra – a rare factory XR8.

... a closer look.

The Chevy small block V8 transplanted into a Ford MkIII Cortina.

A classic factory engine swap; here is the Vauxhall slant four, twin-cam, 16-valve engine in the Vauxhall HS Chevette.

to various road or full race specifications in 1600 or 1700cc sizes. Vegan Tune claims 100bhp at 4000rpm, going on to a peak of 170bhp at 7000rpm.

If you're going to do an engine swap, decide first which engine you want to swap to rather than merely choosing an engine that is readily available. Because your engine swap is likely to involve fitting a larger and more powerful unit, be wary of the ills of a large weight gain at the front of the car which will create difficult-to-resolve handling problems.

The tuneability of the replacement engine is an important consideration, because there's not a lot of point having a 3.5-litre V8 in the engine bay if a similar car with a tuned 2-litre blows you into the weeds. Of course, depending on the car you have, the biggest limitation may well be the engine bay, and this is why alloy V6 and V8 engines, which are relatively short (though wider), are popular substitutes for cast iron four-cylinder units.

You may run into problems siting ancillaries and engine bay components. One particular problem is that of the oil filter. There is a range of take-off plates that can be used to replace the existing filter head and filter. The take-off plate, once fitted, will need to be plumbed to a remote filter head, and, quite possibly, via an oil cooler. See chapter 7 for further details.

ENGINE MOUNTINGS

Whatever engine you have fitted in your vehicle, and in particular if it's an unusual engine swap, you can run into problems with engine mountings. One company that specialises in compliance technology (rubbers and mountings) is Vibra Technics. It has a range of suitable performance engine and transmission mountings for all kinds of vehicles.

Chapter 2
Ignition system

INTRODUCTION

Although a modified ignition system cannot deliver much in the way of increased horsepower, a poorly maintained or inadequate ignition system will prevent an engine from realising its full potential. Perhaps more importantly, an efficient ignition system will provide good starting (especially

Top four options for improving ignition

1. Fit good quality silicone-based HT leads.
2. Fit a high energy coil.
3. Fit iridium sparkplugs of the correct grade, bearing in mind the modifications to the engine.
4. Fit a contactless electronic ignition system.

Ignition system options by usage

Intended usage	Sparkplug	HT leads	High energy ignition system	Performance coil	Rev-limiter	Re-curve distributor
Mild road	Consider grade of plug	Silicone	Contactless	Yes	No	No
Hard road	Harder grade of plug	Silicone	Contactless	Yes	Yes and recommended as ignition system feature or separate component	Recommended
Competition	Harder grade of plug	Silicone	Contactless if regulations (eg FIA) permit.	Yes	Yes and recommended as ignition system feature or separate component.	Recommended

from cold), combined with reliability and minimum maintenance.

When in good condition, any ignition system is adequate for a standard engine. However, an engine tuned or modified to produce more power, whether for hard road or competition use, is more demanding in its ignition requirements. This is because the larger volumes of fuel/air mixture (often at higher compression) that are burnt in performance-tuned engines will require a higher voltage at the sparkplugs to ensure complete combustion, higher engine speeds (rpm) also require more sparks per minute.

The total voltage that can be delivered to the sparkplug is the main factor governing whether or not the plugs successfully burn all the air/fuel mixture in the combustion chamber. Voltage shortfalls at the sparkplug can be attributed to coil output, losses due to resistance in the HT leads and, finally, the sparkplugs themselves can also limit spark quality and strength if their initial resistance is too high. **Caution!** A spark from a power-tuned ignition system can cause death.

To enable you to make the right choices for your car consider the top four options and ignition system options tables at the introduction of this chapter.

HIGH TENSION (HT) LEADS (PLUG WIRES)

Unless the standard leads are old or overdue replacement, there isn't any great performance advantage to be had in changing from standard leads to non-standard. Older standard HT leads were generally made from carbon impregnated string, which was detrimental to good spark energy as it has a high resistance value. It's difficult to accurately put a life on the carbon impregnated leads, but once they've seen 20,000 miles or three years' service they will be past their best.

When replacing old HT leads, look for silicone-insulated leads with wires wound around ferrite cores with the lowest quoted resistance. Such

High-performance HT leads from Magnecor. These are racing leads, but the company also does a road set (both sets can be made to measure).

leads are widely available, and come complete with an integral plug cap.

SPARKPLUGS

There are two choices to be made when considering sparkplugs for hard road or competition use.

The first relates to the grade or heat rating of the sparkplug. A totally standard and unmodified engine will require standard grade plugs, while a modified engine will require a plug that is of a colder (also known as harder) grade. Plugs that are too hot for the engine will cause pre-ignition (knocking/pinking) after or during hard use, and may also cause the engine to run-on after it is switched off. Prolonged use of plugs that are too hot can damage the engine. The grade of the plug is nearly always indicated by a number on the plug itself. However, the numbering sequence is not a universal standard. For example, with Champion brand sparkplugs the number '9' is the standard grade, with lower numbers denoting a colder grade. With NGK sparkplugs the standard grade is indicated by the number '5,' with higher numbers denoting a colder grade. If a high energy ignition system is used, then the supplier's recommendations should be followed in respect to the sparkplug gap, and typically this will be a gap of 35 or 40 thousands of an inch, compared to a gap of 25 thousands of inch for a standard ignition system. To find the optimum heat range plugs for a modified engine, start with the coldest

Section of NGK Sparkplug.

plugs you think might be suitable (say, two grades colder than standard), and then work towards warmer ones; this way no harm will come to the engine.

The second choice concerns the metal of the central electrode. Currently, the most likely/standard metal for the central electrode is copper. Platinum and iridium plugs offer enhanced performance, and the electrodes will be of a smaller diameter. It's recommended to use NGK copper core, platinum or iridium plugs in a performance-tuned engine, though it may not be possible to get much more than 9000 miles (14,500km) from a set of platinum plugs.

COILS & PERFORMANCE COILS

The coil produces the spark that, when delivered to the plugs, ignites the fuel/air mixture. The coil has to produce sufficient power to do this under all circumstances, and the standard coil may be fine for a production engine but unsuitable for the same engine when power tuned. Furthermore, coils don't last forever, and their output will gradually deteriorate over time, first at higher rpm, and then completely. One reason coil performance can be inadequate is that it takes time for the coil voltage to rise before being discharged at the plug. As the engine speed rises, there's less time for the coil voltage to build up, until the point is reached when it can no longer produce an adequate spark. This circumstance is often described as saturation, but actually, when the coil is inadequately charged, the correct description is that it is not reaching saturation. On most road-tuned engines it's unlikely that the engine rpm will be such that the coil will be inadequate, but there are still benefits in fitting a suitable performance/sports/high-energy coil.

Some coils need to be used in conjunction with a ballast resistor, and it's worth checking this out before parting with your cash or destroying an electronic ignition system. The respective voltage outputs for some example performance coils are as follows:

Micro Dynamics MS2 – 25,000
Lumenition CEC35 – 37,000
Lucas Sports – 40,000
Mallory 51,000 and 58,000

Note that it's crucial to match the coil resistance to the ignition system. It's possible to err on the side of caution and use a ballast resistor whichever coil

High-performance coil from Micro Dynamics.

Lucas sports coil.

Micro Dynamics' matched coil and electronic ignition system. This one is for reluctor-type ignition, but a version is also available for contact points-type systems.

you fit, but doing so on a performance coil that was designed to run without one will ultimately reduce the output of that coil, and thereby defeat part of the object of fitting it. Lucas produces a sports coil (DLB110) for use with a ballast resistor and a sports coil (DLB105) for use without – some manufacturers produce only one type of coil. If you purchase the ballasted coil and wonder if the fact that it is marked as a 6V coil means it will produce

less output, the answer is "No." The Lucas ballasted sports coil will match the output of the conventional Lucas sports coil because the ratio of primary to secondary windings in the coil is optimized respectively for each coil. The only downside to using a performance coil on a contact breaker points ignition system is that it will decrease points life due to arcing, unless you convert to electronic Transistor-Assisted Contacts (TAC). Make using a good performance coil a priority, because a cheap or standard coil will invariably have low spark energy, which is detrimental to optimum performance, especially at high rpm.

IGNITION SYSTEMS IMPROVEMENTS

The majority of classic cars would have been fitted with basic contact breaker points ignition originally. However, given the regular expense and hassle, plus the frequency of contact breaker replacement (or adjustment), a switch to an electronic system can represent a justifiable expense, and may even yield a long-term saving.

Improvements to your car's ignition system ought to increase contact breaker life dramatically (or completely do away with them), while the higher spark energy at the plug tip ignites all of the air/fuel mixture (all of the time). Some owners may wish to replace their classic's old or obsolete electronic ignition with a more modern product. Very often, though, people are unsure about what they're buying, or what they have already, or which products are suitable/compatible with their cars' existing components. So this section will cover the basic principles

Ignition module for Crane Cams' contact breakerless ignition conversions.

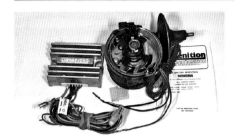

Lumenition kit.

of ignition systems, and offer advice so you can make the best choices for your car.

The first step in an ignition upgrade is to consider why you want to improve it. Is it because you want better starting, better reliability, reduced maintenance, or increased spark energy. The second step is to check whether your car is positive earth polarity. If it is, your choice of electronic ignition conversions is restricted, though some Lumenition kits will work, as will the Crane XR700 and the Pertronix (Aldon) Ignitor.

Looking at ignition systems in isolation from coils and leads, there are two basic objectives when upgrading:

1. To have contactless ignition (maintenance free)
2. To increase spark energy

Note that it's possible for an electronic ignition system to produce less ignition energy than a modified contact breaker system! Also, it's possible to increase spark energy by fitting a performance coil alone. It's because the ignition system can be so confusing that it's important to decide on your objectives at the outset.

Objective 1: Contactless ignition (no contact breaker points)

If you want to replace a contact breaker points ignition system with an electronic system you need to decide on the sort of ignition performance you need. For a high-performance engine you need the highest energy system available,

and this means a sophisticated system that amplifies the ignition signal rather than just switches it on and off. For a standard engine, you'll need a simple electronic ignition system that just switches the ignition signal on and off.

Objective 2: Increase spark energy

If you want a high energy ignition system it doesn't really matter whether you keep the contact breaker points or not, as it's possible to have high energy ignition with either. A contact breaker points-triggered high energy ignition system will work effectively with a standard or performance coil, without reducing points life, while having increased spark energy. Alternatively, you can have an all electronic system with ignition signal amplification and a performance coil.

Now that we're clear about what we're looking for in an ignition system improvement, it's time to look at some different types.

Electronic ignition systems – contact breaker points-triggered

This type of electronic ignition is sometimes known as Transistor-Assisted Contacts (TAC) coil ignition. One product that fits this bill is the Micro Dynamics Electronic Power Coil (EPC01). This unit comprises a points-triggered ignition system and an adjustable rev limiter and coil, all in one compact unit. It will improve the ignition and reduce points arcing (the latter can be a problem when using a high output or sports coil with contact breaker points). A similar but earlier product was the Sparkrite SX2000 – a popular after-market conversion which is no longer made, though secondhand kits do turn up from time to time. Lucas also made some kits marketed as TAC4 which were available for both positive and negative earth cars. The advantage with TAC is improved spark energy, but, in reality, TAC was a first generation electronic ignition design and, while it does the job okay, other electronic systems

are better choices, unless you really want, or have to keep, contact breaker points. The disadvantages with contact breaker points, even when linked to an electronic system, are that it's still possible to have trouble with 'points bounce,' which is detrimental to good ignition, and the nose of the contact breaker mechanism still wears.

Electronic ignition upgrades – original equipment (OE), fully electronic Lucas DE and DM series

If your classic already has electronic ignition as OE fitment, its method of operation will more than likely be either the OPUS (oscillating pick-up) system in a Lucas distributor that includes the designation DE, or its superior successor, a constant energy, variable reluctance/reluctor system in a Lucas distributor that includes the designation DM. The OPUS system had a bad reputation, and replacement parts, if

Here's the top section of the distributor shaft alongside the rotor arm which fits on top. Note the 16-degree marking; the total distributor advance this particular shaft will produce (which is 32 degrees engine advance).

Variable reluctance/reluctor (inductor) type of electronic ignition.

you can get them, are very expensive. If you have an OPUS system, the best thing you can do is either replace the electronics with a Crane Cams XR700-300 electronic (optical) system, which, it is claimed, is specifically designed to replace it, or junk the lot, including the distributor, and start again.

The constant energy, variable reluctance/reluctor distributor and ignition system is very good, and had a long production run, including being fitted to late Rover products in the UK, and used with a Lucas AB14 amplifier. The system can be uprated using a performance ignition amplifier (Micro Dynamics Dynorite 'R' IHN07 or Bestek IG100R) in place of the standard item, or fitment of a performance coil, or both. Better still is to fit a matched performance coil and performance ignition amplifier module (such as the Micro Dynamics EPC03 Power coil that also incorporates a rev limiter). If your car doesn't have the DM distributor, and thus the OE electronic ignition, and you want it, you'll need to source a secondhand unit and have it re-curved by Aldon Automotive for your car's engine and specification. If the electronic ignition 'pickup' inside the distributor fails, it's possible to replace it with either a Lucas part or pattern part from Bestek.

Electronic ignition systems – after- or performance-market, fully electronic

Aside from the factory OE electronic ignition systems there were a few Micro Dynamics electronic ignition distributors and matched amplifier modules. If you come across one of these distributors you will find that it's based on the Lucas DM series, and can be treated accordingly, as outlined earlier.

Electronic ignition systems – after- or performance-market, fully electronic – magnetic type (Hall Effect)

Magnetic type, sometimes known as Hall Effect systems can be regarded

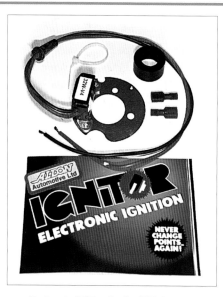

Pertronix (Aldon in the UK) ignitor.

Pertronix (Aldon in the UK) ignitor installed.

Replacement Magnetronic with trigger disc installed.

Replacement Magnetronic without trigger disc installed.

as simple contactless conversions. These are reasonably priced, if not the cheapest of all electronic conversions, and of the systems available two are quite well known, and have the advantage over optical systems in that they are wholly contained inside the distributor cap and without an external black box (which is good for a standard appearance under the bonnet). Both replace the contact breaker and condenser. One system is the Ignitor/Ignitor 2 from Pertronix (Aldon in the UK), the other the Magnetronic from Lumenition. The systems are similar, in that they do away with the contact breaker points and condenser. With the Magnetronic system, however, the trigger magnets pass over the top of the sensor, whereas with the Ignitor, the trigger magnets are mounted vertically. Both can be used with a ballast or non-ballasted coil.

Lucas also made a kit called the Lucas Contactless (Hall Effect) electronic ignition system, though, unlike the Magnetronic and Ignitor, it additionally required an external amplifier (Lucas AB13), and, as far as is known, is no longer made (though new old stock kits do occasionally appear on eBay).

Note that while all three systems should produce better spark energy than contact breaker points, they are not true high-energy systems (except perhaps the Ignitor 2), and need to be used in conjunction with a performance coil to become so.

Electronic ignition systems – after- or performance-market, fully electronic – optical type

Perhaps the most well known fully

electronic systems are the optically-triggered kits from Lumenition, whether the simple budget system 'Optronic PMA50' using the original or a standard coil, or the more expensive 'Performance Ignition System CEK150,' that comes with a matched performance coil. Both systems come with comprehensive fitting instructions with a troubleshooting guide, and conveniently for the Lumenition, the 'black box' that is an integral part of the system can be located on the company's special 'classic' bracket. This bracket locates under the coil bracket and allows the black box to be mounted without having to drill holes in your car. A similar system that hasn't been seen as much in recent years, but which is still available, is the Piranha optical switch system (now produced by Newtronics Systems Ltd) which also works in conjunction with an external 'black box.' The advantage of optical triggering systems (using infra red light), over the magnet (Hall Effect) types is hard to pinpoint, but expect a longer-life system and slightly more spark energy. The disadvantage is the amplifier module might spoil an otherwise standard car, unless you can 'hide' it somewhere.

Distributorless ignition

It is possible to fit a distributorless ignition system controlled by a triggering

Close up of Optronic kit installed in a Lucas 45 series distributor.

device on the crankshaft (crankshaft damper or flywheel). However, an engine lends itself much more readily

to conversion to distributorless ignition when there is a proprietary kit available for it. The advantages to conversion to distributorless ignition are small in comparison to the cost and work involved, so these aren't recommended.

DISTRIBUTORS

If your car has a performance-tuned engine, it may be necessary to modify the distributor so that its characteristics match that of the engine. Also, it's possible to fit an OE electronic ignition system which requires the whole distributor to be swapped. The aim of this section is to explain the differences between distributors.

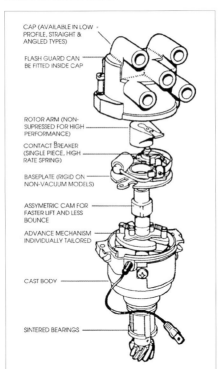

CAP (AVAILABLE IN LOW PROFILE, STRAIGHT & ANGLED TYPES)

FLASH GUARD CAN BE FITTED INSIDE CAP

ROTOR ARM (NON-SUPRESSED FOR HIGH PERFORMANCE)

CONTACT BREAKER (SINGLE PIECE, HIGH RATE SPRING)

BASEPLATE (RIGID ON NON-VACUUM MODELS)

ASSYMETRIC CAM FOR FASTER LIFT AND LESS BOUNCE

ADVANCE MECHANISM INDIVIDUALLY TAILORED

CAST BODY

SINTERED BEARINGS

Components of a high-performance distributor. Such distributors have their advance curves tailored to the engine's requirements. (Courtesy Micro Dynamics)

The function of the distributor

The distributor distributes sparks at regular intervals to the sparkplugs. A single revolution of the engine's

On the left is a Lucas 59DM4 distributor for the A+ engine, with the vacuum advance removed and replaced with a blanking plate. On the right is the Lucas 23 series distributor (long distributor cap clips) cast without provision for vacuum advance.

Lucas 43 series distributor (left) has a significantly different body design at its base when compared to the 59 series (right). Note that the 59 series shown here would normally have a vacuum advance unit/can, but this has been removed and replaced with a Bestek blanking plate.

From left: Lucas 45D4 contact breaker points; US spec MGB Lucas 45DM4 electronic; Lucas Maestro 59DM4 electronic (vacuum advance removed).

crankshaft is 360 degrees of rotation, but the piston's four strokes require

Lucas 45 series distributor re-curved for a modified Sprite/Midget by Aldon Automotive. The vacuum advance has been replaced by a blanking plate, and the body has been drilled and tapped for a screw-fit side entry cap.

Vacuum unit, smooth blanking plate, and Marina-type blanking plate.

720 degrees of crankshaft revolution. Therefore, the firing intervals need to be 180 degrees apart to occur four times in a 720-degree cycle. This is achieved by gearing the distributor so that it runs at half engine speed, and producing sparks 90 degrees apart. The distributor distributes a spark every 90 degrees of its rotation, to a different cylinder each time. Once the engine's crankshaft has

rotated 720 degrees, the distributor has rotated 360 degrees, and the cycle is repeated. The spark is supplied just before the piston has reached Top Dead Centre (TDC), after it has first travelled down the cylinder drawing in air and fuel and then travelling back up the cylinder to compress it. How much earlier in degrees of crankshaft rotation the spark is produced before the piston is at TDC is called advance, and is expressed as the number of degrees of advance before TDC (BTDC). The engine does not require the spark to occur at the same number of degrees of advance throughout its rev range, however, but needs the spark to arrive earlier in the cycle, more advanced, at higher engine speed. However, at a certain engine speed, usually about 3000rpm or 3500rpm, no further ignition advance is required, and the timing is said to be 'all in' or 'fully advanced.' Engines differ in terms of how quickly they require that advance, and the total amount required at various engine rpm until fully advanced. This type of ignition advance is dynamic, so called because it changes in response to engine speed.

Irrespective of by how much and how quickly the dynamic advance takes place, it has to have a starting or reference point – also expressed as a number of degrees of crankshaft rotation before TDC (zero degrees). The starting or reference point is referred to as the static advance. Note that increasing the static advance cannot compensate for a dynamic advance that is too little, too much, too fast, or too slow.

Why distributor swaps might not work

The dynamic advance curve will be specific to a particular engine or state of tune, so, when a distributor is built with a specific advance curve, it will have a specific part number. While there's great scope for swapping a distributor from one engine to another, it's rarely, if ever, likely to have the correct advance curve. A distributor from an 850cc

A-series engined-Mini, for example, may have the same body as that for a 1500 Midget, but the dynamic advance curve will be wrong, and tweaking the static advance settings will not correct it or allow the engine to run properly.

The 'curve,' when plotted on graph paper, is actually closer to a 45-degree straight line than a radius curve. It is produced by the relative limited rotation of the hollow top shaft of the main distributor shaft. This hollow shaft has at its top the four distributor cam lobes (four trigger wheel slots/ four pulse generators, etc for electronic operation) onto which the rotor fits. At the bottom part of the hollow shaft is the action plate assembly, which is connected to a pair of bobweights, the outward movement of which under the centrifugal load applied by the rotation of the main distributor shaft, but acting against springs of predetermined strength, moves the action plate assembly and thus the rotor arm relative to the bottom of the distributor shaft. Put simply, dynamic ignition advance increases in accordance with increases in engine speed. Variation in the weights of the bob weights and spring strengths, as well as the position of the end stop relative to the advance mechanism, is what creates a multitude of potential dynamic advance curves, only one of which is correct for any given engine.

If the distributor body types are the same, but they have different advance curves, it's possible to swap the parts from one distributor to another to change the curves. Also, it's possible to re-curve any distributor, both to change the total amount of advance and the speed of the advance, but this is really a job for an expert, such as Aldon Automotive.

Distributors & performance tuning

Performance tuning an engine changes how quickly and by how much it needs the dynamic (and static) ignition to be advanced. Despite there being a multitude of performance tuning engine specifications, there are usually just two or three basic distributor advance curves available for most modified engines. It's possible to have any distributor re-curved to one of those two basic performance curves, or, of course, you could just buy a new distributor built with that curve. However, any of the two basic performance advance curves can and should be fine-tuned, either after discussing the specification with the engine builder and distributor supplier, or after time spent on the chassis dynamometer (rolling road). For a performance road or race modified engine, it's essential that the distributor is re-curved, or replaced with a distributor that has already been re-curved, to match the new engine's performance characteristics.

The vacuum advance curve

Where fitted – and in the majority of cases it will be – a separate and external vacuum unit is fitted to, or is integral to, the distributor body. The vacuum advance curve is created by movement of the base plate relative to the four distributor cam lobes (four trigger wheel slots/four pulse generators, etc, for electronic operation). The movement of the base plate is produced by a rod in the vacuum advance unit, which in turn is moved by a diaphragm acted upon by the engine inlet or carburettor vacuum (received via a thin plastic pipe).

A particular point to note about vacuum units is that they are not only engine specific but also carburettor or inlet manifold specific. For example, a vacuum unit designed to draw vacuum from a twin SU inlet manifold will have quite different characteristics from a similar-looking vacuum unit designed for a single large carburettor, such as the SU HIF44 – even if the degrees of vacuum produced at the distributor is the same. The vacuum advance operates according to engine load regardless of engine speed. Note that vacuum advance serves to improve economy, and need not be used at

all. Furthermore, if you have a Weber DCOE carb(s) fitted to your engine, you'll find that there's no provision on either the carb or the carb manifold for vacuum advance, so it's redundant and can be removed and replaced with a blanking plate. The base plate inside the distributor then needs to be fixed so it doesn't chatter or move around. For some distributors it's possible to get a fixed base plate for that specific purpose.

Contact breaker points or electronic distributor bodies

For the most part the distributors used in classic cars will either be contact breaker points types or factory electronic units. After-market electronic conversions are quite different to the factory electronic units, but can be fitted to any original contact breaker body, often utilising the same base plate as detailed earlier in the chapter.

Lucas distributors classified by body type

All of the following distributors are Lucas units, and each body type has a designation number that indicates the number of cylinders the distributor is for (DM2 excepted which is for 4-cylinder engines). It's important to note, though, that for any given body type there can be numerous specific models, each of which has a specific number. This information on body type, then, is to aid basic rather than specific identification.

DM2 – The DM2 is one of the earlier Lucas units, and features a smooth body with long clips for the cap, and a vacuum unit with micrometer adjuster. Best kept for a concours car and, for a daily driver, replaced by a later distributor that suits the engine spec.

23D4 – The 23D is a fairly rare unit and doesn't have integral vacuum advance or an aperture for one, while still having long clips for the cap. While fitted to the early Sprite/Midget, it is better known

for being the Mini Cooper S unit.

25D4 – Of the older units this is one of the most common, and, while similar in appearance to the DM2, has a more complicated casting design at the base, while retaining an integral advance unit and the long clips for the cap. Like the DM2, it has micrometer advance adjustment, but was the last type to do so.

35D8 – Contact breaker distributor for V8 engines.

35DE8 – Electronic distributor for Rover V8 engines, with OPUS (oscillating pick-up).

35DM8 – Electronic distributor for Rover V8 engines, with external amplifier.

36DE12 – Electronic distributor for V12 engines, with OPUS.

36DM12 – Electronic distributor for V12 engines, with an external amplifier.

43D4 – Most commonly known as the 1.3 A-Series Austin Marina unit, it doesn't have a vacuum advance, but does have a metal blanking plate fitted. Quite different in appearance and design to the 23D4, it can be readily differentiated by having short clips for the cap.

43DE4 – As for the 43D, but a USA-only spec MGB, with OPUS.

43DM4 – As for the 43D, but a USA-only spec MGB, with inductor electronic system.

45D4 – One of the most common units of all, being similar in outward appearance to the 43D4 with the short clips to the cap, but having a vacuum advance.

45DE4 – A distinctive unit with a unique body that is the OPUS (oscillating pick-up) electronic unit. The electronic amplifier is housed in a squared-off body that looks integral to the main body of the distributor, but is, in fact, fastened on with three screws. The vacuum unit is unique to this distributor, and also part of the amplifier housing and removed with it. When the OPUS unit fails it can be fitted with a Crane Cams XR700 electronic kit. The 45DE4 body cannot be fitted with a standard vacuum unit or even readily blanked off with a blanking plate, since the body is cast different from the 43/45D4 series of bodies in this area. In summary, best avoided as an odd-ball and replaced with something else like the 45DM.

45DM4 – Much improved Lucas factory electronic distributor, operating on the inductor/constant energy principle. The unit can be found on some USA-spec Midgets and MGBs. In external appearance it's close to being identical to the contact breaker 45D, except for the twin wire lead terminating in a

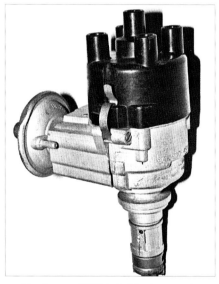

The Lucas 45 DE4 distributor – early electronic design and now obsolete.

socket that exits the unit. The amplifier for the ignition system is external to the distributor, and both factory and after-market upgrades, such as the Micro Dynamics EPC03, can be used.

47D4 – Triumph four-cylinder.

47DE4 – Triumph four-cylinder electronic OPUS unit.

47DM4 – four-cylinder electronic Inductor/constant energy unit.

59D4 – Ital 1.3 A+ design, contact breaker unit, will not fit non-A+ applications without extensive machining to the body and drive dog.

59DM4 – Maestro 1.3 A+ design, electronic (variable reluctance) and a rare unit – needs an ignition amplifier unit, such as the Lucas AB14, or an after-market upgrade, such as the Micro Dynamics EPC03. Will not fit non-A+ applications without extensive machining to the body and drive dog.

65DM4 – Integral amplifier pack (like the DE range) but an A+ design – late 1.3 Maestro, late Metro. A less than ideal unit to modify. Will not fit non-A+ applications without extensive machining to the body and drive dog.

MICRO DYNAMICS DISTRIBUTORS

Micro Dynamics' entire product range, except for the distributors, was bought by Autocar Electrical, and the Micro Dynamics distributors have long since disappeared from sale, though I believe a company by the name of 'Bestek' has the stock. However, if you have a Micro Dynamics distributor, whether contact breaker or electronic, you'll find that the basic body was based on, if not originally manufactured by, Lucas. However, some models were fitted with screw fit rather than clip on distributor caps, but these are still available as a standard Lucas part.

MALLORY DISTRIBUTORS

An alternative to either a Lucas or Micro Dynamics distributor is a Mallory. This is a conventional centrifugal advance distributor only, with dual stabilised

points but a standard advance curve. The dual points eliminate points bounce and erratic timing, which are problems with conventional contact breaker points distributors operating over 6000rpm, especially when the distributor is worn. The key benefit of dual points is an increase in coil saturation time, which, in turn, boosts the output voltage (spark) irrespective of what the coil output voltage is. It's worth noting that if your car competes in motorsport with a full race engine operating at rpm up to and beyond 7500rpm, and where it's mandatory to have contact breaker points ignition, then using a Mallory distributor may prove a significant advantage.

Mallory also has a range of optically-triggered electronic units. There are two main body types: the 45 series, which is without vacuum advance, and the 47 series with vacuum advance. With both distributors, the advance curves are fully adjustable.

PERTRONIX DISTRIBUTOR

The US-made Pertronix distributor uses the company's own electronic ignition system, and is supplied with a generic advance curve that it produced after considerable research. It's also possible to modify the distributor so that two alternative curves can be used. It's a very reasonable approach to take given the huge diversity of ignition curves used in Lucas distributors. However, my personal recommendation is to have the Pertronix electronic distributor curved to

A brand new electronic distributor from Pertronix.

suit your specific engine, and Aldon in the UK or APT in the USA can undertake this work for you. The distributor is also available with or without vacuum advance and, if supplied with vacuum advance, it's designed for a ported source (as oppose a manifold source), and starts advance at 6in of mercury, and reaches a total of 10 degrees at 13in. With a tailored curve to suit your engine, the Petronix will be a perfect brand new performance electronic distributor that will clearly have a long life and is completely uncompromising in its design.

TYPES OF DISTRIBUTOR CAP; GETTING CAPS MODIFIED

Every distributor body has a specific distributor cap, and there's only limited compatibility between some types, and none between others. Caps generally have all the leads coming out of the top of the cap, though side-entry caps are available. Up to and including the 25D series, the caps were designed so the HT leads were secured by a screw which both pierced and then secured the lead. From the 43 series on, all caps were designed for push-fit connecting leads. Aside from the Lucas-based Micro Dynamics distributor, most if not all caps are secured by either the long or later short type of clip, while the Micro Dynamics caps are secured by screws. If you prefer a screw fitting cap, Aldon Automotive can modify any short clip cap distributor (eg 45D4) body, by drilling and tapping it so a screw fit cap can be fitted in place of clips.

REV LIMITER

One benefit of having a well tuned and modified road or race engine in your classic is that it will have a greater rpm potential than the standard engine. In fact, it may have so much potential

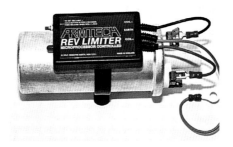

Armteca rev limiter mounted on an ignition coil. (Courtesy Armteca)

Left: rev limiter rotor arm (for a six-cylinder engine). Middle: standard rotor arm 23/55 series distributor. Right: standard rotor arm 43/55 series distributor blue performance rotor for 43/45 series.

that hanging on to one of the lower gears, such as first or second, during a bout of hard acceleration can easily result in excessive rpm being used. Such excessive rpm can be 'fatal' for the engine. The damage is caused by the excessive rpm overloading pistons, conrods, or conrod bolts, leading to complete failure of the component or piston/valve contact (the valve springs simply cannot get the valves out of the piston's way quickly enough). To prevent engine failure or component damage due to excessive rpm, a rev limiter should be fitted.

Rev limiters function in one of three ways: cutting the ignition, cutting the fuel supply, or cutting the ignition and fuel supply. For most cars the after-market rev limiters that are available will work by cutting the ignition. It's possible, though, that cars which

have been fitted with fuel injection and engine management systems (EMS), perhaps as part of an engine swap, will have a rev limiter function that can be programmed within the EMS.

The rev limiters that cut the ignition work by cutting ignition pulses at a preset engine speed, with the preset being set manually once the limiter has been fitted to the car. Micro Dynamics produces a rev limiter that's available either separately or incorporated into an after-market performance electronic ignition system. It's called 'Smooth Cut' because it works electronically rather than mechanically, and will not cut the ignition completely when it comes into operation.

Armteca produces a rev limiter with an integral clip that allows it to clipped onto any cylindrical type coil. Once clipped on, it can be set to the rev limit of your choice.

Finally, it's also possible to use a special rotor arm on many Lucas 4- and 6-cylinder distributors, which will limit rpm (eg to 6500). These rotor arms are available from Aldon Automotive, and are particularly useful on cars with a positive earth electrical system that precludes the use of most modern electronic rev limiters. They were standard fit on early Lotus twin-cam engines, and an after-market option for Jaguar XK engines as well as some Alfa Romeos.

RPM TELLTALE

If you have one of the fine tachometers from Stack it will already have a telltale feature built into it. If you don't have a Stack tachometer, or even another make of tachometer with a telltale function, you can purchase a 'black box' telltale from Armteca, Micro Dynamics, or Lumenition. All products are supplied with good fitting instructions and are easy to install.

Chapter 3

Fuel system

Improvements to the fuel system should increase torque and horsepower and thereby affect two aspects of performance: acceleration and straight line top speed. However, because the improvements may also include an improved throttle response and the elimination of flat spots, cornering speeds may also improve, particularly in very fast bends, by virtue of having more power. The fuel delivery system has some of the greatest scope for power tuning, especially for older engines with small, single carburettors. Note that whether the fuelling is by carburettor or injection, while the modifications are 'bolt on,' it will be the subsequent calibration of the fuel delivery on the chassis dyno/rolling road that ensures the parts yield their full gain. It's important to note that, while any carburettor can be calibrated to deliver more fuel, to the point where the mixture is so rich less power is produced, it's only by fitting a larger or more efficient carburettor that more air can be delivered to the engine. It is the ability to deliver more air, mixed with

the optimum amount of fuel, that allows more power to be produced.

Before you make any decisions about modifying the fuel delivery, you need to understand the basic principle behind carburation. A carburettor in its most basic form can be considered as a tube that, at one point, has a narrower internal diameter (such a tube is referred to as a venturi), and it's at this point that the fuel is introduced. The principle of the venturi is that at the narrow point

the air must increase in speed. The increase in speed causes a pressure drop at the point where the internal diameter is narrower, and the pressure will therefore be less than atmospheric. In a carburettor, the pressure drop creates suction, and this is used to draw fuel out of a reservoir, usually via a jet, and into the venturi to mix with the air flowing through it. The mixture then travels down the venturi to the inlet tract (inlet manifold and inlet port).

(Note that sometimes manufacturers and workshop manuals refer to a venturi as a choke, meaning a restriction in diameter. Do not confuse this use of the word with the carburettor cold starting device choke – a restrictive butterfly that causes the air/fuel mixture to be rich in fuel by air starvation.) Fuel injection is quite different, of course, and doesn't require a venturi to draw fuel out of the injector – it's squirted into either a throttle body or a manifold.

Fuel delivery to the combustion chamber is only ever going to be by one of two means: a carburettor(s) or injection. In both cases there will also be an inlet manifold (with the rare exception of some fuel injection units which fit direct to the cylinder head), and there should also be an air filter. The list below shows, in order of priority and, by coincidence, cost, the power tuning options for the fuel system. The various options, and some 'angles,' will be considered in greater detail.

A performance air filter, such as the K&N items shown here on a flat-four-cylinder Jowett Jupiter engine, will always out-perform the stock item.

AIR FILTERS, AIR FILTER CASINGS & AIR BOXES

The reason for air filtration is to prevent dust, small stones, rubber granules, rock salt, other rubbish, etc, entering the engine. These would be detrimental to performance, and could possibly even prove fatal for the engine. Some racing car engines run without air filters, but they're only able to do this because they need only have a life of a couple of hours before they will have done their job and be ready for a re-build (hardly practical for a road car). In some instances the air filter will be an integral part of a larger assembly, such as an injection system, cold air intake system, or air box, but a simple housing is more usual on classic cars.

There's no reason why an air filter and associated casing or pipework, where fitted, should be detrimental to engine performance, but the reality is that they often are. Because an engine's power output is directly linked to how much air it can breathe, it follows that a less restrictive filtration system, coupled

K&N cone filters on a pair of SU HIF44 carbs on a modified Morris Marina pickup.

with a corresponding increase in fuel to restore the air to fuel ratio, will allow an engine to produce more power.

There are two main categories of performance air filter: foam; and oil impregnated cotton gauze. There are several brands of both type of filter. It's recommended you use a K&N oil

Always use an air filter! Doing so will considerably prolong engine life.

impregnated cotton filter, but whichever type and brand you decide upon, it should not preclude the use of an air box. In independent tests, high-performance air filters have produced gains of 5bhp on medium size engines, right up to gains of 20bhp on big V8s.

RAM PIPES (VELOCITY STACKS/TRUMPETS/AIR HORNS/BELLMOUTHS)

On some carbs or injection systems, at the entrance to the carb or throttle body is what I will call a ram pipe,

The best ram pipes for any carburettor are the full radius (FR) items, shown here on a single Weber 45 DCOE on a manifold for the Triumph Spitfire.

though they are known by a multitude of other names (velocity stacks/ trumpets/air horns/bellmouths). Weber and Dellorto sidedraught carbs have them as standard, whereas SUs and most downdraught or economy carbs don't. However, whatever fuel system is fitted to your car's engine, a change in ram to one of a better design, or more so the fitting of one for the first time, can yield an increase in power. In addition, the ram can improve engine response and flexibility across the rpm range, especially at the bottom end. The restriction on choice is dependent on the fuel system fitted to the engine. If you can't find what you want, it's possible to make your own (or have them made for you). The best rams are the full radius (FR) type, and have to be used for the results to be believed. They are available from such manufacturers as ITG and TWM Induction.

The next most important thing about ram selection is the length. On this point there are two very general rules to be observed: Consider the ram length in relation to the total inlet tract length, long duration cams prefer short rams at high rpm, but long rams provide the best spread of power. However, on

most high-performance engines it may be necessary to compromise on ram pipe length due to the overall space available for the installation.

TYPES OF CARBURETTOR

Before considering a carburettor swap you need to know what type is already fitted. It's recommended to firstly classify carburettor types by whether or not the carburettor has variable venturi or fixed venturi, albeit in some cases of the latter, having the option of being swapped for a different fixed size. Of the two types the variable venturi type is most likely to be an SU, or even a Stromberg. Usually, variable venturi carburettors are used in multiples in high-performance applications, eg twin carbs, but remember that each carb has only a single venturi. It's easy to have period-correct carburettor swaps, whether swapping from a single to twin SUs, or twin to triple SUs, or simply the same number of carbs but of a larger size. Alternatively, swapping to a different type of carb, such as to one or more triple Weber DCOEs, will still be period-correct (some classics were factory-fitted with Weber DCOEs).

The fixed venturi type can be divided into two sub-groups: sidedraught and downdraught. A sidedraught has horizontal venturi, and the downdraught has vertical venturi. Fixed venturi carburettors can come with more than one venturi (two, occasionally three, and sometimes even four, all in a single body).

How many venturis does the engine need, and how big should they be?

Engines may have single venturi carburation supplying multiple cylinders, or carburation with a venturi for each cylinder. It's not the number of carburettors that counts but the number of venturi, so bear in mind that, typically, two variable venturi carburettors, for example SUs, are equivalent to a single twin fixed venturi carburettor, such as the Weber DCOE. The most efficient

installation, generally speaking, is one venturi per cylinder if the inlet tracts are not shared by more than one cylinder. If inlet tracts are shared, then you're restricted to a maximum of one venturi for each sharing set of cylinders. As far as venturi sizes are concerned, consult the experts for your car's engine – but don't use a carburettor or carburettors with venturi any bigger than they need to be, since this can lead to poor low and mid range engine performance without any gain at the uppermost engine rpm range.

The quoted size of a carburettor will refer to the size of the throttle butterfly or venturi, or sometimes by airflow in cubic feet per minute (CFM). Some carburettors (Weber DGAV, for example) have venturi of different sizes within the same body, so both sizes should be considered. Where the carburettor is sized by the throttle butterfly the measurement can be in inches and fractions of inches, or in millimetres (so you may need to convert from one unit to another to compare).

Returning to the number of venturi, a larger number need not necessarily mean greater fuel consumption, and can, in fact, improve it. For instance, an engine with a large single venturi carb may produce better fuel consumption and lower rev range driveability when fitted with two smaller venturi carbs (or a single twin venturi carb). Of course, there may be exceptions that prove otherwise.

CARBURETTER CONVERSIONS

There are two approaches to conversions: one is to fit the same type of carb but of a larger size or quantity, the other is to fit something completely different. At this point it's fair to say that although each carb type has its merits and disadvantages; either of the two types can be made to work well on a performance engine. When you are deciding what carb to convert to bear in mind that in some instances the final selection may be limited by available manifolds (though it's not impossible to make a manifold) and engine bay space. Also consider whether it's necessary to change the carburettors at all. Will an increase in the number of venturi or an increase in venturi size, be beneficial? Is the existing carburation too small? Which type is best for the application – variable venturi or fixed venturi?

Variable venturi (SU and Stromberg)

The calibration of the fuel supply on these carburettors is controlled by a needle and a spring (SU and Stromberg), and can be difficult to set up accurately across the whole rev range. However, a good dyno operator experienced with the SU or Stromberg, and familiar with the needle range, can achieve good results. The advantage

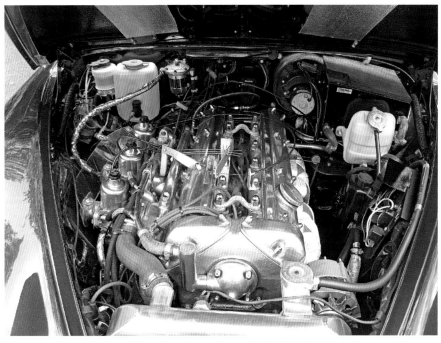

A set of triple SU carbs fitted to a MkII Jaguar (replacing the factory twin SU carb setup). (Courtesy Kev Moore)

Brass hexagon tops on the damper on any SU carb usually indicate they are either H or HD type SUs, though the HD8 always had the black plastic hexagon on the damper.

On the left is a HS6 carb with float chamber, whilst on the right is a HIF6 where the float chamber is integral to the carb body underneath it.

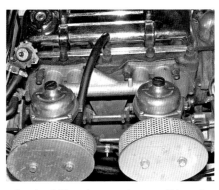

A pair of Stromberg carbs on a Triumph engine.

A pair of HD4 SUs (with chrome dashpot covers) fitted to a V8 in a Daimler SP250.

Sizes (converted sizes) and designations of variable venturi carburettors

SU (Skinners Union)	Stromberg
1⅛in (28.57mm) H1	
1¼in (31.75mm) H2, HS2	1¼in (31.75mm) CD125
1½in (38.10mm) H4, HD4, HS4, HIF4	1½in (38.10mm) CD150
38mm HIF38	
1¾in (44.45mm) H6, HD6, HS6, HIF6	1¾in (44.45mm) CD175
44mm HIF44	
1⅞in (47.63mm) HIF7	
2in (50.80mm) H8, HD8, HS8	

A set of triple DCOE Webers on this six-cylinder Jaguar engine in a racing E-type actually equates to six venturi. Note the FR rams but, sadly, lacking air filters.

The humble Weber DGAV downdraught (left), and the high performance Weber DCOE sidedraught (right).

In this closer look at the bottom of the Weber DGAV, you can clearly see that the primary butterfly is smaller than the secondary.

A quad Weber IDA installation, also lacking air filters, on this V8 engine.

A Holley downdraft carb with four venturi (the choke operates on just two of them). This is similar to the Weber DCD in that half of the venturi (albeit twice as many) open later, but are operated by vacuum. (Courtesy Holley)

Holley 750cfm carb that can be fitted in a pair. Note that there's no facility for a choke on this carb. (Courtesy Holley)

of these carbs is that when used in very mountainous regions they remain correctly calibrated, since they are self correcting in respect of ambient air density. Both types are small and relatively compact, easily used in multiples, and come in a variety of sizes up to 2in (50mm). Furthermore, variable venturi carbs usually have the edge over fixed venturi carbs at low rpm, and may be easier to drive on a high-performance engine in slow traffic. Note that any swap that increases the number of SUs can also use later types of SU, such as the HS or HIF, or use the early carb, such as the HD, with the appropriate manifold.

Fixed venturi

Of the fixed venturi carburettors, Weber, Dellorto and Holley are probably the best known for high-performance applications. There are, however, several makes of fixed venturi carburettor, with sub-classifications by virtue of design. The advantage fixed venturi carbs have over variable venturi carbs is that while the venturi size cannot be varied in operation, on some carbs it can be replaced with a variety of other sizes within certain limits (34mm to 40mm for the 45 Weber DCOE), not least this type of carburettor works well for sudden full throttle operation by virtue of its acceleration jet system, and thereby has the edge for high performance applications.

Progressive (differential) downdraught opening carburettors (eg Weber DGAV & Holley 2305)

The downdraught carburettor with progressive (differential) opening will have two or four venturi, one or one pair of which may be larger than the other or other pair (generally the primary(s) will be smaller). In operation what happens is that the butterfly on one or one pair of venturi opens before the other or other pair. How this works in practice is that as the accelerator pedal is depressed, the first or primary butterfly(s) opens and this is sufficient for the engine to run up to medium engine speeds, say 3000rpm. When the accelerator is depressed further, not only is the primary butterfly(s) opened further, but the second butterfly(s) on the second venturi(s) will be opened, and at a much

faster rate. Such is the speed of the opening of the second butterfly(s), that both or all four reach maximum opening at the same time. The advantage of

Edelbrock twin 500cfm carbs (equals eight venturi) for a small block Chevy. (Courtesy Edelbrock)

A pair of Dellortos (synchronised opening).

the progressive venturi downdraught carburettor is that it provides excellent economy, yet has the capacity to cope with a performance engine operating at high rpm.

Downdraught synchronised opening carb (eg Weber IDA & DGAS, Holley 4160)

The twin, occasionally triple or quad, venturi synchronised carburettor has two, three or four venturi which open simultaneously, and is often used on vee configuration engines, particularly V6s. Although you could use a pair or four pairs on a V8 engine, you also have the alternative of using one carb with four venturi, such as a Holley, or even a pair of Holleys, to achieve the optimum one venturi per inlet tract. A single twin venturi synchronised opening downdraught carb used on V6 engines tends to be very much an economy installation, and can be replaced with an installation comprising three similar but performance carbs. For example, a single Weber DGAS might be replaced with triple Weber DCNF carbs. Something to consider when using synchronised downdraught carbs on vee configuration engines is the overall height of the installation. In extreme cases it may be necessary to have the bonnet 'bulged' in order to provide sufficient clearance for the carburettor(s).

Sidedraught synchronised opening carb (eg Weber DCOE and Dellorto DHLA)

The sidedraught Weber in the DCOE series is just about one of the best carbs you can fit to any high-performance engine. It's the carb seen on probably more racing engines than any other and is still eminently suited to a high-performance classic. One of the myths about Webers is

that they are complicated and difficult to set up. The reality is they have almost infinitely variable fuel metering adjustment (calibration), albeit more expensive than some other carbs, and are equally at home on the shopping run as the race track. Depending on the engine installed in your car and the inlet manifold you plan to use, space may be at a premium. Because space can be so tight, particularly against an inner wing (fender), you often see sidedraught Webers used with no air filters. **Caution!** This is bad practice and almost a guarantee for short engine life – in particular, the life of the pistons and cylinder bores. It should be possible on most cars to relieve the inner wing to allow for an air filter or filter case to be fitted, or fit a very shallow filter.

Note. The Weber DCOE must be mounted with rubber O-ring type gaskets and flexible mountings. This is to prevent fuel foaming caused by engine vibration. Various companies market mountings that will get the job done.

Sizes and designations of some fixed venturi carburettors

Sidedraught	Downdraught
–	1 x 28mm+1 x 36mm Weber 28/36 DCD
–	1 x 32mm+1 x 36mm Weber 32/36 DGAV
–	2 x 34mm Weber 34DGAS
–	2 x 36mm Weber 36DCNF
–	2 x 36mm Dellorto DRLA36
2 x 38mm Weber 38DCOE	2 x 38mm Weber 38DGAS
2 x 40mm Weber 40DCOE	2 x 40mm Weber 40IDF
2 x 40mm Dellorto DHLA40	2 x 40mm Weber 40DCNF
–	2 x 40mm Dellorto DRLA40
–	3 x 40mm Weber 40IDA 3C
2 x 42mm Weber 42DCOE	2 x 42mm Weber 42DCNF
–	2 x 44mm Weber 44IDF
2 x 45mm Weber 45 DCOE	2 x 45mm Dellorto DHLA45
2 x 45mm Dellorto DRLA45	–
–	2 x 46mm Weber 46IDA
–	3 x 46mm Weber 46IDA 3C
2 x 48mm Weber 48 DCOE	2 x 48mm Weber 48IDF
2 x 48mm Weber 48 DCO/SP	2 x 48mm Weber 48IDA
2 x 48mm Dellorto DHLA48	2 x 48mm Dellorto DRLA48
2 x 50mm Weber 50 DCO/SP	
2 x 55mm Weber 55DCO/SP	

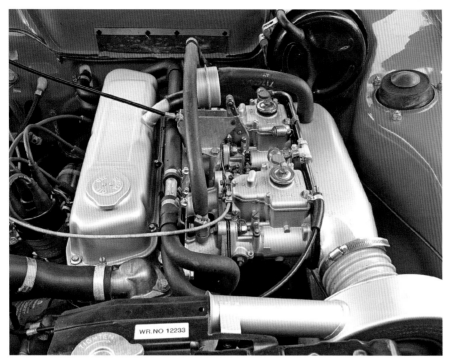

An original equipment installation of twin Weber DCOEs – seen here on the Avenger Tiger.

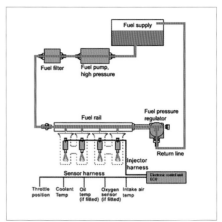

Schematic of a typical fuel injection system. (Courtesy TWM Induction)

The TWM 2000 Series system injection for the Zetec. (Courtesy TWM Induction)

THROTTLE LINKAGE AND CABLES

A throttle linkage may be included if you buy your new or replacement carburation as part of a dedicated kit, but if you've bought separate components you'll need to purchase a linkage separately. There are linkages available for all types of carburation, but not all of them will fit without bonnet (hood) modifications, so check before purchase. Additionally, the cable for a non-standard installation, particularly when the conversion uses a longer than standard inlet manifold, will need to be longer than the standard cable, and may need to be bespoke.

FUEL INJECTION (FI)

Before looking at fuel injection, it's worth looking at the fundamental difference between fuel injection (FI) and carburation. It's often assumed that fuel injection is a modern invention, along with electronic ignition and electronic engine management systems, but

this isn't correct. Early automotive fuel injection systems, often known as petrol injection, were mechanical systems, and diesel injections had injection systems as standard fitting long before petrol engines did. The difference between FI and carbs is

Weber Alpha fuel-injection and ignition system, shown here on a Rover V8. (Courtesy Weber Concessionaires UK Ltd)

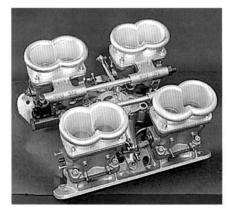

The TWM 3004 Series system injection – shown here for the 308 Ferrari, but a suitable replacement for any Weber DCNF downdraught carburation. (Courtesy TWM Induction)

nothing to do with electronics, but rather how the fuel is introduced to the air the engine is breathing. A carburettor relies upon the venturi effect to draw fuel from a reservoir into the air being drawn into the engine via a system of jets. A fuel injection system doesn't need a venturi because the fuel is not drawn into the airflow, but forced in under pressure as a fine spray. Whether the FI is electronically-controlled or mechanically-controlled, the basic principles remain the same. Most modern production cars with fuel injection will usually have a single butterfly on a plenum chamber, with the injectors fitted in the inlet manifold. These systems aren't readily transferable to a normally-aspirated engine, and there are better alternatives.

Throttle body fuel injection (FI)

The alternative to the typical modern production car, plenum-based fuel injection systems is what is known as throttle body fuel injection, whether the common sidedraught throttle bodies or the less common downdraught throttle bodies designed for an inlet manifold with individual runners. As with carburation, throttle body fuel injection needs a suitable inlet manifold, though many throttle body fuel injection systems have been designed to be a straight fit to inlet manifolds designed for Weber DCOE or DCNF carbs. There are also some throttle bodies designed for fitting direct to the cylinder head (eg on Rover K-series engines).

For a typical conversion to throttle body fuel injection the following major components will be required: manifold, throttle bodies, fuel rail, ram pipes and air filters, throttle position sensor, fuel injectors, high pressure fuel pump and fittings, an Electronic Control Unit (ECU). Add up the cost of that list and you come to the major disadvantage of throttle body injection over performance carbs; the initial cost.

The advantages of throttle body FI over performance carbs, such

as the sidedraught Weber DCOE or downdraught Weber IDA or DCNF, is that FI will be a lot more emissions friendly, and can offer a lot more bottom end RPM flexibility – both important for any road going high-performance classic. As far as absolute top end horsepower goes, there's no significant advantage unless the existing carburation or injection system was undersized or restrictive in some way.

The throttle bodies are available from a number of manufacturers, are available in a range of sizes, and will usually operate with a conventional butterfly throttle plate. One alternative to butterfly throttles is the slide plate throttle, as used on the successful Cosworth DFV Formula 1 engine. These are no longer available as after-market kits, but can be produced as one off conversions by specialist manufacturers. The other alternative, which is readily available, is the roller body kit from Jenvey, Lumenition, or K-series engine specific bodies from Caterham. The advantage of slide or roller action throttling is the absence of a butterfly throttle plate, which would otherwise impede the airflow.

Additional fuel injectors and non-standard fuel injector sizes

With an existing fuel injection system it's often possible to fit an additional fuel injector into the manifold to provide an increase in fuel supply, though this modification is not as popular at it was now that better alternative solutions are available. More often the solution is to fit larger fuel injectors and ensure that they are correctly controlled by the management chip (assuming one is used).

Injection system power boost valves

On an injected engine it's possible to gain mid-rpm range power increases by fitting high-performance fuel valves. They work by providing a higher fuel

pressure than standard in the injection system fuel rail. What this does is allow a greater flow of fuel than standard when the engine is accelerated – they are the equivalent of the pump jet function of a typical sidedraught carb. In effect, the boost valves aid driveability, and can improve acceleration.

FUEL PUMP & PLUMBING

The standard fuel pump on your classic is not designed to cope with more than a moderate increase in engine power and thereby fuel demand, even if it's in good order. Note that some carburettors require high fuel line pressure, while others work better with high volume at a lower pressure. Be guided by the carburettor manufacturer.

To prevent fuel surge (carburated cars), it's usually a good idea to include a pressure regulator in the fuel line. Many of these units usefully also have a built in filter.

Converting to fuel injection may require fitting a high pressure pump as well as a return fuel flow to the fuel tank. More detail on fuel line plumbing is contained in chapter 20.

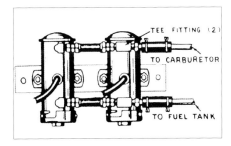

Fuel pumps can be linked in parallel for high flow ...

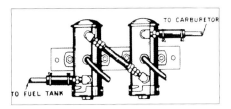

... or in series for high pressure (ie: for forced induction).

A fuel pressure regulator with filter.

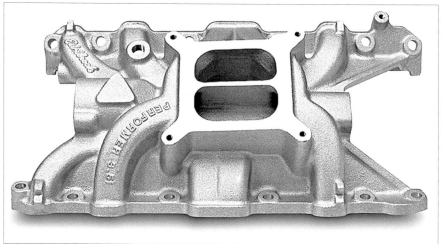

Rover V8 dual-plane manifold from Edelbrock will take Edelbrock or Holley performance carbs. (Courtesy Edelbrock)

INLET MANIFOLDS

Choosing the least convoluted in design, and one which has tracts which closely match the internal diameter of the carburettor venturi or FI throttle bodies.

You need to decide what carb(s) or throttle bodies you are going to use before you choose the manifold (in some instances you need to make the choice simultaneously). For some engines there is a wide choice of high-performance inlet manifold, whereas for others there is virtually no choice at all.

If you're tuning a V8 you have some extra considerations to take into account because, with some exceptions, V8 manifolds are divided into single plane and dual plane types. Usually, the dual plane types produce better low rpm power than the single plane, but the reverse is the case at higher rpm. Because of this feature of V8 manifolds, you'll need to carefully consider the rpm potential of the engine (which means considering the cam) more so than with other engines.

Once you have your manifold, you need to consider if it needs any modification before fitting it. For instance, whatever inlet manifold you have, it's usually possible and beneficial to have an engine tuner clean the inside of the manifold, perhaps even enlarge it a bit. It is also important that the tract diameters of the manifold match those of the carburettor and the cylinder head ports so that there are no 'steps.'

If the manifold is a race bred unit it may not have a brake servo vacuum take-off. If this is the case, and your car requires one, you'll need to get it drilled and tapped and then washed out before fitting it.

HEAT SHIELDS

If the manifold you're going to use is part of a swap from another type of carburettor, twin SUs to single or multiple Weber DCOE carburation, for example, you may find that the original heat shield (if fitted) no longer fits. A carburettor heat shield is used on many engines where the exhaust and carburation is on the same side of the engine, and is designed to shield the carburettors and their float bowls from heat radiating from the exhaust manifold. The solution is to have the inlet manifold, and where possible the carburettor float bowls, coated with a thermal barrier coating.

THERMAL BARRIER COATINGS

Engine bay temperatures can be considerably higher than ambient air temperatures, and this can cause rough running with frequent engine stalls and difficultly restarting the engine when in traffic. Engines with the carburettors above the exhaust manifold will suffer particularly badly, even those where a heat shield is used. The solution is to have the inlet manifold, and where possible the carburettor float bowls, coated with a thermal barrier. The coating is nearly always applied by a specialist manufacturer, and so requires the part, or parts, to be sent away. The coating may be a special paint (CamCoat), or Zircotec's more advanced coating, with a price to match, that's plasma sprayed on. Both coatings will be extremely effective, as well as ensuring that the manifold looks as good as new.

ALCOHOL FUELS

It's unlikely that you'll be using alcohol fuel in a road car. If you are, however, you'll need to seek expert advice from an appropriate carburettor manufacturer, and at least be aware that the carb will need calibrating with very large jets, must have metal (usually brass) floats and jets, and special fuel lines.

Chapter 4
Forced induction

INTRODUCTION

Often perceived as a modern way to tune engines, forced induction has actually been around since the 1920s, first as supercharging, and then, in the 1960s and '70s, as turbocharging. There were many factory turbo cars and after-market conversions, all of which can be inspiration for your own period-correct or period-sympathetic project.

Forced induction can be split into two categories: turbocharging; and supercharging. Very occasionally an installation will incorporate both methods. The principle of both is that the air and fuel mixture (the 'charge') is forced into the cylinders. The operating pressure is usually expressed as a barometric pressure (bar) rather than pounds per square inch (psi). Because more air and fuel is available for combustion, the engine ultimately produces more power (torque and horsepower). Forced induction engines usually have a power curve that is strong in the mid and low rpm ranges and, unlike conventional tuning, the rpm range is not necessarily extended upwards as the cam timing remains unchanged.

Because the power is produced in those useful low- to mid-rpm ranges, there is no loss in flexibility until extreme power gains are sought. All of which make forced induction a good tuning option for a high-performance classic road car. One particular advantage turbocharging has over many other tuning modifications, including supercharging, is that it can actually reduce the amount of noise the engine produces, which is very useful for a road car. Of course, if you want noise it will make it. However, I have known a turbocharged racing engine produce slightly less noise through an exhaust system with no silencer, than a similar non-turbocharged engine which was not only using a silencer box, but produced considerably less power as well!

Every turbocharger or supercharger installation will increase the weight of the vehicle and thus reduce three aspects of performance. Clearly, the power gain should more than balance out the weight gain so there will be improved acceleration and top speed, but there will be a loss of cornering speed and an increase in stopping distance.

SUPERCHARGING

Looking at supercharging first, a supercharger can be thought of as a pump or compressor. It's driven by the engine from the crankshaft by either a vee belt (or belts), or a toothed belt. A variety of designs are available, though some are no longer in production. Of the types still readily available, the most popular appears to be the centrifugal

A massive supercharger on an American V8.

41

This supercharged V8 is fuelled by dual four-venturi carburetors (total eight venturi).

The American classic Judson Supercharger on a Triumph TR.

A modern Eaton Supercharger on a fuel-injected Triumph TR6.

compressor made by Procharger, or the Roots type, usually made by

Weiand, and often found on American V8 engines. The other type is the Lysholm or screw compressor, which tends to be a larger unit, more cuboid in shape, of which the drive may be on an extension from the main body. The supercharger's main advantage over a turbocharger is that the extra power is available the instant the throttle is pressed, with no delay/lag. Another advantage is that until very high boost levels are reached, no charge cooling is generally required. The disadvantages are that engine power is required to drive the supercharger, and the unit and associated components, or a complete kit, can be expensive.

TURBOCHARGING

Like the supercharger, a turbocharger can also be thought of as a pump or

In this close-up of a turbo you can see the waste gate to the right of the turbine.

This HKS GT turbine has been disassembled so that you can see, from left-to-right: the inlet housing, compressor wheel – centre housing – turbine, exhaust housing. (Courtesy HKS)

compressor, but is, in fact, two turbines. The exhaust gas from the engine spins a turbine on one end of a shaft, at the other end of which is a compressor which compresses the induction charge before it's drawn into the engine. The turbocharger's main advantage over a supercharger is that no engine power is required to drive it. The disadvantages are that there's usually some hesitation, known as lag, before it starts to work, and the unit generates a lot of under-bonnet heat.

HOW MUCH IS TOO MUCH?

Before considering what needs to be done to allow a forced induction unit to pass more boost to the engine, you need to decide how much more power you want. I suggest that rather than seek a power increase in a round number, such as looking for a further 25bhp, you aim for a percentage increase of, say, 10 per cent. The reason for this is that it'll be

A turbocharged Vauxhall engine transplanted into an Avenger Tiger.

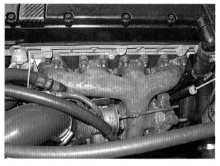

A closer look at the exhaust manifold and turbo assembly in the Avenger.

easier to work within the limitations of other areas of both the engine and car. For instance, it's very easy and relatively cheap to dramatically increase the power of a forced induction engine to find that the clutch, gearbox, and driveshafts (to mention a few components) break with annoying regularity. This is more often the case with forced induction tuning than with other conventional tuning techniques, largely because of the increase in torque produced. This is one reason why manufacturers deliberately limit boost at certain points in the rpm range.

TUNING EXISTING INSTALLATIONS

Once you've decided on how much more power you want, you can look at what's preventing the current installation from realising that amount of power, and then work out a plan of action to increase power. The two options tables can be used as a guide, and the options are listed in an approximate order of power yield, but it must be remembered that these are only guides. For instance, it could be that fitting a

Top three options for tuning supercharged systems

1. Increase boost pressure (by changing supercharger speed or fitting a larger unit)
2. Fit a charger cooler (where possible) or a fuel cooler (where possible)
3. Improve engine breathing using conventional tuning methods

Top five options for tuning turbocharged systems

1. Increase boost pressure (by fitting a modified wastegate)
2. Fit a charge cooler or larger charge cooler (intercooler) either air/air or water/air
3. Improve engine breathing using conventional tuning methods
4. Fit a performance dump valve
5. Fit a modified turbocharger that is optimized for the engine; not just bigger

high-performance dump valve may yield the desired gain in performance (not necessarily more power) without spoiling engine flexibility by introducing turbo lag, and it could be a cheap modification. Finally, with any forced induction engine, never forget that conventional tuning techniques are still generally valid. After the tables there are various sections, each of which look at forced induction high-performance tuning in greater detail.

A Sierra XR4x4 with twin turbos on the Ford V6.

Increase in boost pressure

For an engine with an existing forced induction system, the easiest way to get more power is to increase the boost. However, this can cause problems due to the temperature increase in the inlet charge (more of which later). Also, with any forced induction system there are usually several factors that limit boost. First, there's likely to be some kind of blow-off valve, or, more commonly with a turbocharger, a wastegate. Second, the size and design of the unit itself may be the limitation. Third, higher charge temperatures created by increasing boost can reduce the amount of power that can be produced because the rise in pressure heats the charge. Each can be overcome as follows: The blow-off valve or wastegate can be modified or changed for a different one so that higher pressures can be attained before activation. The turbocharger unit itself can be exchanged for a larger item.

A Tickford Capri with a single turbo on the Ford V6.

Uprated intercooler for the Mazda RX7 from HKS. (Courtesy HKS)

Turbo dump valves from Trans Auto Sport. (Courtesy Trans Auto Sport)

Charge cooling can be improved, or introduced if it did not previously exist.

Charge cooling

The fuel/air mixture, or charge, can be cooled by passing it through either an air/air intercooler, or a water/air charge cooler, or a larger or secondary unit if one is already fitted. Both intercooling and charge cooling do the same job, but the former uses air as the cooling medium, and the latter uses the engine coolant. You're more likely to find charge cooling on a turbocharged application than a supercharged one. Usually the charge cooler will take the form of an air/air intercooler. An intercooler looks very similar to a radiator or oil cooler. It'll nearly always be made of aluminium, and be unpainted. Depending on the engine and turbocharging installation in question, it may be possible to source a suitable intercooler from another model from the same manufacturer, or even from a completely different manufacturer. Lastly, it's possible to purchase a universal intercooler from Allard, Serck, or AH fabrications, possibly even getting them to manufacture a hybrid unit for you. The same applies for installing a larger unit than standard, though you're more likely to need a unique unit specifically designed for your car's engine.

Once you have the intercooler, be it a first time fit or upgrade, it needs to be connected to the turbocharging system. Given that you're seeking to minimise the pressure drop caused by using long lengths of rubber hose (which,

incidentally, should be silicone rubber hose), any long runs of piping should be made using large bore aluminium tubing. Samco is a good source of suitable silicone rubber hosing.

For a supercharged installation it's possible to pump the fuel through a small air-to-air oil cooler unit to reduced the fuel temperature. The theory being that if the fuel is cooler it will cool the air. The most popular way to achieve a cooler charge though, is to fit a large external (to the car body) air scoop (cold air box) to the installation to ensure the air is as cool as it can be.

Turbocharger dump valves

A well known problem with turbocharged engines is that of turbo lag, that is, the time it takes for the turbocharger turbine to accelerate to a speed at which the compressor produces boost. Usually this kind of lag is experienced when the vehicle is being accelerated from low to medium engine rpm. However, it can also be experienced to a lesser extent when changing gear. The lag encountered when changing gear is caused by a build-up of pressure against a closed butterfly valve in the induction system, itself created by the closure of the throttle for the gear change. This build up of pressure causes the turbocharger compressor to slow dramatically, a condition known as stall. When the throttle is opened again, after the gear change has been completed, the turbo has to pick up speed once more before useful boost, and thereby power, is produced. This process takes

time, and is experienced as turbo lag, the turbocharger lagging behind the throttle opening. Most turbocharger installations are fitted with a dump valve that releases the excess pressure caused when the throttle butterfly is closed. If your vehicle's engine's turbocharger installation does not have a dump valve, it's well worthwhile fitting one. If one is already fitted it's worth checking its functionality (leaks would lead to loss of boost pressure) and upgrading to a more robust item.

Fitting original equipment installations to engines without them & wholly after-market installations

It may appear at first glance that the difference between a forced induction engine and its normally-aspirated version is simply the turbo or supercharger unit. On that assumption, it appears that aside from dropping the compression ratio of the engine, the forced induction parts can be bolted on to your normally-aspirated derivative and the job's done. The reality is that, even aside from crucial differences in the fuel delivery system, there's a lot more to it. The engine block, conrods, and a whole load of other components may be differently engineered. Because of this complexity, it's usually easier and cheaper to do a complete engine swap – including the forced induction unit – rather than try and do a bolt on conversion using original equipment parts on the same engine. Where an engine has no forced induction derivative, such as the Rover (Buick) V8, there are two approaches that can be taken. The easiest way is to buy a kit from a reputable tuning company, possibly even having it carry out the fitting as well. The alternative is to design and build your own installation from scratch, using after-market components or adapted production components. In the case of the former, your contractor will do the thinking and work for you, and in the latter, you'll need to seek expert advice and do your own research.

Chapter 5
Exhaust systems

INTRODUCTION

The exhaust system performs two tasks: it removes the exhaust gases and deposits them out of the way of the car, usually behind, but sometimes alongside; and silences the engine's combustion noise. Modifications to the exhaust system can increase power and thereby improve two aspects of performance: straight line top speed, and acceleration. However, as with all increases in power, cornering speed may also be improved. Less obvious are improvements or even detriments to

Side pipe on an early Viva: note it doesn't protrude beyond the bodywork of the car.

Cast iron manifolds on the Jaguar XK engine: heavy and not particularly efficient.

deceleration which could be caused by a change in the weight of the exhaust system.

Modifications to the exhaust system are probably always period-correct, whether using a copy of an early sports manifold and system, or a modern equivalent.

The exhaust system consists of two, or more recently, three, separate components: the manifold (header) which bolts to the cylinder head(s); the

system which will contain the silencer (muffler) box(es); and the catalytic converter, which will (if fitted) be near the front end of the system.

The replacement of standard exhaust parts with high-performance ones allows the engine to produce more power by releasing the exhaust gas more efficiently, and, in doing so, it reduces the pressure of the exhaust gas in the system. This is known as reducing the 'back pressure' or reducing overall engine 'pumping losses.' To understand how this works, think for a moment where the exhaust gas is created – in the engine combustion chamber when the fuel/air mixture has ignited. Combustion produces the power stroke that forces the piston down the cylinder, it also produces exhaust gas. When the piston goes back up the cylinder, it has to push the exhaust gas ahead of it. 'Push' is the key word here, because the exhaust gas has to be forced up the cylinder, out of the exhaust port, and down the whole length of the exhaust system. Energy (power) is required to do this, and if restrictions to the flow of exhaust gas to the atmosphere can be minimised, then the saved power can be used elsewhere – like driving the wheels of the car.

For less power to be required in driving out the exhaust gas the system needs to be less resistant to the flow of gas. One way a performance system may achieve this is for the size, or, more accurately the bore (pipe diameter), of the system to be larger. The bigger bore allows more gas to flow through the system. However, when a gas flows through a larger diameter pipe compared to a smaller diameter pipe, the speed (velocity) of the gas is slower, and too large a bore creates a slow gas speed. A slow exhaust gas speed causes a loss of power because of the way outgoing exhaust gas in the cylinder head aids induction of the inlet charge by creating a flow of gas (it helps suck in the inlet charge). The difficult part about tuning the bore is that there are many variables to consider, including the engine type, camshaft(s) and rpm. All these considerations mean that, although it's difficult to get a very good system optimized for your application, it's very easy to get a bad one. One, more or all parts of the exhaust system can be beneficially modified as follows:

EXHAUST MANIFOLD (HEADER) & TUBULAR/ FREE-FLOW MANIFOLDS

Most classic cars (especially pre-1980), will have a cast iron exhaust manifold. Compared to the modern alternative (tubular design) these may be constrictive and heavy. A cast iron item with very short cylinder runs is usually indicative of a standard manifold that

Four-into-two-into-one Ashley exhaust manifold. (Courtesy Burton Power)

Very neat four-into-one exhaust manifolds for a V8 engine from Edelbrock. (Courtesy Edelbrock)

Nicely chromed six-into-two manifold.

can be replaced with something better. If you find that there appears to be no performance manifold available for your particular car, or very few, it may well be because the standard manifold is actually quite good, or that your car is unpopular for power tuning. Finally, if nothing is available off-the-shelf, it is always possible to have a unique system made – at a price. Note that if you've had to have a bespoke manifold made, most likely you'll need to make or adapt an after-market performance system to go with it, more of which later.

CONTROLLED VORTEX (CV) EXHAUST MANIFOLD

A variation on the standard tubular or free-flow manifold is the Controlled Vortex or CV tubular or free-flow manifold. The CV, or anti-reversion manifold, was developed by Janspeed in conjunction with tuning expert, David Vizard, in 1981, and it became very popular amongst racers. However, the extra cost of the CV manifold compared to an ordinary performance manifold,

Big bore manifolds are not always best, but, in this case, are exactly right for the road legal, race modified Ford Pinto engine in Steve Pratt's MkI Ford Cortina.

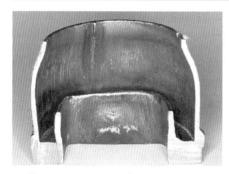

Here you can see a single, sectioned controlled vortex manifold stub.

You can just see the four-into-two joins on this stainless steel manifold fitted to a Ford engine.

made it a less popular conversion for road cars. Additionally, the benefits of the CV are not realised unless used on engines with large carburettor chokes and long period cams, these items being found only on the hottest road cars. Because of the relatively small demand for them, CV manifolds are made on a one-off basis, and Janspeed holds the British patents.

The CV differs from other manifolds in that, at its port ends, it has small cones with a large space around them, and, from the outside, this part of the manifold looks slightly thicker. The reason for the cones is that an engine fitted with a long duration cam allows more fuel and air mixture to enter the combustion chamber, especially so at high rpm (the valves are held open longer than standard cam timing) but creates a problem with lower exhaust gas speed and reverse flow (gas

flowing back through the port and into the combustion chamber) at low to medium engine speeds, both of which cause power loss. The cones in the CV manifold hinder the back flow of exhaust gas. To quote Janspeed: "The controlled vortex manifolds are designed for competition cars running wild camshafts with high induction and exhaust gas speeds. The benefits of a controlled vortex manifold are that the engine gains torque at the bottom to mid-rpm range without loss of bhp at the top end. As a by-product of increasing torque, and hence lowering the usable rpm, you will also find that the car will become far more efficient fuel wise." In his books David Vizard says a great deal about the CV manifold system, but one phrase in particular speaks volumes: "The extra low end torque would be instantly noticeable on the road."

The most disappointing aspect about the CV manifold isn't that it's deficient in any way, but rather that it is so underrated and so little known. A CV manifold on a road car with, for example, a mid range performance cam and Weber/Dellorto side or downdraught carburettor would yield enormous driveability gains and power. If you consider that a road car with a performance-tuned engine not only has to compromise with regard to cam selection but also carburation venturi size, then the benefits of a CV system is obvious. On a Weber/Dellorto side or downdraught carburated engine, the choke (main venturi) will be sized on the small size in order to achieve maximum flexibility required for driving in city and town traffic. The downside to sizing for flexibility is it limits maximum power and power at the top end of the rev range (note that peak power may occur 1000rpm before max engine speed). Attempts to use the optimum choke for power may result in the car being practically undriveable for everyday use because the engine delivers negligible power below 3500rpm. The size difference between the choke

for flexibility and that for power may be at least one size (more likely two). The beauty of the CV manifold is that it allows the choke to be sized for maximum power yet will still allow the engine good low and medium rpm flexibility.

EXHAUST SYSTEM

The original equipment/standard replacement exhaust system will be comprised of tubing and silencer boxes, and ending with a tailpipe. It

Performance rear silencer box from Janspeed. (Courtesy Janspeed)

Two-silencer system from Ashley Competition Exhausts; note the skid plates on the rear silencer box. (Courtesy Ashley Competition Exhausts)

Manifold and system for the Rover Metro 16V 1400 from Janspeed. (Courtesy Janspeed)

will have been designed with cost and noise reduction as high priorities, and performance considerations of little or no significance, more so on classic saloons than classic sports cars or GTs, which may have a slightly better system. If you've fitted a tubular exhaust manifold, replacing a cast iron manifold, you'll have to adapt the exhaust system in length and, most likely, tube diameter, the latter to deal with any mismatch.

The exhaust system is just as important as the manifold, and, in some cases, more power, without loss of flexibility, can be liberated by a good exhaust system than by a change of manifold.

How much of a gain in power there'll be from fitting a performance exhaust system depends both on how bad, or how good, the standard system is, and on how good the performance system is. Janspeed, for example, usually claims a power increase of ten per cent, and often more, for its high-performance systems. With that performance gain you'll usually also get a distinctly sporty exhaust note. Bear in mind that, with some manufacturers' systems, the exhaust noise can be unpleasantly loud, and in excess of the noise limit for motorsport or even circuit track days. Something else to watch for with after-market performance systems is that you can only get what you pay for, and a cheap performance system may not only be a poor fit but also be short-lived.

CATALYTIC CONVERTERS

Before making any decisions about the catalytic converter, it's worth considering what it looks like and how it works. A catalytic converter looks like a small exhaust silencer (muffler). However, inside there'll be a ceramic honeycomb or metal foil spiral roll core, which will have an internal surface area equivalent to several football pitches. This core is coated with an alumina-based washcoat providing a secure base for the catalyst coating

of platinum, rhodium and palladium precious metals. The exhaust gases pass through the core where they react with the metal coating; this chemical reaction converts the gases to carbon dioxide, water and nitrogen. The exhaust system of catalytic converter-equipped cars will also incorporate an oxygen sensor, usually linked to the engine management system of the car.

Very early catalytic converters (probably only seen in the USA) were of poor design, having excessive pumping losses due to their restrictive design. More recent models have minimal or nonexistent pumping losses, depending on make and model car. Porsche was one of the first, if not the first, to produce a solution to exhaust pumping losses through the cat, and came up with an alternative to the ceramic monolith – metal foil. The early metal foil cat that Porsche developed was found to have several advantages over the ceramic cat, including the all important airflow capability. Porsche fitted it to the Carrera 911 model with no loss of power. Porsche also raced cars fitted with cats from the mid-80s onwards.

After Porsche and other manufacturers led the way, it wasn't long before after-market performance cats were available. Of these the Peter Maiden Sebring cat was perhaps the most well known. The Sebring cat had a carbon dioxide sensor connection and heat shield, and is designed to fit a vast range of models. Generally, any large metal foil design of cat in a good casing will produce minimal pumping losses and can be adapted to fit an existing exhaust system.

On certain cars there may be a benefit in fitting a performance cat. However, on cars registered before 1993, although a cat may be fitted, it can be legally removed (at least in the UK) which may achieve the same thing. A final point to consider regarding cats is that some are considerably heavier than a suitable diameter pipe of the same length, and so its replacement can yield a very useful weight saving.

EXHAUST MANIFOLD INSULATING WRAP

There's some debate about whether using manifold insulating wrap will allow the engine to produce more power by keeping exhaust gasses as hot as possible for faster flow and reducing under-bonnet engine temperatures. Some have claimed it works, while others cite clear examples where it hasn't. However, one area of agreement is that the use of the wrap will considerably shorten the life of the manifold by virtue of the higher temperatures. For that reason alone I think that the use of the wrap is to be avoided, especially when there are much better solutions.

EXHAUST MANIFOLD THERMAL BARRIER COATINGS

A far superior solution to exhaust wraps is the use of a thermal barrier coating on the exhaust manifold. The coating can be applied to both the inside and outside, or just the outside, though it's recommended to coat both. The exhaust manifold coating has proved to be very successful at preventing heat radiating from the manifold, and thereby ensuring under-bonnet temperatures are as low as they can be. The coating also serves to protect the manifold from rusting, thereby extending its life, as well as benefiting the overall engine bay appearance. Coatings can be either paint-based, or the more expensive ceramic-based, both of which should be applied by a specialist company. For a particularly demanding (very hot) exhaust system, it's recommended the ceramic coating is used.

BRACKETING & MOUNTINGS

Finally, whatever you do with your car's exhaust, be sure it's all adequately mounted because, if it breaks, loose and is damaged beyond repair, or just simply lost, you will need to purchase a replacement.

Chapter 6
Cooling systems

INTRODUCTION

Performance modifications to the cooling system, as explained in depth later, may produce a small gain in engine power, and thereby affect two aspects of performance: straight line top speed, and acceleration. The increase in power might also affect cornering speed, and, on classic cars, a change to lightweight cooling components, such as an aluminium radiator replacing a copper and brass unit, would reduce vehicle weight, and thereby improve braking performance, cornering, and acceleration. However, improvements to these aspects of performance aren't the main reason for modifying the cooling system; it's rather the need to have a cooling system that prevents the engine overheating and being damaged.

BASIC PRINCIPLES

About a third of all the energy produced by an internal combustion engine is in the form of heat that has to be dissipated by the car's cooling system. Without cooling the engine would overheat and seize. Any engine tuned to

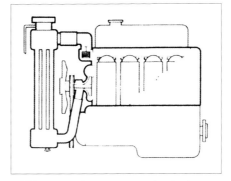

This system has no expansion tank, and is filled via the radiator pressure cap. Excess coolant is vented to the atmosphere.
(Courtesy BARS Products)

produce more power will also produce more heat. The cooling properties of the oil in the engine will be dealt with separately in chapter 7.

Whether you have a slightly modified classic saloon or a full engine transplant street rod you must ensure the cooling system can adequately cool the engine in whatever circumstance and use it's put to. Any automotive

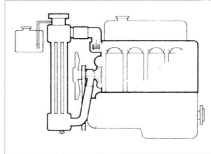

Similar to the previous system, except that expanded coolant passes to a non-pressurised tank. Coolant returns to the radiator on cooling.
(Courtesy BARS Products)

cooling system in its simplest form will consist of a radiator and a water pump, and, more than likely, an overflow tank which may be an expansion tank. If your car has an overheating problem at driving speeds of 35mph and below, look to airflow for the solution – the fan. For overheating problems above 35mph look to the radiator size for a solution. The same principles apply if you do not have an overheating problem but want

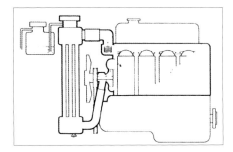

This system utilizes a remote radiator header tank, identified by the connection of two or more hoses, and is filled via the header tank pressure cap.
(Courtesy BARS Products)

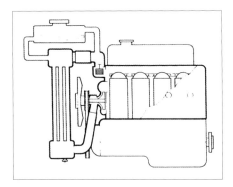

This system uses a pressurised expansion tank with a pressure cap fitted. The tank, not in circulation, is filled via the access cap or plug, located at the highest point.
(Courtesy BARS Products)

Cooling system problems & solutions

Overheating in traffic (assuming a standard cooling system in good order)	Fit electric cooling fan
Overheating at speeds above 35mph (assuming a standard cooling system in good order)	Consider water pump efficiency and large size water pump pulley Fit competition radiator with expansion/recovery tank system Fit wing vents to trailing edge of wings

Note that just because the pulley looks different doesn't mean it's a different diameter – the middle and right-hand items are the same diameter, but both are larger than the one on the left.

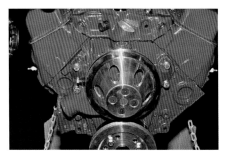

A non-standard lightweight aluminium pulley on a V8 engine.

to drop the coolant temperature.

Having power tuned the existing engine, or transplanted another, it's now necessary to select the major cooling system components: the water pump; water pump pulley; and radiator. No matter what engine you are using in your car, it's extremely likely it'll be using the standard water pump for that engine. The engine builder may, however, specify a slight deviation from the norm, but unlike the pump itself, the pulley drive for it may well deviate from the norm for that engine.

WATER PUMP PULLEY
The water pump pulley is important because it controls the speed at which the pump runs for any given rpm.

Changing the pump's gearing by using a smaller pulley may improve water flow at low engine speeds, but can have a negative affect at high rpm by causing cavitation of the impeller – a water 'wheel spin' effect that results in no real movement of the coolant; a situation to be avoided. To reduce cavitation and improve coolant flow it may be necessary to fit an oversize pulley. In

back-to-back tests with one particular car I found that with a larger pulley the engine ran five degrees cooler than with the standard pulley, and that was at moderate engine speeds. The reason was that there was less or no cavitation when the water pump was driven more slowly using the larger pulley. However, because pumps can vary so much, you may need to experiment to find the optimum pulley size, particularly if you've tuned the engine so it has a much higher rev range than standard.

RADIATOR
Radiator size is crucial – not only in its overall fluid capacity but its physical dimensions as well. While most production cars have a radiator large enough for the worst scenario, and still have spare capacity, this is unlikely to be the case for classics, which weren't designed to spend time in today's traffic jams. Therefore, the older your classic the less likely it will be you can use the original equipment radiator for your given choice of engine or engine tuning and not have cooling problems. Additionally, three further points arise: first, you may wish to run a much lower coolant temperature than the production model (more of this later); second, when using the donor car's original equipment radiator with a transplanted engine, the airflow to it may be less than the airflow it received in the original car; third, there may be a space constraint which prohibits the use of an original

A high-performance aluminium radiator is significantly lighter than its copper and brass equivalent, and reduces the coolant temperature – this one is from Pace for the Jaguar XK150.
(Courtesy Pace)

This aluminium radiator has brackets for an electric fan. (Courtesy Pace)

equipment radiator in the case of engine swaps.

On the face of it, assuming the original equipment radiator can cope with the additional loads placed upon it by the tuned engine, there are no further problems. However, it's generally agreed that for optimum power and torque, engines require a working temperature of around 70 degrees Centigrade (158 degrees Fahrenheit). This isn't the optimum temperature for economy (which requires a higher temperature), and the car is likely to have been designed to run at the most economical temperature. The original equipment radiator may not be capable of dropping the temperature to 70 degrees Centigrade but, assuming it copes in every other respect (the engine will not boil the coolant), the situation can be

lived with. If, however, you do want to run the engine coolant temperature at the power efficient (but uneconomical) 70 degree mark, a change in radiator, or the addition of a secondary radiator, will be required.

A look back now, to the second point in our list of potential problems, that of airflow to the radiator possibly being inadequate. Quite often, the problem with airflow to a radiator is not so much getting enough air into it as getting air out. Put another way, if the air, once it has passed through the radiator, cannot leave the engine bay it cannot allow any more air to follow it. Air needs to leave the engine bay easily to generate a cooling airflow through the radiator. The biggest radiator intake ducting in the world will not work if the air stalls once it's inside the engine bay. The simplest solution here is to cut or fit louvres in the bonnet to release hot air from the engine bay (at the same time creating a neat period-correct look, like the E-type Jaguar).

Another interesting solution is one passed to me by Ford Motorsport; it told me that the air fans bolted to the front wheels of a race car that provide brake cooling also help radiator cooling by sucking air out of the engine compartment. The original Minilite wheels assist brake cooling in the same manner, so it's a reasonable assumption they might also help remove hot air from the engine bay.

The last problem on the list was that of a space constraint prohibiting the use of the original equipment radiator. Whatever the reason, for example, following an engine swap, the solution is to find something suitable from another car or have something made from scratch.

Assuming none of the three solutions suggested solves an overheating problem, it will be necessary to engineer-in more cooling. The simplest method to achieve this is by fitting an auxiliary radiator. It's also possible to use two smaller radiators of similar size rather than a standard

size radiator and an auxiliary radiator. An auxiliary radiator, like the main or primary radiator, must be positioned where it will receive sufficient airflow to achieve its purpose. An increase in coolant capacity on its own will simply create longer warm-up times. Kenlowe, best known for its range of electric fans, is one company that produces off-the-shelf auxiliary radiators. Naturally, it also manufactures an electric fan to go with any auxiliary radiator.

A neater solution to using two radiators is to use a single larger-than-standard radiator. In this instance, it may be possible to use a radiator from another production car that has a larger coolant capacity. If you can't get such a radiator, or prefer not to, it's possible to fit a racing radiator. A true racing radiator manufactured in aluminium will be much more efficient than a conventional production copper and brass (or even plastic) radiator, for a number of reasons. The principal reason is that an aluminium radiator is likely to have a much higher ratio of water tubes per centimetre than a conventional radiator and, in itself, this dramatically improves cooling. Further, the core of an aluminium radiator is of different internal construction, whereby it has built-in turbulators which improve efficiency; it may also have a greater core thickness. An additional bonus in using an aluminium radiator is that size-for-size, it is considerably lighter than many production radiators and, coupled with the customer choice of unique dimensions, it's a solution hard to fault. Serck Marston has a racing division which is a leader in the field of race car radiators. It can make one for your road (or race) vehicle (a complete one off, for example, dimensionally similar, but with a thicker core, to the original unit). Another expert company in the UK is Pace Products which has a wide range of performance aluminium radiators for classic cars.

SWIRL POTS
In certain installations, steam pockets

or airlocks may form in the cooling system, the latter being very much more likely when the radiator height is lower than that of the engine block. In order to remove excess air from the cooling system, a swirl pot (with an inlet at the top and an outlet at the bottom, at right angles to the inlet) can be fitted. The passage of the coolant through the pot de-aerates it.

THERMOSTATS

Cooling system thermostats allow the engine to reach its operating temperature quickly by cutting-off water circulation to the radiator. Thermostats are made to open at a specific temperature, which varies with the requirements of the cooling system. Although it's not possible to change the opening and closing parameters of the thermostat, it's possible to exchange it for one which opens at a lower (or higher) temperature. Another option is to carefully drill holes in the body of the thermostat to increase the flow of water through it when it's open, and allow some water to flow through it when it's cold. Note that the best cooling system in the world will not allow the engine to run cooler than the opening temperature of the thermostat. It's possible to do away with the thermostat altogether, but this can cause the engine to run too cool, as well as lengthening engine warm up times. In certain instances removal of the thermostat can be detrimental to coolant flow through the system. If in doubt seek expert advice from a reputable specialist for your classic.

RADIATOR & EXPANSION TANK PRESSURE CAPS

The operating pressure of the car's cooling system is determined by a pressure cap, fitted either to the radiator or the expansion tank. The cap seals the cooling system against the atmosphere via a sealing ring, usually of rubber, which is part of a spring-loaded assembly. The pressure rating

These radiator (or pressure caps) look identical but have different pressure ratings – a worn spring or wrongly rated cap can cause coolant loss – and acute embarrassment – at traffic lights.

Two racing caps from Stant that are perfect for any high-performance classic; the cap on the left is a lever vent cap.

The lever vent on the Stant racing lever vent cap compresses the spring and seal assembly to release pressure from the cooling system.

of the cap varies from car to car, with a trend towards higher pressure ratings the newer the model. Aside from the differences in pressure rating, there are differences in the cap designs. Older

cars tended to have a 1in deep radiator neck, while the caps fitted to later cars and expansion tanks is designed for a ¾in deep neck.

The significance of the pressure rating of the cap is that, by pressurising the cooling system, the coolant's boiling point is raised. Each pound per square inch (6.9kpa) of pressure will raise the boiling point by 1.7 degrees C (3 degrees F). The accompanying table provides information on boiling points with no radiator cap or a faulty cap (that does not pressurise the cooling system) as well as some higher than standard rated pressure caps.

Pressurising the cooling system means the coolant reaches a higher temperature before it boils. This provides a useful additional margin against coolant loss due to overheating, whether in a traffic jam or on the starting grid of a race. This is important because, once coolant has been ejected and lost from the cooling system, it will become increasingly unlikely that the coolant temperature will drop, as there's less of it to actually be cooled. **Caution!** If at any time the cooling system overheats and expels coolant, never ever remove the pressure cap or depressurise the system in any way, as doing so will lead to an almost instantaneous ejection of steam and boiling coolant. The reason for this is that the depressurising further drops the boiling point of the coolant, which is already at boiling, worsening the problem. You must wait for the temperature to drop before any fresh coolant can be added (pouring cool water on the radiator may help speed this up).

On the face of things the quickest upgrade to a cooling system is to fit a higher rated pressure cap, but there a number of reasons why this isn't the case. First and foremost, running the cooling system at a higher pressure doesn't allow the engine to run cooler, it simply allows higher temperatures to be reached before the engine boils over. Next running the cooling system at a

Pressure rating of cap	Boiling point in C	Boiling point in F	Comment
Zero/atmospheric	100C	212F	At sea level
4psi	106.8C	224F	
7psi	111.5C	233F	
10psi	117C	242F	
13psi	122.1C	251F	
15psi	125.5C	257F	
16psi	127.2C	260F	

Note: the following Stant caps are all 16 psi: 10331/11331, racing swivel cap 18231/28231, racing lever vent 18331/28331

Kenlowe's electric fan (ducted design) is available as a complete kit for most classics.

higher pressure than it was designed for can create problems with core (freeze) plugs in the cylinder (engine) block being blown out, or damage a copper/brass radiator, both which can be the cause of a dramatic and rapid loss of coolant. Older conventional rubber hoses may also fail if subject to higher pressures than they were designed for. There are, however, slightly higher pressure caps that can be safely used, as well as caps engineered to a precise limit – both from Stant.

Non-standard radiator & expansion tank caps

Irrespective of the pressure rating for caps designed for a three quarter inch deep neck, it's possible to use racing caps, lever vented caps, and a racing lever vented cap, all of which come from Stant. There are two important things to note about the Stant range, and the first is that there are no racing caps, nor lever vented caps, available for the 1in neck fitting radiators (Note: It's possible to have a three quarter neck fitted to any radiator). Second, in the United Kingdom, usually only a very high pressure rated lever vented racing cap from Stant is listed in motorsports products catalogues, so it's recommended you visit the Stant website and deal direct. Stant has a wide range of products, racing and non-racing, with the racing caps manufactured to closer tolerances than non-racing products. Also Stant has a lever vent design available in racing and non-racing formats. The lever vent

cap allows cooling system pressure to be released before the cap can be removed. Not least, the racing cap range has a brighter, longer lasting finish when compared to other caps, so will complement a tidy engine bay.

ELECTRIC & ENGINE-DRIVEN FANS

If you want to reduce the engine's coolant temperature by increasing the airflow through the radiator when driving slowly in traffic, or even when stationary in traffic, you'll need to fit a more effective cooling fan. More effective means: a larger fan; or two fans; a fan or fan with more blades; a fan running faster; or a more efficient design of fan blade.

Note that any engine-driven fan is drawing horsepower that could be used

to drive the car, and thereby increase its performance. In addition, an engine fan that provides sufficient cooling in traffic is not really doing much at normal or highway driving speeds, because the airflow through the engine bay is doing all the real work then. If you have a cooling problem when driving hard, it's more likely to be cured by an increase in radiator size than fan size.

All of this may make you wonder why bother to change the fan at all. The answer is, of course, to reduce the power the fan draws from the engine, and the solution is to fit an electric fan (or fans). Of course, if your car already

A Kenlowe fan fitted to an XK Jaguar.

Some things just look right – twin electric fans on this modified Morris Minor.

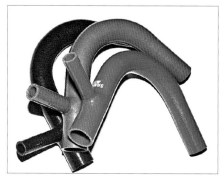

A selection of SAMCO silicone hoses, available in a range of colours for most retros/classics.

uses an electric fan, but has a high engine temperature in traffic, then it may need a second electric fan, or perhaps a larger single fan.

A trip to your local breaker's yard should result in an electric fan that can be pressed into service on your car. The most difficult part of such a solution will be fabricating brackets for it. An alternative is to purchase an off-the-shelf fan. There are several makes, with the Kenlowe recommended as being effective, durable, and having a very long service life. Kenlowe produces fans with blade diameters of ten, twelve and fourteen inches, and both the smaller sizes can be used in dual applications. There's also a choice of fitting brackets, and the fan-to-body mounting, also known as general adjustable bars, is recommended. This type of fitting usually comes with two bars, though if you need a third, Kenlowe can supply it. Once fitted, the activation of the fan can be by a thermostatic switch, direct switch, or a combination of the two.

Warning! As many people have learned from bitter experience (in the form of an under-bonnet fire), you must always use a rubber grommet when passing a wire or wires through any part of the car body.

The Kenlowe, and probably most electric fans, can be made to run in either direction. However, because of the pitch of the fan blades, only one way is correct. With the Kenlowe, fans can be used as push or suction, so decide what side of the radiator the fan will be mounted before ordering.

CORE (FREEZE) PLUGS
On some engines that are tuned for more power (the Ford Pinto, for example) the engine core (freeze) plugs may pop out, immediately releasing most of the engine's coolant. The solution is to drill and tap three holes around each core plug (evenly spaced) so that a washer and bolt can fasten over the edge of the core plug to prevent its release. A more common problem on a classic car is that the core (freeze) plugs will rust away and leak, so they should be replaced during an engine build or if they appear corroded.

HOSES
All the original cooling hoses on classic cars are conventional rubber, and will need replacing when they have either perished through age, or softened and perished due to contamination by fuel or oil, or some other rubber solvent.

In recent years an alternative to rubber hoses appeared, first for the performance after-market, and more recently the classic and performance classic after-market, in the form of silicone rubber hoses. At first they were mostly available in blue but are now available in a wide range of colours

The advantage of silicone hoses over rubber hoses is not that they're available in colours other than black or look cleaner for longer. The hoses have a greater heat resistance, greater vibration resistance, higher pressure rating, are more durable, and will simply outlast a rubber hose.

COOLANTS
In most instances the engine coolant will be a mixture of water and antifreeze (usually consisting of ethylene glycol). Aside from obvious anti-freezing properties and important anti-corrosion properties, ethylene glycol has a higher boiling point than pure water and typically contains anti foaming agents, sequestering agents to prevent precipitation caused by the use of hard water, and silicate stabiliser to protect aluminium components. **Caution!** Never use water on its own.

Chapter 7

Engine oil systems & oil cooling

INTRODUCTION

As with the cooling system, performance modifications to the oil system may produce only small gains in engine power, or none at all, but its importance in preventing damage to the engine cannot be overlooked. An efficient and adequate oil system is an essential requirement because engine oil is a coolant as well as a lubricant.

The more power an engine produces the more heat it produces, which is also very much the case when an engine regularly runs at a higher rpm, due to performance tuning, than it was designed for when standard. Because some of that heat, such as that generated at bearing surfaces, is absorbed by the engine oil, the oil will heat and, as it gets hotter, will gradually lose film strength. If this continues, it will no longer be able to prevent the two metal surfaces from touching, at which point seizure and damage occurs.

OIL TEMPERATURE GAUGE

To establish whether the engine oil temperature is such that film strength is likely to be lost, it's necessary to measure it. Without an oil temperature gauge it's very difficult (but not impossible) to find out what the operating oil temperature range of the engine is. The use of a temperature indicator strip is one method that can be used. However, the real solution is to fit an oil temperature gauge, and further details are given in the electrics and instrumentation chapter. Note that the oil gets hottest when the top end of the engine's rpm range is used, even if for quite short periods.

OIL COOLERS

Having discovered the temperature

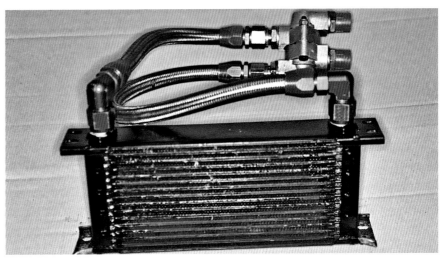

Oil cooler with Goodridge braided steel hose, fittings, and a thermostat.

range of the engine oil, if you find it's regularly hotter than 230 degrees F (110C), the next priority is to fit an oil cooler. An oil cooler is a radiator that exchanges heat between the oil and a cooling medium (usually the cooling medium is air, but it can be the engine coolant). The flow of the cooling medium through the matrix of the cooler unit cools the oil passing through it. Fitting a cooler also increases the total oil capacity of your engine and lubrication system by the capacity of the unit you fit and its associated piping. Before fitting a cooler, the optimum size must be determined. This can be decided by considering how great a reduction in oil temperature you are looking for.

Air-cooled units

Air-cooled oil coolers come in a variety of shapes and sizes, with the most common having a width of nine or thirteen inches (229 or 330mm), and a height of ten rows. All other cooler sizes will have the same width, but more rows (thirteen, sixteen, nineteen, etc). For a well tuned road car, a thirteen inch by ten row cooler is usually adequate. For more highly tuned engines it may be necessary to use a thirteen or even sixteen row cooler to keep the oil temperature around the 212 degrees F (100 degrees C) mark.

It's worth doing some research on your make and model of car to see if it's more demanding in this respect than the average. In other words, does it have a reputation for being hard on oil, or does it tend to run hot? If either or both of these scenarios apply, you should consider erring on the large side for the cooler. Most, if not all, turbocharged engines will have some form of oil cooler already, but if you're planning a considerable increase to the power output of the engine, you may need to fit a bigger cooler. Because an oil cooler will reduce the temperature of the oil across the temperature range, to prevent over cooling of the oil in cold weather, and to assist initial

engine warm up, it's very strongly recommended an oil thermostat is fitted; more of this later.

Oil coolers are usually bought as a kit that usually contains the following: cooler unit, piping, fittings, and mounting brackets. A lot of these kits are universal fittings, but, if a kit is specific to your make and model of car it is preferable to a universal kit. Alternatively, buy all the parts you need separately.

Whatever cooler you buy, assuming it's a standard air-cooled radiator type, it will need to be positioned in a good airflow. If there is space next to the radiator, that will usually be ideal.

Water-cooled units

An alternative to the conventional air-cooled oil cooler is a water-cooled unit. The advantage with this type is mainly that it doesn't require siting where there is a suitable airflow. The disadvantage lies mainly in the cost, which is approximately three times that of air-cooled units. If you fit this type of cooler because siting of a conventional cooler is a problem, be sure to check that your existing water radiator can cope with the extra demand placed on it. If it proves not to be coping, see the chapter on water cooling for a solution.

BRAIDED STEEL HOSE FOR OIL LINES

Generally, most off-the-shelf oil cooler kits are supplied with rubber hoses. In some instances, though, there may be the option of a braided stainless steel line; if this is the case opt for it. The advantages of braided stainless steel hose is the higher burst rating

In-line oil thermostat fitted with Goodridge braided steel hose and fittings.

and higher chafe resistance. Goodridge offers a range of stainless steel braided hose with coloured hose fittings. If you're using braided hoses be sure to use proper P-clip type rubber-lined hose clamps to secure them so they can't move around and chafe anything adjacent to them. Note, in UK motorsports, only braided steel or steel reinforced oil lines can pass through the driver/passenger compartment, and only threaded joints may be used in that area (eg, to a bulkhead).

OIL THERMOSTATS

The only drawback with an oil cooler is that in countries with very cold winter weather it's possible for the oil to be overcooled at that time of year. To prevent this and to shorten the length of time it takes to warm the oil, the solution is to fit an oil thermostat. You'll need to decide at the planning stage whether or not you want to fit a thermostat. The first thing to consider is whether the thermostat can be incorporated into a sandwich plate (a plate with oil inlet and outlet take-offs that fits between the oil filter and its housing). If your cooler installation does use a sandwich plate then this is the neatest solution, and is recommended. If your oil cooler installation doesn't use a sandwich plate then you'll need to fit a separate thermostat unit. There's a further choice here because the unit will use either push-fit or threaded hose connectors. With threaded fittings and braided steel hoses the chances of hose separation from the thermostat, with potentially expensive consequences – are

A sandwich plate, with an integral oil thermostat, enables fitment of an oil cooler.

considerably reduced. However, with care and regular checks, standard hoses and worm-drive clip type fastenings are adequate.

When you start the installation, it's crucial to find the union stub marked 'inlet' for the oil to feed into the thermostat from the engine. Likewise, look for the union stub marked 'outlet' (or 'return') for the oil to return from the thermostat to the engine. **Caution!** This may sound obvious, but if you get it wrong you could end up with a massive build up of oil pressure and a blown cooler. The reason for failure is that when the oil is cold it would be entering into the unit without being unable to exit because the thermostat is in the closed position. For a sandwich plate-type thermostat you generally can't go wrong because it will work in either direction. Finally, while most coolers are unidirectional, check whether yours has a preferred flow, such as left-to-right.

OIL FILTERS

There are two types of oil filter: the modern canister type; and the older element type that fitted into a canister. The element type is always problematic to change, and invariably messy. Fortunately, for popular engines it's often possible to fit a canister filter in place of the original element type by using a later engine-specific filter housing or a conversion kit. Alternatively, a remote filter housing could be used. Think Automotive, and many marque specialists, stock a wide range of suitable kits.

Remote filter & housing

If you've done an engine swap and found the engine oil filter on the new engine is where another component needs to be, for instance, the space that needs to be occupied by the steering rack, the solution is to fit a remote oil filter where there is a suitable space for it. However, try to keep the oil line runs as short as possible to minimise oil pressure drop, and fasten in place with P-clips to obviate chafing. With some engines, you'll need to fabricate your own blanking plate for the space left by the filter, for others they'll also be available from Think Automotive. For those engines that are a popular choice for transplanting, such as the Rover V8, the standard pump also incorporates the filter mounting which can be swapped for a special blanking unit. The blanking plate makes it easier to plumb in an oil cooler.

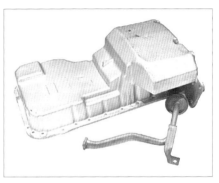

Wet sump for the Ford Pinto engine used in the RS2000 but with development by Burton Power to reduce surge by having modified baffling.
(Courtesy Burton Power)

pick-up pipe, passed through a filter, and delivered under pressure to all of the bearing surfaces via castings in the engine block and head (known collectively as galleries) and via drilled oilways in the crankshaft. The oil galleries also allow the engine oil to drain back down to the sump by gravity. The sump is designed to contain an oil reserve even when oil is circulating as the engine is running. The reserve has to be adequate to cope with sudden demands on it, caused perhaps by a sudden increase in the oil pump's demand due to increased engine rpm. This type of sump and system is known as a 'wet sump' system and tends to be the norm.

Having considered the wet sump, think about what happens inside it when the engine is running. Oil is being sucked out, flowing back in, and the crankshaft is rotating at high speed flicking oil about. As a result of all these factors, the crank is running in a constant mist of oil which can actually cost a little power. Obviously the amount is small but, nonetheless, every little bit counts in the quest for power. The solution to this power loss is to dry sump the engine (more of which later), or to fit an effective windage tray. The purpose of the windage tray is to separate the reservoir of oil from the crank. There are few commercially

A spin-off filter conversion from SNG Barrett for the Jaguar XK engine.
(Courtesy SNG Barrett)

Remote filter fitting with braided steel hose helps the 2000cc Ford Pinto fit in Steve Pratt's MkI Ford Cortina.

OIL SUMP
Wet sump

The engine sump contains the reservoir of engine oil. The oil is sucked up from the sump by the oil pump via a

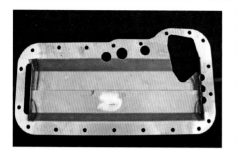

A Fiat X1/9 sump baffle from Vick Autosports. (Courtesy Vick Autosports)

available windage trays, so if you decide on having one you may need to either make your own or approach an appropriate race engine builder to have one made for you.

The sump also needs sufficient oil so that, as centrifugal forces acting on the oil, side-to-side (in cornering) and fore and aft (acceleration/deceleration), cause the oil to accumulate in a particular point in the sump, there is still sufficient depth of oil to be picked up by the oil pump, via the pickup pipe. If the oil level is low, or the centrifugal forces extreme, the pump will pick up nothing but air, and oil starvation will occur, resulting in damage to the bearings and failure of the engine (if it seizes). One way to prevent this potentially disastrous series of events is to limit excessive movement of the oil by baffling the sump. A baffle is a plate with some holes in it, or, at its most sophisticated, one-way flap gates which prevent rapid movement of the oil without restricting the flow to the part of the sump the oil pickup pipe draws from. Burton Power produces a suitable sump baffle for the Ford X-flow engine. For other engines and sumps you may have to fabricate your own, or approach an appropriate race engine builder to have one made. Finally, on certain cars, such as the Mini, where the transmission gears prevent a baffle being used, the solution is to use a special oil pick up pipe, which draws

A typical dry sump, cast in aluminium alloy, from Pace for the Ford X-flow. (Courtesy Burton Power)

Dry sump pump. Courtesy Burton Power)

from the centre of the sump rather than from one side. For some engines, such as the Ford Pinto, it's possible to use an alternative and lighter sump, such as the one designed for the RS2000, with an improved version now being manufactured by Burton Power. Both Burton Power and A Frame Engineering produce non-standard sumps for engines being used longitudinally when they were designed for transverse installation. A further drawback to the wet sump is that the depth of the sump adds to the overall height of the engine, with the result that the weight of the engine and the bonnet line are both higher than they might otherwise be.

Dry sumps

The alternative to a wet sump and the problems it poses is to remove the sump and site it remotely from the engine. This is known as dry sumping because the engine sump does not contain the oil reservoir (and, in fact, isn't really a sump at all). To achieve this a second oil pump is required, and an oil reservoir or tank must be plumbed into the oil system. For popular motorsport engines (such as virtually all Fords), it's possible to purchase a complete dry sump kit from a leading manufacturer/ supplier such as Burton Power.

The disadvantage to dry sumping an engine is the gain in power is likely to be small (single figure increase in bhp) and the cost high. The system will be heavier than the wet sump arrangement, without considering any extra oil the system may require. The undeniable advantage lies in being able to site the engine lower and having a lower bonnet line, as well eliminating oil surge and windage problems. On a classic car that low bonnet line may be not exploitable. So, on balance, this mod is worth consideration, but not the top priority for oil system modification.

Finally, many front engined, front-wheel-drive cars do not lend themselves to dry sumping because the transmission gears run in the sump, which also acts as the gear case.

LUBRICANTS

For high-performance use, or even extending the life of your classic car's engine, it's strongly recommended you use a good quality oil, including synthetics and semi-synthetics, checking first that it will be suitable for your car's engine. Note that many synthetic oils are too 'thin' for classic engines, so check the viscosity rating as part of your research.

Chapter 8
Flywheel & clutch

INTRODUCTION

High-performance modifications to the flywheel and clutch centre on weight reduction, and, because the parts are rotating masses, have benefits over and above any saving in mass alone. Weight savings to the flywheel and clutch improve three aspects of performance: acceleration, deceleration, and cornering (more so than you expect in respect of acceleration).

Warning! Performance aspects aside, there are safety considerations when modifying the flywheel.

For the clutch, modifications to increase clamping pressure and reverse loading improve no performance aspect, but are necessary if clutch problems and failures, due to increased engine power output, or increased rpm (including changing down gears), are to be avoided.

FLYWHEEL

The flywheel is fitted on the end of the crankshaft to store energy from the firing stroke of every cylinder. In addition, it carries the toothed ring gear

A lightened flywheel being balanced, along with the crank, at Burton Power.
(Courtesy Burton Power)

that the starter motor pinion engages to turn over the engine. Last but not least, it provides the mating face for the clutch plate and fastening surface for the clutch cover.

Lightening & balancing

You may have heard that lightening the flywheel will cause problems with engine tick over. There are two responses to this: (a) it probably won't, and (b) tick over is hardly important on a tuned engine anyway. The fact is, changing the cam to one with a greater overlap than standard will have a greater effect on tick over than just about anything you can do to the flywheel. In addition, if the flywheel is balanced after lightening, the tick over may well be smoother than it would be with a standard, unbalanced flywheel.

The reason why flywheels are lightened is that not only are they are a heavy mass (weight), but, as part of the reciprocating mass of the engine, they have to be accelerated in their own right. Less weight requires less energy to move, and therein lies the improvement in performance.

A weight reduction of the flywheel can be equivalent to 15 times the weight reduction of the all-up weight of the car. In practical terms, ten pounds off the flywheel can have the same effect as reducing the weight of the car by 150lb. However, this is only the case for acceleration in first gear – pretty important for a racing start in motorsport, less so for traffic light grands prix. An approximate formula for working out the benefit of flywheel weight reduction is:

$$0.5 \times r^2 \times g^2 + R^2 \text{ divided by } R^2 =$$
weight of the car lb/1lb flywheel weight

(r = radius of gyration, g = gearbox ratio x final drive ratio, R = radius of wheel + tyre)

If you're lightening the flywheel yourself note that the most important place for the weight to come off is the outer radius rather than the centre. **Caution!** If you wish to reface the clutch mating face of the flywheel, the removal of a large amount of metal will cause problems with clutch setup heights, and is, therefore, to be avoided.

Balancing is beneficial because it reduces vibration, and thus stresses on the engine. **Warning!** It's not unknown for unbalanced flywheels to disintegrate; this can also happen with poorly lightened or excessively lightened flywheels. Parts of a disintegrating flywheel can tear through the bellhousing and bodywork like shards from a grenade.

Steel flywheels
Most classic car flywheels are made of cast iron, which places a limitation on how much it can be lightened before it is liable to disintegrate in use. Also, a cast iron flywheel can disintegrate, even when balanced, if very high rpm is used. So, it's a good idea, therefore, to replace the cast iron flywheel with a steel item, greatly reducing the risk of disintegration (to almost zero), while increasing the potential for lightening. The only negative aspect to using a

The back (non-clutch surface) of this steel flywheel has had some detailed machining to ensure as much weight as possible has been removed from the outermost edge.

steel flywheel is that it's more expensive than a cast iron one. There are a variety of tuning companies that can supply you with a steel flywheel, but if you're tuning an unusual engine and are having trouble locating one then Farndon Engineering can make you one.

Aluminium flywheels
Although a steel flywheel can be made lighter than a cast iron one, a lighter option again, however, is an aluminium item. Aluminium flywheels are not made solely from aluminium, but have a steel centre for the clutch mating surface and to bolt to the crankshaft. They are not as widely available as steel flywheels.

Flywheel bolts
Whatever flywheel you use on your car's engine, always use the correct flywheel

ARP flywheel bolts are used on this steel flywheel. Note that the bronze bushing is the crankshaft spigot bush.

bolts (never ordinary 'S' grade bolts). Alternatively, and for minimal extra expense, it's recommended you use an uprated flywheel bolt set, such as that manufactured by ARP.

CLUTCH
The car's clutch will consist of three components: the release (throw out) bearing; the cover; and the plate, or driven plate. If your car's engine is modified and is producing more power, especially more torque, and is likely to operate at a higher rpm than the standard engine, you'll almost certainly need to change the clutch for an uprated item (assuming one's available). If your car's engine power output exceeds the design parameter of the clutch, failure can be in any one of a number of ways. Clutch slip is likely to be the most common failure, and may well be accompanied by a strong smell of burning (the slip causes the clutch plate friction material to overheat). Total failure of the plate may also occur, even to the extent of complete disintegration, which can also damage the flywheel. Depending on your car's engine, it may be possible to get an uprated plate and cover, or just the plate. The release bearing is unaffected by increases in engine power, though alternatives to the stock item are available for some gearboxes, and are discussed later in the chapter. Uprated clutches can vary in their design and composition.

Clutch cover type
The clutch cover will be sprung either by coil springs or a diaphragm. The coil spring design weighs more and has a heavier action than the diaphragm design. For older classics originally fitted with a coil spring cover design, it's possible to replace it with a later diaphragm cover. Conversion kits are available for a whole range of classic engines, including many Fords and the Jaguar XK. If no specific kit appears to be available, then specialist manufacturers, such as AP Racing, can advise on a suitable alternative.

'DS' TYPE COVER ASSEMBLY

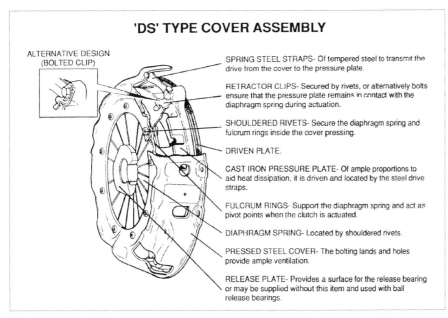

ALTERNATIVE DESIGN
(BOLTED CLIP)

SPRING STEEL STRAPS- Of tempered steel to transmit the drive from the cover to the pressure plate.

RETRACTOR CLIPS- Secured by rivets, or alternatively bolts ensure that the pressure plate remains in contact with the diaphragm spring during actuation.

SHOULDERED RIVETS- Secure the diaphragm spring and fulcrum rings inside the cover pressing.

DRIVEN PLATE.

CAST IRON PRESSURE PLATE- Of ample proportions to aid heat dissipation, it is driven and located by the steel drive straps.

FULCRUM RINGS- Support the diaphragm spring and act as pivot points when the clutch is actuated.

DIAPHRAGM SPRING- Located by shouldered rivets.

PRESSED STEEL COVER- The bolting lands and holes provide ample ventilation.

RELEASE PLATE- Provides a surface for the release bearing or may be supplied without this item and used with ball release bearings.

Components of an AP Racing DS clutch – a suitable performance clutch for a road car. (Courtesy AP Racing)

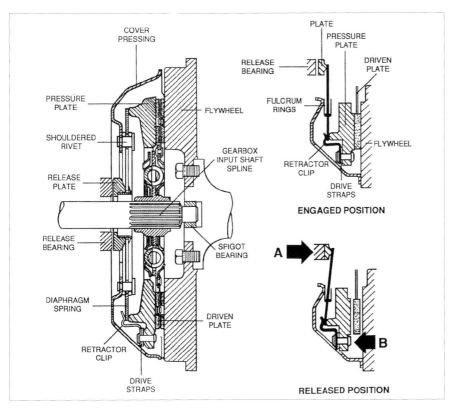

ENGAGED POSITION

RELEASED POSITION

A cutaway view of the same AP Racing DS series clutch, also showing engaged and released positions. (Courtesy AP Racing)

Clutches with organic lining material

Most clutches are described as organic if the clutch lining, the part on the clutch plate that contacts the flywheel, was made from a naturally occurring material, such as asbestos or, in recent years, fibreglass. Most organic clutch plates can be replaced by an uprated organic clutch plate, suitable for road and race use, from AP Racing. It can also advise you if any modifications are required, such as machining the flywheel, before you try fitting the uprated clutch. Note that while a racing clutch can be used in a road car, it will be very 'positive' and unsuitable for driving in traffic, let alone a stop/start traffic jam.

The AP uprated units are based on the standard original equipment Borg and Beck item. AP Racing produces a handy booklet which details uprated options to replace standard clutches. When you're considering an uprated clutch, it's important to consider the use the clutch is going to be put to, as well as the power it's expected to handle. As far as the actual power output is concerned, it's the torque rather than horsepower of the engine that must be considered, so forced induction engines will be particularly demanding on the clutch. For some engines, an uprated plate only is available, whilst for others, an uprated cover is available as well.

Organic friction material clutch plate. (Courtesy Rally Design)

Paddle clutch plate

If an engine is highly tuned and burning out clutch plates, and it's not possible to modify the flywheel to take a larger diameter organic plate, the next step – and it's an extreme one for a road car – is to fit a paddle clutch plate. This is a fully circular plate, but with contact patch areas of lining material, each approximately the size of a small brake pad. These contact areas are known as paddles, and vary in number for any given plate: usually four, but sometimes just three. The lining material is metal based, as opposed to conventional organic material. The rest of the plate is sometimes solid and undamped, sometimes fully damped, as is the case with most organic material plates. The paddle plate is not as smooth to use as a conventional plate, being very much in or out, and therefore needing a lot of slipping when driven in stop/start conditions (heavy traffic). The action can be less fierce if a conversion is used that uses twin (two) plates, but this will require a completely different clutch cover.

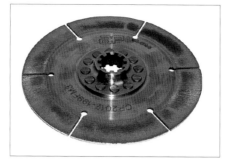

A metal clutch plate is even less suitable than a paddle plate for a road car, unless you never, ever, have to drive in traffic. (Courtesy AP Racing)

Paddle clutch plate suitable for handling large amounts of power, but not a suitable road clutch, other than as a last resort. (Courtesy AP Racing)

Sintered metal (cerametallic) clutch plate

The sintered metal (cerametallic) clutch plate is a single disc of material with no added lining, and is really only suitable for racing cars. The action is very much in or out, with nothing in between. It's also undamped, but does have the virtue of being extremely lightweight and almost indestructible.

Clutch actuation mechanism

Once you start to use modified flywheels and clutches, you can come across problems with the clutch not fully engaging (not having enough 'travel'). The solution is to consider the method of actuation and adjust it accordingly. This is straightforward for an adjustable cable-operated clutch, but difficult for an hydraulic one. It's possible, though, to modify the length of the operating rod, or create an adjustable rod for the slave or master cylinder on an hydraulic clutch to get the travel right if you have problems. The alternative is to vary the size of the clutch master cylinder, which will not only alter the length of travel at the pedal end, but also pedal pressure.

HYDRAULIC CONCENTRIC & COAXIAL RELEASE BEARING CONVERSION

For several classic gearboxes there is a conversion kit to replace the standard method of clutch release – throw out bearing (and carbon bearing if used)

For several gearboxes it's possible to fit a coaxial or concentric hydraulic clutch release bearing – this one from Burton is for the Ford Type 9 gearbox ...

... and here it is fitted to the gearbox.

of an actuated rod or lever – with a wholly hydraulic system. Typically, this is called a concentric or coaxial release bearing conversion. One such example is available for the Ford Type 9 gearbox, whether or not the gearbox is going into an older Ford, Morris, MG, Triumph or Fiat. Available from Burton Power, the conversion provides a neat solution with minimal if not zero lost motion, resulting in smoother operation. There's also a useful weight saving of 0.5kg over the standard bearing guide sleeve (or 0.25kg if your gearbox has been fitted with the aluminium alloy guide sleeve used on the Caterham six-speed gearbox).

Chapter 9
Gearbox

INTRODUCTION

Because the gearbox is a torque multiplier, and because torque makes acceleration, acceleration is the aspect of performance most affected by gearbox tuning. That aside, an engine swap may open up a choice of gearbox,

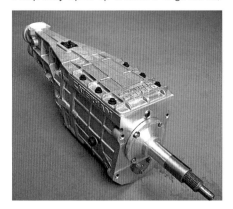

The more ratios the better, six from Caterham and in most Fords, if your wallet can take the strain. The Caterham six-speed gearbox can be fitted with the Ford bellhousing conversion, and has the following ratios: 2.69, 2.01, 1.59, 1.32, 1.13, and 1.00. (Courtesy Caterham)

as is the case when fitting the Rover V8 engine. On the other hand, there may be a lighter or more performance-orientated gearbox, or gearbox part available that would be worth fitting in place of the standard item. On that basis, it's possible to improve one, two, or even three aspects of performance.

Gearboxes fall into two clear groups for the purposes of this chapter: manual and automatic. Of course, there are continuously variable transmission (CVT) boxes, but there isn't much you can do with them by way of modification, and they aren't performance-orientated.

CLOSE-RATIOS

A gearbox exists to multiply the torque (turning force) of the engine, and it's the ratio magnitude, and overall number of ratios, that are the key to unlocking the power of the engine. In case you're sceptical about the importance of gears, when next out for a drive just try accelerating in too high a gear or using every other gear on the way up the gear ratios.

Which is quicker?

Having established how important the gears are, it's equally important to consider the ratios in conjunction with the overall gearing of the car, which means including the final drive or differential (diff) ratio in the calculations. Most classic gearboxes will have three or four ratios, plus reverse, and the occasional gearbox will be equipped with five forward ratios. Some gearboxes will also have an overdrive unit (considered later in this chapter).

However, it's not necessarily the case that your car needs more gears to go faster. Rather your car needs closer ratios in order to accelerate faster. To find out why this is the case you need to look at the engine. Every engine produces power and, more especially, torque in relation to the speed at which it's running. This power output can be plotted on a graph as power output against engine speed (rpm). The plot will look like a mountain in that it starts at nothing, climbs to a peak or plateau, then drops again. Depending on the engine and how it's tuned, this

Excellent for the race track, but straight cut gears – here shown in a sectioned Tran-X Ford box – are noisy and expensive for road use.

'mountain' may be steeper, narrower, etc, and the same can be said to apply to the power band of the engine. For instance, a highly tuned racing engine may be said to have a narrow power band, and this is where the gearbox comes in. In order to keep the engine operating within its optimum power band, it needs different gears. As the car accelerates and engine speed rises, another gear is selected that will ideally drop the engine speed such that it is now once more below the maximum speed (rpm) of the engine, but still at a point in the power band where useful power is produced.

It follows that the narrower the power band of the engine, the greater the requirement for closer gears will be if the engine is to be kept working within its power band. Likewise, the broader the spread of power the engine produces, the less important close gear ratios are. Unfortunately, power tuning, with the exceptions of forced induction (turbo and supercharging), usually reduces (narrows) the power band of the engine.

Whatever the gearbox in your car, there'll always be one ratio (usually on fourth gear), which has a ratio of one-to-one. The exceptions to this are usually found on racing gearboxes and other special units. The one-to-one gear is the one gear that remains the same when the gearbox ratios are changed, so, for the ratios to be closer, the bottom three gears, and any higher than this one, need to change in magnitude to get closer to the one-to-one ratio. What this means in practice is that each gear below the one-to-one gear gets larger, and fifth and sixth may get smaller (though they frequently stay the same). This has the drawback in that first gear ends up being quite a bit higher in a close-ratio box when compared to a standard box. This poses no problems on a racing car, where first is often only used for starting, and then with a low overall gear ratio by virtue of the car's diff ratio. An overly high first gear may pose a problem for a road car, though, and more so if you have to do any city driving, as this can require excessive clutch slip whenever starting from stationary, resulting in a shortened clutch life. The problem is exacerbated by a highly tuned engine with that little bit less power at the bottom end of the rev range. Care must be taken then not to choose too high a first gear when selecting close-ratio gearsets for a road car.

To sum up, then, the greater level of engine tune, the narrower the power band and the greater the need for close gear ratios, but the more difficult it will

Alternative Ford Type N or 9 ratios						
BGH GearTech – 2.0 Long 1st	2.98	1.97	1.37	1.00	0.82/ 0.87	Helical
BGH GearTech – 2.0 Sporting Close	2.92	1.86	1.295	1.00	0.83/0.85/0.87	Helical
BGH GearTech –2.8 Long 1st	2.83	1.81	1.26	1.00	0.825/0.85/0.87/0.89	Helical
BGH GearTech – 2.8 Sporting Close	2.66/2.75	1.75	1.26	1.00	0.82/0.84/0.86/0.89	Helical
Tran-X	2.48	1.69	1.27	1.00	0.87	s/cut
Tran-X	2.38	1.69	1.27	1.00	0.87	s/cut
Tran-X	2.25	1.53	1.16	1.00	0.83	s/cut
Tran-X	2.29	1.62	1.23	1.00	0.83	s/cut
Tran-X	2.16	1.46	1.16	1.00	0.87	s/cut
Quaife	2.39	1.54	1.21	1.00	0.87	s/cut
Quaife	2.745	1.69	1.21	1.10	0.93	s/cut

be to set off from stationary. The reality is a bit less grim, and even moderately closer gear ratios than standard bring improvements in acceleration and driveability.

Close-ratio & other ratio conversions

For some popular gearboxes there are a wide range of alternative ratios available, for others nothing may be available at all. Some of the Ford four- and five-speed gearboxes are very well catered for by BGH GearTech, Quaife, Tran-X and other companies. You'll need to consult marque specialists to find out what's available for your car. The accompanying table shows just some of the available ratios for the Ford Type 9 gearbox.

Calculating rpm drop for any given gear ratio

You'll find details of how to calculate vehicle speed for any given tyre/rear axle combination in the next chapter. However, if you want to work out the rpm drop for any given gear change there's an easy way.

To calculate the rpm drop from first to second gear, divide the first gear ratio by the second gear ratio, then use that figure to divide the change point rpm figure; this gives you the rpm drop. For example, on a standard Ford Sierra gearbox, changing from first to second gear at 6000rpm we calculate 3.65 (1st gear) divided by 1.97 (2nd gear) = 1.852. Dividing this figure into our chosen rpm produces 3239rpm. This is a useful formula when you're choosing the camshaft for your engine, because you know that with the standard gearbox you need a cam that has a powerband that is broad enough to cover at least 3239rpm, and preferably with some margin. However, if you have a close-ratio gearbox, you can probably afford to compromise less on the camshaft. For example, staying with our Sierra box but with BGH Gear Tech sporting close-ratios of first 2.92 and second 1.865 we have a rev drop at 6000rpm to

3833rpm – a reduction of about 600rpm over the standard ratios. Although 600rpm doesn't sound much in the grand scheme of things, it can be the difference between the engine staying 'on the cam' and pulling or chugging up the revs till it's back in the powerband. The difference in day-to-day driving is significant, especially with a 'cammy' engine. Engine camminess aside, the closer ratios will keep the engine performing in its strongest range, which considerably improves acceleration.

GEAR TYPES

In gearboxes there are two types of gear in use: straight cut, and helical cut. Straight-cut gears absorb less power than helical gears, but are much noisier. Helical-cut gears absorb more power than straight-cut gears, but are much quieter. From those simple facts you can see why straight-cut gears are used in racing cars, where power counts for everything and no one minds about the noise. In a classic road car, noise does matter, and, even with all the sound deadening material in the world, you wouldn't want to drive far in a car equipped with straight-cut gears.

DOG BOXES

These gearboxes are for racing cars and use a form of gear engagement known as 'dogs.' The dogs replace the conventional synchromesh mechanism.

OVERDRIVE UNITS & OVERDRIVE CONVERSIONS
What an overdrive unit is

An overdrive unit is a sun and planet gear assembly contained within a casing that fits on the back of the gearbox, such that the gearbox and overdrive unit are treated as a single assembly. While many classic gearboxes were available with overdrive, generally speaking the gearbox casing for an overdrive gearbox is different from the standard gearbox casing, or has a special adaptor between the gearbox and overdrive unit.

The sun and planet gears in the overdrive unit are either: a) locked together to create the overdrive ratio; or b) freely rotate around each other to provide direct gear action. The function is controlled by an internal double-sided clutch that engages a cone, switched in or out by a solenoid, which is operated either by a dashboard-mounted, or gear lever-mounted switch, without the use of the car's clutch. The overdrive action may be inhibited so that it operates only on certain gears, usually third and fourth gears (on older three-speed gearboxes second and third gears), to provide a four-speed gearbox with six ratios. The overdrive ratio will vary with each specific unit. For example, 0.756:1, 0.778:1, 0.797:1, and 0.820:1 which, in use, reduces engine rpm for any given speed by approximately 20 per cent. The most common overdrive units were made by Laycock (sometimes known

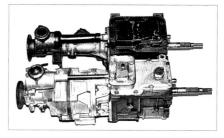

An overdrive gearbox (front), and its non-overdrive (standard) version (rear).

The Hi-gear five-speed conversion being fitted to a car. Note that the tail casing moves the gearlever position considerably further forward of that of a standard Type 9. (Courtesy Hi-Gear Engineering)

as Laycock de Normanville) in varying types (A, D, LH, J and P), found on a hugely diverse range of cars, including Volvos and some Ford Transit vans and Land Rovers. Borg Warner also made some overdrives, and these were used on some Ford Type B gearboxes, including those used in the Consul, Zephyr and Zodiac.

Overdrive conversions

The most straightforward way to provide your car with overdrive is to first establish if your particular classic, or one very similar, was ever fitted with an overdrive gearbox. If it was, source one, have it overhauled, and then fit it (along with a suitably shorter propshaft, and wiring, etc). If your or similar classics weren't fitted with an overdrive, you'll need to consider a complete gearbox and overdrive conversion or suitable after-market conversion kit (scarce).

Overdrive modifications

There's very little that can be done to modify an overdrive unit other than re-working the operating action so that it will be quicker but, consequently, less smooth on engagement. For a classic racing car such a modification

might prove worthwhile, though it's not recommended for a road car.

CASING SWAPS

Some standard boxes can be improved upon by swapping the casing for a lightweight alloy item that is not only

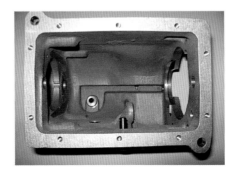

Interior of the Quaife casing showing a drainage channel for the oil drain plug, and the location for the metal particle collecting magnet.

Frontline adaptor plate for fitting the Ford Type 9 gearbox to the Triumph/MG 1500 bellhousing.

Side view of a Quaife Ford Type 9 gearbox case – stronger and lighter than the standard unit.

Five-speed conversion kit including bellhousing and Hi-Gear's own tail casing. (Courtesy Hi-Gear Engineering)

Right angle speedo cable conversion from Caterham – can be used on the Ford Type 9 gearbox.

Type 9 long input shaft (diesel in this case) box on left, four-cylinder engine (petrol) on the right.

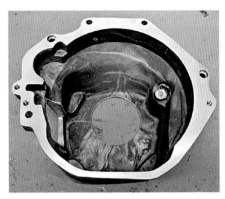

A hybrid bellhousing for the Vauxhall XE to Borg Warner T5 gearbox, with cable-operated clutch from A Frame Engineering. (Courtesy A Frame Engineering)

lighter, by as much as 3.7kg, but stronger than the standard cast iron case. Quaife manufactures aluminium alloy main cases for the Ford Rocket four-speed gearbox and Ford Type 9 five-speed box (as fitted to the Sierra). A more recent lightweight alloy main case is produced by Canley Classics for the Triumph three-rail gearbox.

Gearbox conversions

There are a variety of reasons why you may be looking to use a non-standard gearbox in your car. The standard gearbox may too weak for projected power output, for example, or your car's gearbox is a four-speed and you want a five-speed, or even because the engine you're planning to use *can*

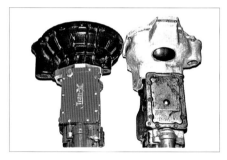

A pair of Ford Type 9 gearboxes. The one on the left has a Tran-X aluminium alloy top cover plate, and a bellhousing for the 1500 engine using the Frontline adaptor plate. The one on the right is fitted with the Morris Minor centre bellhousing for A-series engines.

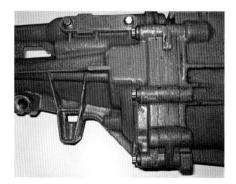

ARP metric stainless steel bolts for bolting the Type 9 extension housing to the gearbox and the reverse lock-out cover.

be fitted with a better gearbox. If you have a Ford Escort with a Crossflow or Pinto engine you might want to use a Sierra five-speed gearbox or a derivative (Caterham six-speed). An alternative would be to use the Cosworth T5 Borg Warner gearbox. A diverse range of other classics, including Morris Minors, MGs, Triumphs, Fiats and Lancias, all have hybrid bellhousings or adaptor plates available to allow the Ford Type 9 five-speed, and derivatives, to be fitted them. There is also a conversion from Dellow Automotive which will allow the T5 box to be used with the Rover V8 and Chevy V8. Broadspeed has a conversion kit to fit the T5 gearbox to classic Jaguars.

FOUR-WHEEL-DRIVE CONVERSIONS

Any four-wheel-drive conversions is going to be difficult, but it's usually less complicated to use the complete engine and four-wheel-drive assembly in one go, whatever it's come out of. An exception would be if you're using Range Rover four-wheel-drive, in that you can hang a Chevy V8 on the front of it via a special Dellow conversion. Other four-wheel-drive conversions might be based on the four-wheel-drive variant of the Ford Type 9 gearbox, or Range Rover engine (usually Rover V8 engine) and drivetrain.

QUICK-SHIFT GEAR LEVERS, SHORTER GEAR LEVERS & GEAR KNOBS

For a variety of Fords, other classics like the Mini, and gearboxes such as the Borg Warner T5, it's possible to replace the standard gear lever (and linkage where applicable) with parts that produce a much faster gear change. B&M makes a lever for the T5 gearbox, and Quaife makes one for the Ford Type 9 and other gearboxes. The quicker gear change can significantly improve the car's overall acceleration. The parts are usually, if not always, a direct swap for the standard parts, and, once fitted,

From left: standard five-speed Sierra gearknob; polished aluminium gearknob; SNG Barrett gearknob.

A quickshift gearlever from B&M for the Borg Warner T5 gearbox.

are an absolute delight to use.

If you have limited funds that don't stretch to quick-shift, a simple and cheap, but second best alternative is to shorten the gearshift lever so that it falls readily to hand. Most standard gear levers are on the long side, but how much you will need to shorten the lever will depend on your seat, seat position, and arm reach. You should be aware, however, that shortening the lever reduces the leverage it provides and, in some cases, this can make the change a bit heavier, but not necessarily slower.

You can approach the job in one of two ways: a) remove the required amount from the middle of the lever and then weld the two halves back together; or b) remove the required amount from the top of the lever, and then re-thread the 'new' top. The method you choose will be dictated only by the tools and equipment at your disposal.

With a gearbox swap you're often obliged to fit the gear knob that came with the gearbox or an after-market alternative, whether in polished wood or aluminium. One interesting alternative for the T5, Getrag, and Type 9 gearboxes is a black gear knob with the five-speed gate pattern etched in and painted white (a near copy of a classic MG/BMC/Triumph or Jaguar four-speed gear knob). One company that can supply them is SNG Barrett.

AUTOMATICS

An automatic gearbox is one which, instead of a having a clutch and flywheel with a conventional gearbox, has a driveplate (flex plate), which also carries the ring for the starter motor to engage for starting. It has a torque converter with a special design of gearbox where gear ratios can either be manually selected or are automatically selected according to a preset of variables the automatic box recognises, eg engine

Aluminium alloy bellhousing for the Spitfire and 1500 MG Midget from Bastuk. (Courtesy Bastuk)

rpm, road speed, throttle position.

Generally, an automatic gearbox is only a performance option for very large engines (which typically might be an American V8). There are, however, a couple of things that can be done to improve the performance of an automatic gearbox.

First, for a wide range of automatic gearboxes there's a range of performance quick-shift gear selector mechanisms available. Second, consider the torque converter stall speed, which isn't designed for a performance road car or engine modifications. A modified torque convertor will ensure that higher rpm can be used when the engine is in gear and held on the footbrake (known as the stall speed), and this will enable a more rapid start when the brake is released. In fact, with a modified engine a higher stall speed may be necessary if power tuning has reduced the engine torque at low rpm, even though it's ultimately much greater at high rpm. Third, it's possible to get an uprated driveplate, which is stronger and more rigid than a standard item.

Automatics often have what can

be termed a 'lazy' gear change, which ultimately results in slower acceleration compared to an equivalent manual gearbox car. It's possible to eliminate that lazy gear change for a sharper shift by fitting what is described by B&M as an 'improver' or 'tranpack kit.' It's also possible to modify fundamental characteristics of the gearbox, such as the road speed at which first gear can either be re-engaged or the rpm any gear can be held to.

Finally, some modifications for automatic gearboxes are to prevent premature failure of the unit or its components by ensuring the operating transmission fluid is kept cool, and there are both cooler kits and larger capacity oil sump units available.

GEARBOX LUBRICANTS

For high-performance use, or even extending the life of the gearbox in normal driving, it's strongly recommended that you use a synthetic oil. In fact, some modern gearboxes specifically require it. However, one important exception is an overdrive unit in which you must **never** use a synthetic oil. Gearboxes usually, but not always, require the use of gear oil.

Readers are recommended to take a look at Richard Michell's *Which Oil? Choosing the right oils & greases for your antique, vintage, veteran, classic or collector car* (also from Veloce Publishing – *ISBN 978-1-845843-65-6*). The book contains everything you need to understand your car's lubrication requirements, and to relate them to modern lubricants. You'll be able to make correct and safe choices, or to seek out appropriate specialised lubricants if necessary, using step-by-step instructions. Answers are also given to many of the most commonly asked questions about suitable oils for classic cars.

Chapter 10
Drivetrain

INTRODUCTION

Performance modifications to the drivetrain will change two, perhaps three, aspects of performance. Changes to the overall gearing can increase, or even decrease, the straight line top speed. A change from an open type differential (which is the conventional fitting), to a load/speed limited-slip differential (LSD), or fitting a viscous coupling (where this is possible), may improve acceleration and perhaps cornering speeds – it will depend on whether traction is a problem. Aside from the aspects of performance, it's important to ensure that the vehicle's drivetrain doesn't break, and has the

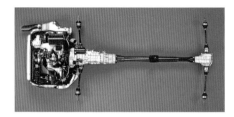

An unusual drivetrain configuration – 4WD with the engine at the back – on this Porsche 911 Carrera 4. (Courtesy Porsche)

right final drive ratio for the use the car is being put to, taking into consideration anticipated changes to the overall wheel and tyre diameter.

Before considering any drivetrain modifications, you need to find out what the existing drivetrain configuration is on your car. It will be one of the following: front-wheel-drive (FWD) with the engine at the front; rear-wheel-drive (RWD) with engine at the front, middle or back; four-wheel/all-wheel-drive (4WD/AWD) with the engine at the front or the back. All of these drive configurations will use driveshafts (axleshafts) to transmit the power to the wheels. However, if the car is RWD with the engine at the front, and has a live axle (a rigid axle case with the driveshafts contained within it), the driveshafts are usually known as 'halfshafts.' On a 4WD/AWD vehicle, driveshafts are usually much the same as other configurations, the main difference being that some 4WD/AWD configurations will have as many as two or even three differentials; more of which later. Once you've established what the drivetrain configuration is on

your car you can now begin to consider the modification options.

PROPSHAFT

Only front engine RWD or 4WD/AWD cars will have a propshaft in the drivetrain configuration, and its purpose is to transmit power from the engine to a final drive unit (RWD) or centre diff (4WD/AWD). A final drive unit includes a differential and, in most cases, a final drive ratio as well. The propshaft may be in one piece with a universal joint at each end, or it may be in two sections with a central bearing. Whatever form it takes, the most important thing is to ensure that it's in good order and have it overhauled if it isn't. Once you have the propshaft in good order, and assuming it's lubricated as necessary, it will be unlikely to break or give any kind of problem. The only thing you can do to it from a high-performance point of view, is to have it balanced by an expert company, such as Reco Prop.

HALFSHAFTS

Halfshafts are the driveshafts used in

It's time for competition-quality halfshafts when the spline on the standard one twists like this (middle), before failing completely (left).

live axle cars. If your classic's been power tuned to any extent, it's likely the increased torque will damage the standard halfshafts. What usually happens is the shaft breaks, though it may twist first. If the shaft breaks there is generally significant damage to the differential, and extraction of the broken portion of the shaft can require complete disassembly of the unit. There are two ways to avoid this scenario; the first is to have the shafts crack tested and, assuming they're OK, them heat treated to make them stronger; the second is to purchase stronger halfshafts from a company such as Quaife. If no uprated shafts are available for your car, then Quaife can manufacture a pair for you in a suitable steel, by using one of your car's old shafts as a pattern. A point to note is that if you're upgrading your car from an open differential to a limited or torque sensing type, the halfshaft will be under greater stress by virtue of the loaded wheel being under greater load, so the strength of the halfshaft needs to be considered – more on diff action later.

DRIVESHAFT

Just like halfshafts, driveshafts can break or twist when subjected to torque that is beyond their design limit, and everything that applies to halfshafts can apply to driveshafts. They can also bend under load or mistreatment. The solution, again, is to buy uprated units.

FINAL DRIVE RATIO

Perhaps the most important decision to make when modifying the drivetrain, is what final drive ratio to use. The final drive ratio is determined by the ratio of teeth on the differential crownwheel to those of the differential pinion. The limitation here is likely to be what is available for the final drive unit you're using, or perhaps any final drive assembly that can be swapped from another model from the same manufacturer. In certain instances it's also possible, within certain limits, to have a specialist gear cutter make up a crown wheel and pinion in the ratio you desire. Before you make this choice, or perhaps in conjunction with it, you need to have decided upon the gear ratios for the car, and have an idea of what top speed you're aiming for (be realistic), and what engine rpm is required to achieve the desired speed.

This crown wheel and pinion has shed a tooth, due to being overloaded, and is now scrap.

First, you'll need to work out the effect of ratio changes using the following formula:

60,000 divided by final drive ratio x wheel revs per mile = mph per 1000rpm in 4th gear (assuming 4th is one-to-one)

To calculate miles per hour in gears other than one-to-one you multiply the top gear mph by 1000rpm and divide by the relevant gear ratio.

Note that you'll need to contact your tyre dealer to obtain the wheel revs per mile (wrpm) figure for your chosen tyres.

Assuming wrpm of 820 (195/60 VR14 tyre) we get:

60,000 divided by 820 x 2.95 = 24.804

Dividing by 3.75 for 1st gear = 6.614mph per 1000rpm
2.235 for 2nd gear = 11.098mph per 1000rpm
1.518 for 3rd gear = 16.339mph per 1000rpm
1.132 for 4th gear = 21.911mph per 1000rpm
0.928 for 5th gear = 26.728mph per 1000rpm

A point to remember when choosing a final drive ratio is that a numerically high number is actually a lower final drive ratio. If you don't know exactly what any final drive ratio is, it can be calculated by counting the number of teeth on the crownwheel and dividing that number by the number of teeth on the pinion. For example: 41 teeth on the crownwheel divided by 11 teeth on the pinion produces 3.727. What the ratio actually means is that the gearbox output shaft turns 3.727 turns for each revolution of the wheels.

DIFFERENTIALS

Any typical classic car, except some high performance models (fitted with one of the limited slip types of diff), is always going to struggle to put down all its available power through two or even four wheels, at the same time, and especially mid corner. The simple reason for this is that the differential doesn't allow it, and that goes for four-wheel-drive cars (4WD) that can have three diffs, one for each pair of driven wheels and one for the split front-to-rear.

When a car is cornering the outside wheel has to travel further than the inside wheel and, in practice, it achieves this by turning faster. The drive from the engine to the wheels (except for some vintage cars) is always to both driven

An open (standard) diff assembled with the CWP in a diff carrier.

wheels, whether the car is FWD or RWD and to all four wheels in a 4WD/AWD drive car. However, the driven wheels need to turn at different rates when the car is turning a corner, otherwise the outer wheel (which is travelling further than the inner wheel) would tyre scrub and single wheel, wheel-spin.

The solution is a mechanical system of sun and planet gears which can allow one wheel (or, in a 4WD/AWD, a pair of wheels) to turn faster than the other when it needs to, but also allows both wheels to turn together the rest of the time, all things being equal. Of course, all things are not always equal, especially when one wheel is more lightly loaded than another due to cornering forces and body roll. The differential in its most basic form is described as being 'open,' and is 'dumb,' allowing the power passing through it to always take the course of least resistance, and that means the wheel with least grip. Ultimately, the wheel with least grip spins progressively faster, since once it's spinning it has no grip and the diff is happy to feed all the power to it, taking the course of least resistance. That spinning wheel, which isn't gripping, causes a general loss of momentum until grip is re-gained and momentum is reduced, usually after the car has slowed down because centrifugal forces and body roll have reduced as a consequence of less momentum.

The same scenario applies for a standing start which will result in one wheel spinning excessively and the other producing wheelspin to a lesser degree. Aside from a loss in acceleration, the diff doesn't take kindly to being excessively wheelspun, and can fail completely.

The solution to these problems is to replace the standard 'open' differential with a type that will prevent or reduce wheelspin. These are known as Limited-Slip Differentials (LSDs) though, for some types, the term is a misnomer. LSDs can be classified into two distinct types: those that operate by sensing load, sometimes known as Torque sensing (TorSen), and those that operate by sensing speed. A third alternative which performs a similar task to a limited slip diff is a viscous coupling.

LIMITED SLIP TYPES

Depending on what classic car you have, an LSD might be already fitted as either original equipment (OE) by the manufacturer, or by a previous owner. Even if your car does have an OE LSD, it may still be possible to swap it for a different type or a different model, depending on your preference and, perhaps, the use to which you intend to put the car. For those cars equipped with an open differential you'll have to find out what's available for your make and model.

Dealing with load sensing types first, the most common after-market fitting will be the Quaife, and, as an OE fit, the TorSen (first seen in the original Audi Quattro in the 1980s and still used in Audis and other performance road cars today). Of the speed sensing types, these will be clutch pack/plate types. As after-market options for road cars, there's generally a choice between the Tran-X or Gripper, the more recent Jack Knight, and the, no longer available new, Salisbury Power-Lok. Original equipment clutch plate types for road cars are most likely to be ZF, as fitted to some BMWs and Ford Capris. Other

diffs you hear less of are the Cam and Pawl (ZF or Jack Knight).

When looking for an LSD bear in mind that, quite often, the manufacturer of your car will often have a higher spec OE LSD for use in a higher specification model or as an option (eg Sierra 4x4, TVR, etc). Make sure you know what type of LSD it is: load sensing or speed sensing, as well as knowing the brand name because brand names can be misleading. Also, note that several manufacturers have used a variety of different LSDs in their models over the years – not just switching makes but type as well. BMW, for instance, has used ZFs clutch packs and TorSen gears.

A point to check when buying secondhand, is that if the final drive ratio isn't the one you need, then your existing crown wheel and pinion will have to be swapped, and setting the backlash is a job for an expert.

Torque sensing (TorSen)

As mentioned earlier, one of the most widely available after-market torque sensing diffs is the Automatic Torque Biasing (ATB) Quaife. It consists of floating, helically-cut gear pinions meshing with sun gears, producing a progressive limiting action which is free on wheel overrun and never fully locks. This type is slightly more expensive than some others, but if you

The same CWP and diff carrier but with a Quaife ATB (automatic torque biasing) diff.

A sectioned Quaife ATB (automatic torque biasing) diff.

Clutch pack/plate

The most common type of speed sensing (or non-TorSen) LSD is the clutch plate/pack type – a true 'slipper' or 'slippery' differential. ZF calls it the 'Multiple Disc Self Locking,' and the diff consists of the normal sun and planet gear arrangement like an open diff, but is, crucially, stronger, in having two pinion pins and four planet gears instead of just the regular one pin and two gears. The limiting action is achieved by the design of a series of clutch type plates. The ZF, Gripper, and Tran-X have a two-pin, four-gear design, but the Xtrac Salisbury type has a three-gear design. When the differential is in use these plates lock or release according to the loading on the differential in conjunction with pre-set friction limits. The limiting action of the plates allows drive to be transferred to the non-spinning wheel. This type of

... and here's a closer look at it.

plan to keep the car for many years, or drive high mileages, in the long-term, it should represent the best value for money. It's also probably the most suitable type for a classic road car. In use with a full throttle standing start, a Quaife locks almost instantly, which, in rear-wheel-drive cars does produce a quick flick out of the rear end which needs correction with opposite lock. Mid-corner the action also locks (but not solid), across both wheels, so no forward momentum is lost except where a driven wheel lifts (likewise for the TorSen except for the very latest ones which have built in pre-load). The reason for this is the Quaife requires residual torque, and, with a driven wheel in the air, it doesn't get any. Momentum is lost till the airborne wheel lowers providing residual torque again. Of course, if your car doesn't lift a driven wheel, this simply doesn't matter. With a Quaife in a front-wheel-drive car on a standing start you need only a finger light touch on the steering wheel and the car simply pulls forwards in a straight line. In other driving conditions there will be less understeer compared with a clutch pack plate diff. Quaife aside, TorSen has an after-market performance range, but this is primarily aimed at the US market. A final point on TorSen diffs, whether the original or the ATB from Quaife, is that because they work by a system of gears and not clutch plates they are not truly a limiting slip diff, and are not 'slippers' but 'whirly gears.'

Anatomy of a clutch plate limited slip diff – this is the Gripper for the Jaguar and shows (from left): the clutch pack assembly; the diff carrier, and the bevel or side gears.

In this sectioned clutch plate diff carrier you can see the clutch plate type diff ...

differential is likely to have a higher wear rate than a Quaife ATB or TorSen diff, and will need periodic re-building with replacement plates, whether an OE diff from ZF or a Tran-X. A key difference between a clutch plate diff and the TorSen is the former doesn't have a locking action such that both wheels have near equal power transmitted to them, but switches power to the wheel with most or all the grip. The ratio of the slip can vary according to what you ask for, but typically might be 30-70 per cent. So, with one driven wheel fully airborne, the other wheel is still fed up to 70 per cent of the available power and, mid corner, almost full momentum is maintained, unless, of course, you break a halfshaft or driveshaft. From a full throttle standing start with a clutch plate/pack diff, acceleration is much more rapid than with an open diff, and wheelspin is possible, which produces a dramatic but stable fish-tailing or snaking action in a rear-wheel-drive car that shouldn't be corrected – let the diff sort itself, point the front wheels straight ahead, and feather back on the throttle until grip is regained. On a front-wheel-drive car, the car can weave from side-to-side slightly on full throttle starts.

A final point on slipper diffs is that they can be tuned to suit your driving style and your car, at the point of manufacturing or rebuild, particularly the latter, with significant differences in the settings between front-wheel-drive and rear-wheel-drive cars.

Cam and pawl

The cam and pawl type LSD was invented in the 1930s, and was first produced by ZF. More recently other manufacturers made cam and pawl LSDs, including Jack Knight. The cam and pawl is better suited to the race track, than the road, by virtue of its maintenance and wear characteristics, and is, therefore, not recommended for road use. Further, some users have even described it as 'ratchety' and harsh. It's a relatively rare diff, and generally much more expensive than other LSDs.

Welded diffs and spools

If you have very limited funds, or happen to be a drag racer, you can do without a diff action altogether and weld up the sun and planet gears to get what is, perhaps not surprisingly, known as a 'welded' diff. A neater alternative is to have something similar made, which, by virtue of design, will be a lot lighter. Known as a spool, the welded diff is 100 per cent locked all the time, and, from a standing start, drives like a TorSen or Quaife, only more so. Mid-corner, however, it is closer to a slipper. If you have to drive it slowly round town, it will be unpleasant, noisy, and jumpy, because one wheel will be snatching and scrubbing all the way through a corner, especially a tight one.

Viscous couplings (VC) (Ferguson)

The viscous coupling (VC) was invented in 1969 and was used on 4WD and FWD cars, such as Lancias, the original Jensen FF, and some very specialised rally, touring, and Indy cars. A Ferguson VC is usually placed between one driveshaft and a driven wheel; as grip is lost at one wheel due to wheelspin, the coupling provides increasing resistance and ensures drive is transferred to the other wheel. On 4WD cars, a viscous

A stripped down Ferguson viscous coupling. (Courtesy FFD Ricardo)

coupling is sometimes used instead of a central differential, to control the amount of driving force (torque) transmitted to either the front or rear wheels, depending on which has the most available grip. There are no after-market viscous coupling conversions.

Phantom Grip

Something different in the diff world is the Phantom Grip. This achieves a very similar result to an LSD, but for a fraction of the price. There's no catch,

The Phantom Grip unit.

but you get what you pay for and, while with a true LSD you purchase a completely new diff with the limited action, with this product you keep your old diff, adding the parts to change the way it works. The product is called Phantom Grip and, when fitted to any conventional open diff converts it to a limited slip action.

The Phantom Grip unit is sprung, and two spring ratings are available: gold for street use; and green for competition or more aggressive use.

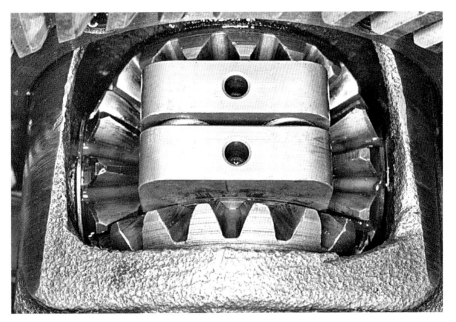

The Phantom Grip installed in what was a conventional open diff.

Also included with the unit and the alternative springs are comprehensive illustrated fitting instructions (these assume the diff you're going to use is in good condition). Because the Phantom Grip modifies your car's existing open differential, it requires the old one to be removed from the car (be sure to have the necessary gaskets, tools, including a torque wrench, and confidence to undertake the job before proceeding).

A typical installation of the Phantom Grip will require partial dismantling of the differential, since the unit is installed with the diff cross-pin running through its centre, with each side positioned to work against the sun gears. The sun gears benefit from having their rough surface facing smoothed off with emery paper, to aid the break in process of the Phantom grip, otherwise the differential can be re-assembled and re-fitted. However, given that unlike the fitting of a conventional LSD, the Phantom Grip uses all of the existing differential parts, you might want to give consideration to having the differential overhauled at this point.

In use, and from a standing start, the action falls somewhere between an open diff and the Quaife, which, in practice, means it's progressive in action but very driver friendly. When cornering, where grip levels are exceeded, the unit is again very driver friendly, allowing a steady four-wheel drift to be maintained, and the car driven and steered on the throttle. In summary, you get what you pay for and, while this product isn't a match for a pure LSD, it's a good budget alternative.

MAKE YOUR SELECTION – WHAT TYPE OF DIFF AND WHY

Assuming there's more than type of diff action to choose from for your classic, your selection needs to based on the type of driving you're going to do, the type and weight of your car, and how much you can afford and how often, eg for rebuilds. Generally, a load sensing diff like a Quaife is more suited to road

use than a clutch pack/plate because it will wear well and is reliable, but is held to be less effective than speed sensing types if the car will be cornered on three wheels (eg on the racetrack). That said, a lightweight but powerful car with a high degree of roll stiffness may lift a wheel on the public highway. There is no such drawback with the speed sensing diffs that are available, but because the plates can wear very quickly, even with very regular diff oil changes, they can work out very expensive in the long run. If you bear those two factors in mind, and base your decision accordingly, you should get value for money. The welded diff or spool is the cheapest of all, but with the most drawbacks and is for track use only. The other budget option – the Phantom Grip – is road user friendly, inexpensive, but ultimately not as strong as true LSDs. Last, but not least, the viscous coupling is not available as an after-market option. However, if may be possible to transplant one from a higher or sporting specification model similar to your own car, assuming you have a base model. In short, it's simple but effective.

DIFF CARRIER

Some classics, and in particular Fords, use a cast iron differential carrier or housing. If your car has a cast iron differential carrier it's worth the money to have it replaced with an aluminium alloy item, bearing in mind it's not just a weight saving but an unsprung weight saving. Burton Power can sell you one.

Recently, Weslake has produced

Alloy diff carrier from Burton Power to replace the cast iron item on the Ford English axle. (Courtesy Burton Power)

diff conversion using BMW open and BMW limited slip diffs in conjunction with Weslake manufactured components to produce a straightforward bolt in diff swap for Triumph Stags and TR6s. The diff is available with standard BMW ratios of 3.72 to 1, 3.64 to 1, and 3.46 to 1.

AXLE CASING BEARING SURFACE REPAIRS USING A SPEEDY SLEEVE

While axle casing problems aren't a performance consideration, a regular loss of diff oil will cause problems, and this short section will provide a useful solution not found in other books. So, if you find that you're regularly getting an oil leak from a rear wheel hub on a live axle, and replacing the hub seal

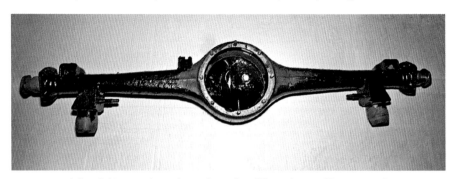

A 'banjo' type axle casing, where the diff can be readily swapped.

The bolt-in BMW-based diff conversion for the Triumph TR6 from Weslake. (Courtesy Weslake)

Speedy sleeve.

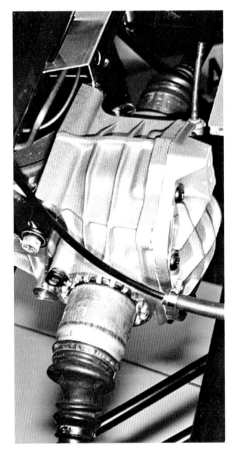

RWD diff carrier with drive shafts (ie: not a live axle).

(or gaskets and O rings) isn't solving the problem, it's likely the axle casing itself has a worn or damaged surface where the oil seat runs on it. You may be able to see an indication of wear on the exact point that the oil seal should run, and may find a fine wear groove. It's this groove that prevents the oil seal doing its job effectively for very long. With a worn axle casing, replacement of the oil seal will not prevent oil or grease escaping for long. New axle casings haven't been available for some time for most classics, so you have to search around for a secondhand casing in better condition and swap the whole casing, or effect a repair.

The repair is made by using an axle casing repair section (wear sleeve) which is known by the brand name of 'Speedy Sleeve' by Chicago Rawhide, and retailed via any SKF bearing supplier. The sleeve repair sections come in a variety of sizes, complete with full installation instructions. Before fitting the repair sleeve, it's recommended you remove the brake backplate and

then check that the axle casing shaft is clean and shiny (if not, it will need to be cleaned so that it is without burrs or rough spots). If you find burrs or rough spots they will need to be carefully filed off with a file or emery stone. If there's a deep groove where the old seal has run (there is bound to be some groove) the installation instructions advise a light smear of sealant at that point, or even some kind of powdered metal glue. An installation tool is provided in the kit but may not be suitable for all axle casings, in which case a suitable size of pipe will be needed instead. If you're extremely careful, and the sleeve is not really tight on installation, it is just possible to lightly work around the flange of the sleeve with light taps of a nylon-headed hammer until the Speedy Sleeve is installed in the required position without damaging the sleeve.

Now that you have the sleeve fitted, it only remains to re-assemble all the parts, including a new oil seal.

Chapter 11
Brakes

INTRODUCTION

Improvements to the braking system of your classic car will change one, and, possibly, two additional aspects of performance. Primarily, the improvement will be to the deceleration (braking), with acceleration and handling improved if the weight of the braking components are reduced. Because the braking components comprise unsprung weight, the advantage in reducing weight is greater than would first appear.

Warning! Braking might well appear an uninteresting part of your car's performance. However, when modifying a classic car, it's more important that it will stop fast than accelerate fast. The brakes on your car are what makes it stop, which seems a pretty obvious statement to make; think about what you're taking for granted, though, and then give some thought to the demands you place on the brakes, and what they have to do.

The key principle when thinking about brakes is understanding they do the opposite to the engine, in that they decelerate the car. The quicker you want the car to decelerate, the harder the car's brakes have to work. In terms of overall performance, while a car's rate of acceleration is determined by its power-to-weight ratio, its rate of deceleration is determined by its braking power (torque)-to-weight ratio. Similarly, a car's rate of deceleration is determined by its braking power (torque) to weight ratio. A further consideration is that the brakes need to be consistent in delivering the braking torque; in other words, they work as effectively for a low speed stop as for a very high speed stop with no weakening in performance or feel – ie, they don't fade.

Given that a car's braking performance is determined by its braking power to weight ratio, then two changes to the car will stop it quicker. The first is more braking power, the second is less weight. Note that second point about weight because, although no one usually fits less powerful brakes on a car, they often put more weight into it.

Another aspect of braking is that, just as a more powerful engine will require more cooling, so more braking power will require more cooling. The harder the brakes work, the more heat is generated. Sometimes, the only reason more powerful brakes are fitted is that they are easier to cool by virtue of their design, more of which later. However, the most efficient solution is to use the smallest brakes, and thereby lightest, that will get the job done, and have a small safety margin in reserve.

Another limiting factor in braking performance also bears comparison to acceleration and that is grip, or lack of it. Just as excessive power can cause the tyres to lose grip, with resultant wheelspin and loss of acceleration, so the reverse is true of excessive braking power. Once the wheels are locked and the tyres are skidding, deceleration is largely lost. Put another way – you need to match braking power to grip. An increase in grip can shorten the braking distance if the braking system can utilise that grip.

Disc brakes, especially at the front of the car are preferable to drum brakes, as they are far more resistant to brake fade by the nature of their design, so are a very desirable upgrade.

1. Replace brake fluid with new fluid of DOT 4 or 5.1 rating, and regularly replace at 12 month intervals or more frequently.
2. Replace all rubber flexible brake hoses with braided steel flexible brake hoses.
3. Replace friction material (pads/shoes) with high performance material.
4. Replace front drums with discs, or fit larger front discs, vented and grooved if possible.
5. Fit larger and lighter brake calipers.
6. Replace rear drums with discs or grooved type brake drums, as applicable.

All of the above factors make it quite hard to plan what the braking upgrades need to be. However, following each section of this chapter in order will prevent unnecessary expenditure. To help you make those choices consult the top six options.

BRAKE FADE & OVERHEATED BRAKES

Reduced braking efficiency, long brake pedal travel, and a strong burning smell are all symptoms of brake fade, which can be caused by overheating of the friction material, or fluid, or both. When the brake fluid boils, the symptoms will be a soft brake pedal (which sinks to the floor in extreme cases), coupled with a drop in braking power. When the friction material overheats, the pedal will remain firm, but there will be a drop in braking power. A strong burning smell does not mean that the friction material is fading, but it is close to overheating.

On a classic car with uprated friction material, the most likely cause of brake fade is fluid overheating, and a change to a DOT 5.1 fluid, or a racing fluid on a classic racing car, eliminates the problem.

If brake fade occurs even with competition friction material and brake fluid then it's recommended to upgrade the brakes to a larger and thicker disc (more of which later), except where class regulations in motorsport require standard brake discs or drums to be used. In that instance it will be necessary to provide a flow of cooling air from appropriate ducting.

BRAKE FLUID

The brake fluid you use in your car's braking system is as important to braking performance as the brake components themselves, and in many respects is more important, and so merits consideration before the rest of the braking system. The best braking system money can buy will perform poorly if the brake fluid isn't appropriate for it. A modified classic car that uses the brakes more demandingly than a standard car, will require a better brake fluid than that normally specified. This is because, as the brake components dissipate heat when in use, some of that heat is passed to the brake fluid. When the temperature of the fluid reaches its

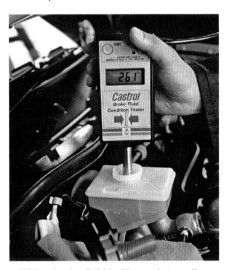

With a brake fluid boiling point reading this low, using a Castrol brake fluid tester, the biggest improvement to the brakes will be fresh brake fluid. (Courtesy Castrol)

boiling point it vaporises. The vapour is compressible, resulting in a depressed brake pedal compressing vapour instead of displacing fluid, the net effect being no, or very poor brakes. The solution is to use an appropriate fluid of one of three main categories: mineral, silicone, and polyglycol based.

You are only likely to find mineral fluid in classic Citroëns and Rolls-Royces. If your car is one of these and is using mineral fluid you mustn't use anything else, and be particularly careful about any changes made to the braking system, checking with the supplier of any non-standard hydraulics parts before fitting, to check that they'll work safely and satisfactorily with mineral fluid.

For all other cars, either silicone, or more conventional polyglycol, fluid is used. The principal difference between silicone and polyglycol fluid is that the former is not hygroscopic (it does not absorb moisture from the atmosphere). Silicone brake fluid may preserve the interior of hydraulic pipes, it also has a long service life, but is expensive and isn't suitable for most performance applications (the reason being it becomes compressible at high temperatures and does not have a 'dry' boiling point as high as racing fluids). Silicone fluid may not be hygroscopic, but if any moisture or water is present, or is introduced, it remains 'free' water, and can produce vapour lock at temperatures as low as 100C (212F). When changing from polyglycol to silicone fluid, or vice versa, you'll need to thoroughly clean the system, and possibly renew the pipes and seals, though not everyone agrees on this point. This is because, although silicone and polyglycol fluids are compatible, they are not miscible (they will not mix). There are problems with brake seals when silicone fluid has been used, especially on older cars, and some brake parts manufacturers specifically don't recommend it.

All fluids are graded in relation to the way they are affected by

	DOT 3	DOT 4	DOT 5.1	AP racing 551
Dry	205C	230C	268C	269C
	401F	446F	514F	516F
Wet	140C	155C	191C	151C
	284F	311F	375F	304F

temperature. There are four common standards: DOT 3 (J1703); DOT 4; DOT 5 (silicone); and DOT 5.1 – DOT 5 (silicone) values aren't included in the accompanying table since its use isn't recommended. The DOT value relates to the wet and dry boiling points of the fluid. The dry boiling point is measured using fresh fluid. The wet boiling point is measured after the fluid has been exposed to a controlled humidity and has, therefore, absorbed some moisture. The respective dry and wet boiling points for DOT 3, DOT 4, DOT 5.1 and a racing fluid are as shown in the chart above.

It can be seen from the chart that a higher DOT number equates to higher dry and wet boiling points. The 'dry' standard is the important one because frequent changes ensure the fluid never comes close to being classed as 'wet.' Fluid changes every 12 months or less (monthly for cars used in motorsport) is recommended. Consult AP for fluid change intervals if you are using that company's racing fluid (because of its low 'wet' boiling point it requires changing at more frequent intervals than conventional fluids).

Castrol DOT 4 and AP DOT 5.1 will give good service when used in a classic car whatever brake components are fitted. Don't be tempted to use a race fluid in a road car – it's not designed for such use, since it has a comparatively low wet boiling point. Put another way, a race fluid goes off (to the wet value) much more quickly than a normal fluid.

Although DOT 3 brake fluid is recommended for some classic cars, at least in the USA, a number of problems have been reported when using it. The solution to any problems that might be experienced using DOT 3, is to use Castrol LMA DOT 4 fluid, which, apparently, does not give any problems, and, in fact, has the benefits of a higher DOT rating.

SPEED BLEEDERS

One useful upgrade to any braking system is to replace the standard zinc-plated steel nipple with a stainless steel speed bleeder nipple. There are a couple of advantages in making this change. Firstly using a stainless steel nipple removes the problems of nipples corroding in the calliper or the wrenching head, both of which can cause problems when they need to be removed. Secondly, the speed bleeder nipple has a built-in check valve so that the brakes can be bled by a single person.

Speed bleeder valves are available in a range of sizes, and can also be used on non-standard braking applications.

The Speed Bleeder brake and clutch bleed nipple doesn't only allow effective single person brake bleeding, but is also available in stainless steel, so it won't end up seized in position, as might be the case with the standard nipple. Note the smaller wrenching head on the Speed Bleeder, and the rubber dust cap.

BRAKE HOSE

The standard rubber brake hoses can be replaced by stainless steel braided hoses, such as those from Goodridge. The fittings for the hose may be of steel, stainless steel or anodised aluminium alloy. Using this type of hose results in a much firmer brake pedal that not only provides better braking 'feel' but a faster action on the initial application. It's possible to buy an off-the-shelf kit for many classic cars. If, however, you can't find an off-the-shelf kit, it's not much more expensive to have the hoses custom-made. If you're using non-standard callipers on your car, you may need to have custom-made hoses anyway. **Warning!** Whatever hoses you use, especially when brakes, wheels, and suspension components have been modified, make sure there's no contact between hoses and anything else through full suspension articulation and steering movement. If there's contact you must re-route the pipe or use a different length of pipe to remove the problem.

From top-to-bottom: steel braided hose with banjo type fitting; Goodridge steel braided hose; rubber hose.

WORKING TEMPERATURE RANGE OF BRAKES

It's essential that you establish the working temperature range of the brakes on your classic so you can be sure that both the friction material and brake fluid will be operating within their design limits. To do this it's necessary to use thermal paint (available from

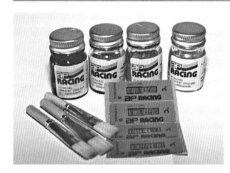

The sure way to determine whether the brakes are operating within their working range is to use the AP Racing heat sensitive paint kit.

Grooved and vented disc, with temperature-sensitive paint on a 1975 Chevron B36 classic endurance racing car.

AP Racing and its stockists) on the brake discs and or drums (though it can also be used on the edge of pads and shoes). Alternatively, AP Racing temperature indicator strips can be used on the brake calipers and drums.

Full instructions are included in the kits, which, if used correctly, will provide you with vital information concerning the temperature range of your car's brakes. The green paint, for example, turns white at 430C.

FRICTION MATERIAL

Brake friction material, sometimes known as brake lining, is the material bonded or riveted onto the metal part of a brake pad or shoe. The friction material makes contact with the brake disc or drum friction surface when the brake pedal is pressed. This contact creates friction which ultimately slows the car. The friction, in turn, creates heat, and it's this heat that can cause problems. The harder the brakes are used, either because of the speed or weight of the vehicle or the level of deceleration being attempted, the greater the heat developed. For a high-performance classic that's been power tuned, the standard brake friction material may not have a sufficiently high heat rating to cope with the use it's being put to. There are two solutions: one is to improve heat dissipation of the brakes by fitting larger or more effective components, such as grooved and vented discs; the second is to fit a friction material that has a higher heat rating. In some instances, the only choice will be to choose the latter and, in others, the problem may be such that both approaches will need to be adopted. However, this section deals only with friction material. **Warning!** Too high a temperature range friction material will result in glazing of the pad surface, and poor, if not dangerous, braking performance (such a material will not work well at the relatively low temperatures generated by normal road use). Put another way, don't be tempted to use racing friction material on a road car in the mistaken belief that the brakes will work better. The reason for this is that any friction material has an effective working heat range that includes a lower limit as well as an upper one. With racing friction material, although the upper limit is higher than that of road material, so is the lower limit, and when working outside its working range it's ineffective. Simply, racing material doesn't work when cold. The solution is to buy a performance friction material suitable for road use. This is straightforward enough when buying pads for disc brakes, but for drums you may need to have the shoes re-lined with a suitable material (specialists like Cambridge Motorsport can do this).

An interesting point about friction material is that some material can outperform another not just by having greater resistance to fade, but by having superior grab and bite at initial application. In this respect the Hawk compounds are particularly impressive.

GENERAL HYDRAULIC PRINCIPLES

If you're contemplating changes to the hydraulic components of your car, bear in mind the basic principle of an hydraulic system: the pressure put into the system (depression of the brake pedal) will produce an equal pressure elsewhere in the system. However, the equal pressure exerted elsewhere is proportional to the area in which it is applied. For example, a system pressure of 1000psi would produce 1000lb on a one inch square piston, but only 500lb on a piston half the size. That same 1000psi on two square-inch pistons would produce 2000lb. What that means, when you are modifying the brakes, is that if you increase the sizes of the slave end of the braking system, ie, the brake caliper piston area by size (or quantity), or the drum slave cylinder piston area, you'll end up with more brake travel than you had originally, because more fluid is required to fill the larger voids left by the displaced pistons. An example would be fitting

A remote master cylinder from AP Racing. (Courtesy AP Racing)

General principles of hydraulics

Change	Effect	Solution
Increase in slave piston size because of larger piston size or number	Longer brake travel, softer pedal	Increase master cylinder size
Increase in master cylinder size because of larger piston size or number	Shorter brake pedal travel, harder pedal	Fit brake servo or increase servo size
Reduction in slave piston size or area	Shorter brake pedal travel, harder pedal	Fit brake servo or increase servo size
Reduction in master cylinder size (in isolation of any other change)	Longer brake travel, softer pedal	Don't reduce master cylinder size

large-piston, four-pot calipers on the front brakes to replace drums.

Alternatively, if you change the master cylinder size you achieve the same effect in reverse. For instance, if you find that the new pedal travel is excessive, then, to restore the status quo of the system, you'll need to fit a larger master cylinder. However, if you replace a single master cylinder with twin cylinders, increasing master cylinder area may be unavoidable, and you will increase brake pedal loadings. The only way to reduce them back to something more manageable will be by fitting a brake servo, or, if your car already has one, fit a larger servo, or even twin units.

The input pressure is derived from the pedal effort exerted by your right foot multiplied by the leverage ratio of the pedal.

PEDALS

There aren't many instances where you might want to change to a different brake pedal. However, if you do, note that not all pedals have a similar leverage ratio. The range is normally from about 3:1 up to 5:1. If you assume a pedal pressure of 100lb, you will have hydraulic input of 300lb or 500lb depending on the pedal ratio, so it does

make a big difference. What one person considers a 'firm' pedal another may consider 'soft.' However, 100lb appears to be an agreeable figure, with less for servoed brakes. In any event, maximum required pedal pressure should not exceed 300lb for a man and 200lb for a woman. I mention these figures because they may be useful if you're calculating what size servo may be required.

MASTER CYLINDER(S)

You might need to change the brake master cylinder to one with a larger piston, or to fit dual master cylinders, as part of a conversion to have adjustable brake bias (more of which later), or to solve an engine bay clearance problem. In any case replacement may be difficult. The reason for this is that on most cars the brake master cylinder is likely to be mounted as part of a purpose-designed assembly in conjunction with the brake pedal. On some later classics this will take the form of a combined master cylinder/ servo unit. The assembly is not easily replaced other than perhaps by something very similar (larger bore in the master cylinder) from the same manufacturer. For some makes, such as Fords, it's possible to buy an off-the-shelf conversion kit. If there's no kit for

your car it may be possible (and easier) to adapt a kit from another car than to fabricate one from scratch.

For straightforward master cylinder swaps take a look at the range from AP Racing, and note that quite often the fluid reservoir may be sited remote to the cylinder. Be careful about sizing the cylinder, and seek expert advice if in any doubt.

SERVOS, INCLUDING REMOTE TYPES

Brake servos are sometimes known as 'power boosters'; an accurate description. However, what gets 'boosted' is the power of your leg rather than the hydraulic pressure exerted. As such, a brake servo does not improve the efficiency of the braking system; it reduces the amount of pedal pressure required from the driver to achieve a given amount of hydraulic force. Put another way, a brake servo makes hard braking achievable without having to press as hard on the brake pedal. In itself this might not seem a significant improvement, but it's particularly useful in making the transition from driving a classic without servo assistance to a modern car that has. Having said that, having full hydraulic pressure available with a firm push without herculean effort does allow the full utilisation and potential of the car's braking system, which might not be available instantaneously for non-servo-assisted braking systems, particularly so once wheel and tyre sizes have increased.

As mentioned in the master cylinder section, some cars have a servo built into the brake master cylinder assembly, while others are a wholly separate unit plumbed into the brake system. Turning to the rating of the servo itself, if you assume a typical manifold vacuum versus atmospheric pressure across the servo diaphragm giving an applied vacuum pressure of ten psi, then multiply it by the area of the diaphragm, you get the value of pressure assistance. The size of the diaphragm is usually expressed as a

Remote servos, while standard fitting on the Avenger Tiger as seen here, are available in a range of types and sizes for any classic, and avoid the hassle of fitting a modern combined servo and brake master cylinder unit.

diameter, such as ten inches, rather than an area, or occasionally a boost ratio such as 1.9:1. To calculate the area, first halve the diameter to get the radius and then multiply the radius squared by pi. Note that if a non-standard carburettor or fuel injection manifold is used it might be the case that the servo draws on vacuum from one inlet rather than all the engine inlets, so that it operates at less than full capacity.

If you want to change to a different brake master cylinder, perhaps to fit a twin master cylinder setup, you may need to fit a different combined master/servo unit or fit a remote servo to restore acceptable pedal pressure.

An engine swap, for instance, might place a demand on space in the engine bay. It might even be the case that the servo cannot be sited in its original location and, perhaps not in the engine bay at all. If this is the case, then it's important to size both the master cylinder and servo correctly. Refer to the accompanying General Principles

of Hydraulics table if you've made other braking system changes which will have a bearing on the size of the components you select. The choice of remote servos is somewhat limited, though it's possible to use them in pairs. Finally, it's possible to do away with the servo altogether – if you can live with the pedal pressure required.

BRAKE BIAS ADJUSTMENT

Because of the weight transfer from the rear to the front during braking, some cars, especially front engine front-wheel-drive cars, have a pressure limiting valve to ensure that the front brakes lock a fraction before those on the rear. With modern cars fitted with anti-lock brakes, this is all taken care of by the system. For most classics, however, the front-to-rear brake bias is part of the braking design of the car, with the brake sizes (including slave pistons) such that the front brakes lock before the rears.

Warning! Modifications to the

braking system can cause problems with anti-lock systems so seek expert advice before modifying cars so equipped.

Where a limiting valve is fitted, it will, in most cases, be unable to respond to improvements you make to the braking system, weight, or balance of the car. So, if you've considerably lightened the car, or even increased its weight, you may find you have a braking balance problem. For instance, consider a typical iron block, front engine rear-wheel-drive car. The standard engine is replaced by alloy Rover V8 that sits further back in the car. The weight, and weight bias, of the car will have changed considerably – a recipe for brake bias problems. However, on many cars, the front brakes are usually sufficiently larger than the rears for things not to get out of hand. But, if you want spot-on brakes, you'll need to adjust the brake bias. The easiest and best way to do this is by fitting an adjustable bias or proportioning valve. Once you have the valve installed, all that remains is for it to be set so that in dry conditions the front wheels always lock a fraction before the rear wheels.

The alternative method, with the advantage of being more readily adjustable, sometimes in the car, of allowing brake bias adjustment front-to-rear is to fit twin master cylinders in conjunction with a balance bar. This type of installation is a lot more involved and expensive than using a bias valve. If a proprietary kit is available then use it, and, where one is not, you'll need to build something from scratch. The advantage of having in-car adjustable brake bias is only realised in motorsport where the bias would be changed according to local track conditions – wet, damp or dry (the car's tyres responding to the different levels of grip and therefore having different amounts of weight transfer).

LINE LOCKS

A line lock is a piece of equipment that, when plumbed into the brake hydraulics, allows the front brakes to be isolated from the rears, and, in effect, allows the use of two-wheel braking.

There are two situations when you might want to do this. The first is that in a rear-wheel-drive car you can switch all the braking force to the front wheels, put one foot on the brake pedal to lock them and the other foot hard on the throttle and perform a drag racing-type burn out with the car remaining stationary. The second situation is where all the braking force is switched to the rear wheels. The foot brake can then be used to lock the rear wheels in isolation, giving the same effect way as using the handbrake to perform handbrake turns.

If you plan to fit a line lock, you'll need to look at the schematic for the braking lines on your car to ensure that they're suitable. If the system has dual circuit brakes it may not be possible to fit a line lock.

BRAKE DISCS

It's the brake disc size (diameter and thickness) that ultimately determines braking power. However, disc diameter is limited by the diameter of the wheels used on the car. For a vehicle with thirteen inch diameter wheels the choices are very limited, but if your classic car uses fourteen inch or larger diameter wheels, or can be modified to take them, then the choice is wider.

Disc diameter is important because the further the calipers are from the centre of the wheel, the greater the leverage ratio applied to their action (force x distance applies). Because braking friction produces heat, which the disc absorbs but has to dissipate, the larger and thicker the disc the greater the physical mass of metal and the greater the heat energy that can be absorbed for any given temperature rise. Disc thickness is secondary to disc diameter in importance, because while an increase in thickness and therefore mass, aids heat absorption, it does nothing for dissipation (which an increase in disc diameter does). Because dispersion

Drilled and vented disc from Tarox. (Courtesy GGB (Engineering Spares) Ltd)

Grooved and vented disc from Tarox. (Courtesy GGB (Engineering Spares) Ltd)

Grooved and drilled disc on this Datsun Z series.

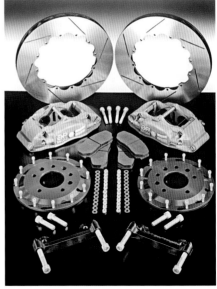

Everything you'll ever need in a brake conversion kit. (Courtesy AP Racing)

The Coopercraft four-piston caliper conversion for the MkII Jaguar. (Courtesy Kev Moore)

of heat is so important to disc design, some disks are vented (ventilated) to aid cooling. Sometimes, a vented disc is made from two halves, and in others it's one piece. A problem with early designs of vented discs is that they had a tendency to warp when overheated. **Warning!** The design of the vanes in a vented disc can be such that they're handed for each side of the car, and this is a point to watch when fitting vented discs for the first time.

Some discs, whether vented or not, have grooves in the friction face. The grooves are designed to aid the release of hot gases generated during braking. Some discs are drilled to aid brake cooling, and, although it's possible to have a set of discs drilled after purchase, this has been known to lead to problems with cracks propagating from the drilled holes during service life.

ROAD & RACE CALIPERS

There are three main differences between road and race calipers: race calipers are much more expensive; they are made from aluminium alloy (or magnesium alloy), sometimes with titanium pistons and are, therefore, lighter (road calipers are usually cast iron with steel pistons); they don't have dirt/dust seals.

However, it's no longer the case that aluminium calipers are exclusive to racing cars. AP Racing and others have produced a range of affordable aluminium calipers for road use which, while not quite as light as race calipers, are still considerably lighter than cast iron calipers. The weight advantage is very useful but, that aside, because the calipers come in a range of sizes, it's relatively easy to upgrade both disc and caliper for a whole variety of cars.

The AP Racing road calipers also have the all important dirt/dust seals. Racing calipers do without these seals because the calipers used on a race car are frequently stripped, cleaned and reassembled (after each race, usually). Also, their usage, though hard, is limited to track conditions that are clean in comparison to the public highway. Ingress of dirt is, therefore, not a major problem, and those regular re-builds ensure even slight piston or cylinder wear is remedied by replacement or scrapping as appropriate. On a road car the reverse conditions apply and, therefore, racing calipers should only be used with caution, and this should be borne in mind when making your purchase.

The size of the caliper is important

because an overly ambitious choice, especially in relation to the disc size, whether or not standard size discs are used, can lead to wheel clearance problems. The other consideration is that a larger caliper will weigh more and increase unsprung weight, though switching to an aluminium caliper redresses this problem somewhat, if not completely.

CALIPER PISTONS – HOW MANY & TYPE

A disc brake caliper may have one, two, or even four or more pistons, sometimes known as pots. The single caliper piston is an economy design which has a mechanism to replicate the action of a pair of pistons both being pushed onto the disc during braking. It's more likely to be found on a rear disc brake assembly than a front disc brake assembly, and isn't a high-performance option. Perhaps most common of all

Twin-piston lightweight caliper from AP Racing. (Courtesy AP Racing)

Two different sizes of four-piston lightweight caliper from AP Racing. (Courtesy AP Racing)

is the two- or twin-piston caliper, with a piston acting on each side of the brake disc. While the design is sound it prevents the use of large or long brake pads, even if each piston is increased in size. An improvement on the twin-piston caliper is the four-piston caliper which has two pistons on each side of the discs and a relatively long brake pad. If there is a conversion for your classic that replaces twin-piston calipers with four-piston calipers it's worth consideration.

The piston in most standard brake calipers is steel, sometimes coated or chromed. Over time that coating will corrode and can lead to sticking in the caliper cylinder. For some classics, for a slightly higher cost, it's possible to get stainless steel pistons; recommended, since they'll be less trouble in service.

DRUM TO DISC CONVERSIONS
Front brakes

For some popular classics with very long production runs, the classic Mini, for example, the first models had drum brakes while later ones, or performance versions, had disc brakes. Therefore, with careful selection of parts, it's possible to convert from front drums to discs. For other cars, such as a variety of Fords, it's possible to use parts from a different model, with an adapter kit to upgrade from drum to disc. For other classics, such as the Morris Minor and XK Jaguars, there are dedicated kits from classic specialists to convert from drum brakes to disc brakes.

Rear brakes

If the rear of your classic is fitted with drum brakes, then, in the vast majority of cases, it will be difficult to replace them with discs. The reason for this is that although it's relatively straightforward to fit discs and calipers in place of drums, as is the case with many racing cars and modern road cars, a road car must have a handbrake (parking brake). So, fitting a small disc and caliper setup to the rear axle of your

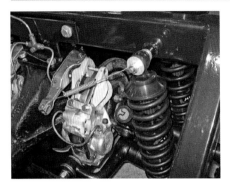

A problem with fitting discs to the rear of a road car (in the UK) is that of having a separate handbrake mechanism. This isn't something a racing-orientated conversion will have, but the car shown here does.

Braking distances

On a good dry road an average car should be able to stop in the distances detailed in the table below a modified road car in less. On a wet road you could probably double the distances.

Speed	Speed in feet/second	Braking distance in feet
30	44	45
45	66	101
60	88	180
70	102	245
90	132	405
100	147	500
120	176	720
130	191	845
140	205	980

One mile = 5280 feet
60mph = 1 mile a minute, or 5280 feet a minute, or 88 feet per second.

car may infringe legislative requirements unless it incorporates a working handbrake. For some cars, suitable rear disc conversions do exist.

DRUM BRAKE MODIFICATIONS

For some models it's possible to replace the standard cast iron drum with aluminium alloy items. The advantage is in the reduction in the overall weight of the car and, in particular, the unsprung weight. Aluminium drums will usually be the Alfin type with cooling fins, or the Minifin type with ribs rather than true cooling fins.

Much more widely available than aluminium alloy drums are cast iron Tarox drums, with grooves machined

Datsun copied the Alfin drum to create its own finned aluminium alloy drums for the Z series, as seen here on this 240Z.

into the braking surface. The grooves allow hot gas and brake dust to be released, and this permits the brake shoes to operate at maximum efficiency. However, if you have done the brake testing recommended later in this chapter, you may find that the car actually doesn't need any more braking force on the rear (assuming the vehicle is disc/drum – front/rear), so such a purchase would not be necessary.

BRAKE DYNO TESTING & ROAD TESTING

After each modification to the braking system on your car you should do a static check. For this you will need to have the engine running to provide a vacuum for the servo and, with the car stationary, press and hold the brake pedal firmly down. Check that the pedal is not only firm, but stays firm and doesn't sink. If the pedal is 'spongy,' there is air in the system that will need to be bled out. If the pedal slowly sinks there is a fluid leak that must be stopped. **Warning!** Under no circumstances drive the car until the problem is fixed. If the static check

is satisfactory, a low speed (15mph) emergency stop can be undertaken. If the car pulls to one side, check that the brakes on the opposite side of the car to which it pulled are working properly and are not seized.

If the low speed check is satisfactory the car should be driven to a vehicle testing station and the brakes checked on the roller brake tester. The braking torque figures should be noted and any problems rectified. The final check can only be undertaken at a reasonable speed and, therefore, for safety reasons, done on a private road or race track. Emergency stops are undertaken such that the wheels lock. **Warning!** The front wheels need to lock first. If the rears lock first a tail slide will follow, leading to a spin. This problem is most easily rectified by fitting a brake bias valve and adjusting the front-to-rear setting. An alternative approach would be to increase the size/power of the front brakes or reducing the size/power of the rear brakes. Once all that has been done it's possible to measure stopping distances from 60mph to zero using a G-Tech performance meter.

Chapter 12
Suspension general

Changes to a car's suspension will affect the cornering speed aspect of performance. However, to a lesser extent, the other three aspects of performance may also be affected. Acceleration and deceleration both cause a weight transfer to take place, and the suspension plays a part in limiting these effects. Straight line top speed may be improved because a reduction in ride height has reduced the coefficient of drag.

The general principles and advice on suspension are contained in this chapter; subsequent chapters cover specifics with regard to front or rear suspension. Although the means of achieving suspension modifications vary in relation to the type of suspension the car being modified has, the general principles are the same for all types of design.

Before you can get the best results from modifications to your car's suspension, you first need to put the car through a total alignment check to find out what condition it's in. For instance, are components old and worn, possibly

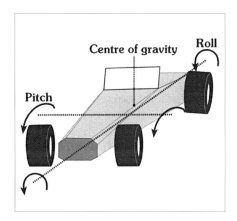

The principal forces applied to a car are roll and pitch.

even damaged, poorly set up? Once you have a clear starting point you can plan, cost, and then carry out the modifications in a logical sequence as suggested by the 'Order of decision' table (page 88). You may, however, still want to evaluate the effect of each change before undertaking another. Part of that evaluation will also require you to have at least a rudimentary understanding of what the car does,

and how the suspension responds to it, why it does it, and what it's called. Useful advice on how to solve or reduce undesirable effects can be found in the 'Solving Handling Problems' table (page 88); but first the basics.

UNDERSTEER & OVERSTEER

Whenever a car turns, its tyres create a sideways or cornering force. This results in the tyre running with a 'slip angle' (the angle between the direction in which it is pointing and the direction in which it's being forced to travel by the inertia of the car). The front and rear tyres rarely run at the same angle when the car is cornering. When the front tyres run the greater slip angle the effect is known as 'understeer,' and is usually felt by the driver as the front end of the car wanting to run slightly wide of the cornering line. If the rear slip angle is the greater, the condition is known as 'oversteer.' The driver usually feels the rear end of the car wanting to run slightly wide of the corner.

Generally speaking, a front-wheel-

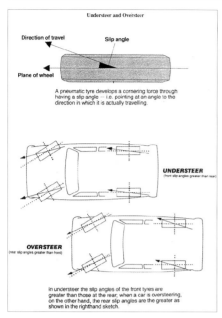

Understeer, oversteer and slip angles graphically illustrated. (Courtesy Michelin)

drive car will tend to understeer, and a rear-wheel-drive car will tend to oversteer. If you want to know what the difference feels like in practice, go for

Double wishbone with an adjustable coil-over shock on the Caterham 7.

a drive in a front-wheel-drive car, and then, straight afterwards, a rear-wheel-drive car, or vice versa.

There's a lot of talk about whether it's better to have understeer or oversteer, the truth is it's better to have neither. A neutral handling car, or, in our case, tuned suspension, is the ideal to aim for. Note that the generalisations about understeer and oversteer are just that. It's possible to have a car that will have slight understeering properties when cornering hard, but cornering harder will produce a sudden and large amount of oversteer. That sounds awful, but in practice the handling may be predictable and perfectly safe. **Warning!** Predictable handling rather than precise but nervous handling is preferable; but it's your car and your choice.

ROLL

As a car is cornered there's an outward weight transfer which the car body reacts to by rolling about its centre axis. The amount of roll is dependant on many things, including the height of the car (more specifically the centre of gravity), the weight of the vehicle, its resistance to roll (a feature of suspension), the amount of grip, and the speed the corner is being taken at. However, the greater the roll the greater the reduction in grip at the wheels due to camber changes induced by the roll. Put another way, as roll increases, the tyre contact patch with the road is reduced in size, and so the car is less able to respond to steering input and proceed in the manner intended. Furthermore, the lighter-loaded wheels, which will be the innermost ones in relation to the corner, will have little or no useful grip, possibly resulting in the driven wheel spinning. Roll, therefore, is one of the greatest enemies of good cornering.

PITCH

As a vehicle accelerates or decelerates there's a weight transfer – either front to rear for acceleration, or vice versa for deceleration. The effect this has

is to either load or unload the driven wheels (except for 4WD vehicles), and the steering road-wheels. In practice, because increases in load increase grip, it means that a FWD car with a rearward weight transfer under acceleration has less grip at the driven wheels and steered road-wheels, being therefore likely to lose traction and steering. For a RWD car the traction will increase under acceleration, but the steering will be less affected than it would in a FWD car because the front wheels are being asked to steer only, and not transfer tractive force as well. All of this explains why purpose-built dragsters are RWD.

COMPLIANCE

Because the vehicle suspension is usually (but with some exceptions) mounted in rubber bushes or other moving joints, such as trackrod end bearings, there is some give and take. This give and take is known as compliance and, when bushings and joints age and wear, the compliance can become excessive and lead to sloppiness or vagueness in handling. The remedy is replacement of the worn parts.

DAMPING

When a car spring has a load put into it, for instance under braking, the spring absorbs energy and compresses. Once the load has been released, the spring decompresses. A spring, by its very nature, will want to repeat the cycle, known as oscillation, which is undesirable and dangerous. The spring is prevented from oscillating by the damper (shock absorber), which, as its name suggests, damps the action of the spring. Springs and dampers need to be matched, and a change in spring should be accompanied by a change in damper (other than for very minor differences from the original fitment). The reason for matching is that a spring that's overdamped is prevented from working effectively, and the damper overworks, leading to premature wear and perhaps fade, the latter a condition in which it

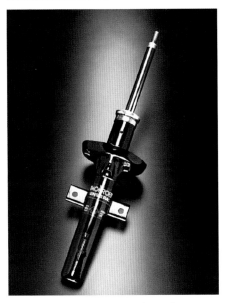

Some dampers, as shown here, form part of a suspension strut. (Courtesy Tenneco Automotive)

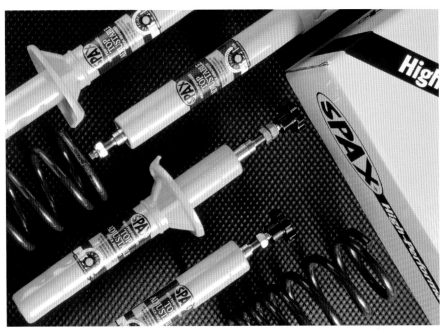

It's often easier to ensure the spring and damper are matched by buying the components in a kit; like this one from Spax. (Courtesy Spax)

Adjustable coil-over shocks from Edelbrock. (Courtesy Edelbrock)

overheats and then ceases to function properly. If the damper is too weak for the spring, then oscillation can occur. For these reasons, it's recommended that you purchase springs and dampers as a single package, or purchase adjustable dampers.

CAMBER

Camber is the angle at which the wheel and tyre sit in relation to vertical (in relation to the centre line of the axle). Camber is important because it needs to be correct in order to maximise the grip from the tyres, especially at the front. Ideally the camber should be zero. However, because the camber of the front wheels changes as the car rolls it's desirable to have a slightly negative static camber, so, as the car rolls, the wheels move from negative to zero camber, and maximum grip is realised from the tyres.

Lowering the ride height of the car often changes the static camber setting and, because the lowered ride height of the vehicle causes a reduction in sideways weight transfer, body roll is reduced, so less static negative camber is needed to maximise tyre grip in a turn.

UNSPRUNG WEIGHT

The majority of the car's weight is supported by the springs, and this is known as 'sprung weight.' The weight of all components not supported by the springs, including the springs themselves, is known as 'unsprung weight.' The unsprung weight, therefore, typically includes: wheels, tyres, brakes, springs, and half the weight of the damper (shock absorber) and suspension links. Note those parts that connect from the vehicle body to the suspension (or form part of it) only count as half weight because one end is part of the sprung weight of the vehicle, the other end unsprung as part of the suspension. It's possible to reduce the unsprung weight by careful suspension design (using such devices as rockers to work with inboard springs and dampers, and therefore comprise sprung rather than unsprung weight).

Increasing the ratio of unsprung

to sprung weight, especially when it's achieved by reducing the unsprung weight, will improve the general handling of the car and traction (grip) in acceleration and braking, particularly on bumpy road surfaces. The reason for this is that weight creates inertia, and the less inertia the unsprung components have, the more easily will the springs keep the tyres in contact with the road. Reducing the car's sprung weight will worsen the ratio, though there are many benefits in reducing the overall vehicle weight. Increasing the car's weight will improve the ratio, but the benefit will be negated by the poorer handling and general performance. The preferred solution, therefore, is to reduce both unsprung and sprung weight by careful selection of components and thereby achieve as high a ratio as possible.

TOTAL ALIGNMENT CHECK

A total alignment check involves considerably more than just checking the tracking of your vehicle. Although this type of service is relatively common in the USA, it's scarcer in the UK, though Pro-Align in Northampton is one company that can undertake it. A total alignment service is based around the use of computerised infrared measuring heads fitted to each wheel. The wheels are then checked for run-out (buckling). The next series of checks produces a computerised printout of: toe, castor, king pin inclination, and wheel set-back

The bare minimum alignment check should be the front wheel tracking as being done here.

Solving or minimising handling problems

Excessive roll	Fit or uprate anti-roll bar
	Reduce ride height
Excessive pitch	Increase spring rates (stiffness)
	Reduce ride height
Excessive spring oscillation	Fit new or uprated dampers
General vagueness	Increase compliance (renew or uprate bushes and suspension joints)
Understeer	Increase negative camber
	Increase toe-out at front
Oversteer	Increase toe-in at front
	Stiffen front anti-roll bar

The laser tracking gauge from Gunson, used here on a wire-wheeled Sprite.

for the front wheels, and toe, thrust angle and camber for the rear wheels. A copy of the information is yours to keep for reference, and should form the starting point for any rectification you need to undertake.

TRACKING – GAUGES

It's always been possible to check tracking yourself (assuming you had a suitable gauge). Unfortunately, a typical optical tracking gauge is likely to be prohibitively expensive; in the order of between 15-20 times the cost of having the job done professionally. More recently, Gunson has produced a laser tracking gauge that potentially pays for itself after being used as few as three-four times. The gauge is easy to use, portable, and will work on wire-wheeled cars.

ORDER OF DECISIONS FOR CHANGES TO THE SUSPENSION

Having covered the basics on car

suspension, it's time to move on to planning some solutions:

1. Identify major problems (alignment and suspension checks)
2. Make wheel and tyre selection
3. Ride height
4. Spring stiffness (front and rear)
5. Roll stiffness (front and rear)
6. Damping
7. Compliance (bush) stiffness
8. Camber changes
9. Steering system changes

RIDE HEIGHT

Reductions in ride height will reduce body roll because the centre of gravity is lowered. There's also a benefit in that pitch will also be reduced. Lastly, there may also be a reduction in the amount of air travelling under the car, thereby improving the coefficient of drag and increasing straight line top speed. Ride height is mostly controlled by the springs (whatever form they take:

This Eibach pro kit includes all the major suspension components to lower and stiffen the suspension. (Courtesy Eibach)

torsion bars, hydragas units, etc) though the wheel and tyre combination can also affect it. If the car has coil springs, a change in their height (or the heights of their mounting platforms) will alter the ride height of the car. Whatever the spring rate on your car it should be possible to purchase a set identical in every respect other than overall height. However, since most lowered springs also have uprated spring rates, you may well need to establish spring rates in conjunction with ride height. If you're happy with a spring rate, but cannot get springs in the height you want, and aren't keen on the expense of having a set of bespoke springs made, you can consider lowering their installed height by some kind of spacer to lower the spring pan (where the springs are coil springs). If you're really desperate, you can cut a set of coil springs to shorten them but it's not recommended.

Other types of spring can be set lower, as is the case with torsion bars and hydragas units, by re-setting them in accordance with the workshop manual, or the work can be done by a specialist.

SPRING RATES

The spring rate – the strength of the spring (usually expressed in pounds) – particularly on the front of the car, should be considered as part of the overall modifications to the car, and not just suspension modifications. This is because changes to the overall weight of the car change the degree to which the springs have to work. For instance, if as part of your modifications you are swapping engines – such as cast iron four-cylinder to aluminium alloy V8 – the all-up weight of the car may be lighter because the aluminium alloy V8, which, although a larger engine, is lighter than the original. On the other hand, if you're fitting a larger cast iron engine, the overall weight of the car can increase. That said, the amount of increased spring stiffness you can live with will depend largely on your own preference and the type of roads you spend most time driving on (smooth dual

carriageway, or bumpy country lanes).

In addition to the all-up weight of the car, the springs need to be considered in relation to the anti-roll bars (where fitted). It's always better to reduce roll by increasing roll stiffness by increasing anti-roll bar size (diameter), than spring rates. This is because the roll bar stiffness has much less affect on straight line driving, almost negligible, than increases in spring stiffness.

Before buying springs, take a look in the workshop manual for your car and find out what the standard rate is for your model. Consider, then, whether the existing springs are so old that they might have gone soft, and ask yourself whether all the car really needs is new springs of the original rate, rather than something harder? It's possible to have a spring checked to find out what its rate is. If you find that none of your local garages has the necessary equipment, try a local racing team or specialist spring supplier.

With or without details of your old spring, you can still ask your spring supplier what spring rates are on offer.

ANTI-ROLL BARS

One of the most obvious ways to reduce roll is to increase roll stiffness, and one of the best ways to do this is by fitting an anti-roll (sway) bar. These are commonly found on the front of

the car but are sometimes fitted on the rear suspension, too. The anti-roll bar works by resisting loading (weight transfer) on the outside wheel, as the car corners, and thereby reduces roll. The reduction in roll reduces changes in tyre camber that are detrimental to the size of the tyre contact patch. The key advantage of the roll bar isn't just that it reduces roll, but that it only has a pronounced effect when the car does roll. This is unlike the situation of fitting stiffer springs, which will reduce roll, but will have a pronounced response to road bumps, even when travelling in a straight line.

Once fitted, an anti-roll bar links both sides of the suspension (front or rear) on a single axle. Often, but not always, the anti-roll bar is additionally mounted at a central point on a subframe or chassis section. For cars that already have anti-roll bars fitted, it's often possible to further limit roll by increasing the thickness (diameter) of the bar. In addition to the use of a thicker bar, in some instances it's possible to have the rubber in the roll bar mounting replaced with a less compliant material, like polyurethane, nylatron, or even aluminium alloy.

Ride height and spring stiffness must be set before selecting an anti-roll bar. The reason for this is that the lower and stiffer the front end of the car is, the

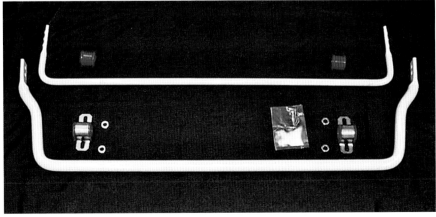

A couple of anti-roll bars (with the performance option of polyurethane bushing). (Courtesy Flyin' Miata)

less weight transfer there will be, and therefore less work for the anti-roll bar to do.

Anti-roll bars are rated by thickness, expressed in fractions of an imperial inch or in millimetres. Note that only a few millimetres or sixteenths of an inch can double the stiffness of the bar, so, when testing for the optimum bar size, only go up a size at time. The reason for this is that stiffness increases as a fourth power of change in diameter. Put another way, you have to multiply the thickness four times to calculate a stiffness value. As an example, a 22mm bar gives an end value of 234,256, while a 26mm bar has a value of 456,976 (26 x 26 x 26 x 26). You can see that while a 26mm bar is only slightly thicker than a 22mm bar, it is almost twice as stiff.

Should you find your requirement is for something in between the diameters commercially available, locate a specialist supplier able to make a one-off bar for your classic.

BUSHES & JOINTS

When suspension bushes or joints are old and worn, the suspension will have more compliance that it was designed to have, and handling will suffer. Replacing worn out parts will produce an instant benefit. For improvements beyond fitting new parts, and for certain makes and models, it's possible to get uprated bushes with less compliance than standard. A stiffer and better medium

Some dampers, like the AVO item shown here, are on-car adjustable.

for bushes than rubber is polyurethane, and several suppliers exist that have a wide product range so can accommodate most makes and models. Nylatron and similar hard plastic materials are also widely available for many applications. However, the use of Nylatron as a bushing material is not recommended for road use, as it's much too stiff. Likewise, spherical rod end bearings (rose joints) are also not recommended for road use because they are insufficiently compliant.

SHOCK ABSORBERS (DAMPERS) GENERAL

At each 'corner' of the car there will usually be a shock absorber to go with each spring. The shock absorber's job is to damp the oscillations of the spring to ensure that the wheel and tyre stay in contact with the road. If uprated springs are fitted to a car, an increase in damping stiffness will be required to go with them. However, even on their own, changes to the shock absorbers can produce useful benefits in ride, handling, and braking. In fact, you can radically improve the overall performance of your car not so much as by fitting uprated shock absorbers but by replacing standard units that are worn. If just one shock absorber is faulty (perhaps working at only 50 per cent efficiency) the ride, handling and braking will suffer to a marked degree. With just one defective shock absorber, a car will typically require an extra 8.5ft to brake to a standstill from 50mph. With worn shock absorbers, aquaplaning (loss of grip in the wet), can start at speeds 10mph lower than a car with good shock absorbers. When cornering on a tight bend (at 50mph) the rear end of the car can break traction at 5mph less than a car with good shock absorbers. Finally, consider that once a car has covered 40,000 miles the shock absorber should be checked for wear every 12,000 miles.

Warning! If a shock absorber does need replacing, always replace the other shock absorber on the same axle. When

you come to choose a replacement unit consider the difference between ordinary and gas units. Contrary to popular belief both ordinary and gas units will have oil in them. It is the action of the shock absorber piston (with its associated valving) travelling through the oil, that damps the action of the spring. With a conventional unit the interaction between the oil and air causes the oil to foam, thereby reducing damping action and leading to the phenomenon of shock absorber fade (a marked reduced efficiency). With a gas unit there is no foaming and hence no fade. However, under very extreme conditions, such as special stage rallying, fade can still occur with a standard gas unit.

SHOCK ABSORBERS (DAMPERS) UPRATED

When fitting uprated shock absorbers you are increasing ride control at the expense of ride comfort. The only exception to this rule is the Monroe Sensatrac. The Sensatrac is unique in that the action of the piston in the shock absorber tube is not just controlled by the valves in the piston. It has a vertical groove in the wall of the shock absorber which allows the oil to flow between the top and bottom of the shock absorber tube thereby by-passing the piston which allows for a faster and therefore softer damping action. However, in order to retain a slower and therefore firmer damping action the groove only exists at the comfort zone' of damper travel where the wheel movements are small. When wheel movements are large, the piston moves into the 'control zone' where no groove exists and normal piston action occurs and with the Sensatrac this means a firm damping action. In use the Sensatrac truly offers the best of both worlds – race stiffness with road softness.

LEVER ARM/ ARMSTRONG DAMPER UNITS

On some classic cars, instead of a

Rare original, adjustable Armstrong lever-arm shock absorber.

Front Armstrong lever-arm damper, professionally modified by the leading Armstrong expert Peter Caldwell of Worldwide Auto Parts.
(Courtesy Peter Caldwell)

telescopic shock absorber, Armstrong lever arm dampers were fitted, each unit being designed specifically for a particular make and model (eg Austin-Healey 3000, MGB, etc). There are no readily available uprated variations of these dampers, though some are sometimes sold as having an uprated action. Whether new or reconditioned though, it's possible to modify some units to uprate the damping action, with the simplest method to use a thicker than standard oil in the damper which increases the action in both bump and rebound. Note, though, that too thick an oil can result in damage to the unit, especially in cold weather when the oil will be at its thickest and damping action stiffest. There is a benefit in using a synthetic oil as it will aid fade resistance; also be aware that motorcycle fork oils can provide a useful selection of oil grades to choose from. The damping action is to some extent controlled by two springs internal to the damper and accessed by removal of the 7/8in nut on the top of the unit. The valve can be withdrawn (it looks like a small metal rod with a small integral spring) and a large spring the valve seats on can then also be withdrawn from the damper body. The large spring controls the bump action of the damper and can be replaced with a stronger spring from a different Armstrong unit (for some models), or it can be shimmed in relation to the valve by placing spacers between it and the valve, or both, for increased effect. The small spring, integral to the valve, controls the rebound action of the unit, and can be adjusted by tightening the small nut. If you don't feel up to modifying a unit yourself, and want an upgraded unit a bit more specific than '+30 per cent,' then Worldwide Auto Parts of Madison/Nosimport in the USA can supply to order, or rebuild and recondition your existing unit.

ADJUSTABLE ARMSTRONG DAMPER UNITS

Now obsolete and scarce, you might nevertheless chance across the adjustable Armstrong lever arm shock absorber that was a BL Special Tuning part for some classic cars. They are very similar in appearance to the standard items, except for a large adjusting knob. Old units are still reconditionable, and worth buying if you find them. Fitting is straightforward as they are a direct replacement for the standard part.

More recently, Peter Caldwell of Worldwide Auto Parts of Madison/Nosimport in the USA, the acknowledged expert on the Armstrong damper unit, has developed adjustable units based on standard units. While quite different in appearance to the original factory adjustable units, they are fully functional and, since they're not based on a unique casting but the standard casting, will have excellent availability. What Caldwell did was to make a bypass circuit for the original valve that is adjustable by means of a full flow needle valve. This allows some changes to the original valve, which itself is then re-worked to be able to be very stiff. The volume of oil that is metered by the altered valve does the damping, the rest runs through the needle valve and is not involved in damping. The standard of engineering, as with the quality of the reconditioned dampers, is very high, and underlines the company's position as the world authority on the Armstrong damper.

Chapter 13
Front suspension & steering

INTRODUCTION

Performance modifications to the front suspension (in isolation) and steering will improve the cornering of the car. However, other than with a few exceptions covered in this chapter, guidance in the preceding chapter will stand good for front and rear suspension.

CAMBER CHANGES

If your car has MacPherson strut front suspension, it's possible to change the camber by means of an adjustable top mount. Several companies manufacture special top mounting brackets that will allow adjustment for camber changes; for example, Burton Performance makes them for Fords.

However, with some non-standard shock absorbers it may be necessary to purchase top mounts that you are certain will be compatible. The new adjustable top mounting will replace the old, but setting-up will require access to a camber gauge, or will need to be carried out in conjunction with a follow-up alignment check. Those classic

Most Japanese cars can use a similar adjustable top mount. (Courtesy HKS)

cars that don't have MacPherson strut suspension are likely to be of an older design that utilises a trunnion or similar top linkage on the front suspension stub axle, or use a wishbone. For both types it's usually possible to fit a negative camber trunnion or bushes, or adjust the wishbone length or bushing to achieve camber adjustment.

TRACKING

Sometimes known as 'toe' (as in pigeon toed) because tracking refers to how much out of parallel one wheel is to the other on an axle. Although rear wheel toe is often not adjustable, front toe always is. If the fronts of the wheels are closer to each other than the rears, they are said to 'toe-in,' while if the fronts of the

Some classic cars will have top and bottom wishbones on the front suspension, with a trunnion at the top or bottom which can be changed for one that will produce negative camber (left).

wheels are farther apart than the rears they are said to 'toe-out.' Generally, as little toe-in as possible is recommended. However, each car will be different, and you should be guided by the standard setting for your car and any suspension modifications you undertake. The tracking can be set as part of a total alignment check, or by yourself, or a garage, with tracking equipment.

STRUT BRACES

Strut braces are often regarded as merely a fashion accessory, for show under the bonnet, but they do, in fact, serve a vital function. What the strut brace does is link the top of the front suspension towers together, usually on a car with MacPherson struts. What this linking does is reduce chassis flex, thereby reducing spurious wheel alignment changes mid-corner.

STEERING GENERAL

To a large extent how well a car responds to steering input will depend on its suspension and tyres. This section, therefore, is about the steering input part of the equation. In practice, this means the steering wheel, steering column, and steering rack.

Steering wheel

A car's steering wheel is one of the primary control devices of the car, and one often taken for granted. Size matters with the steering wheel, and the smaller the diameter of the wheel the quicker the driver can input steering commands – and the heavier

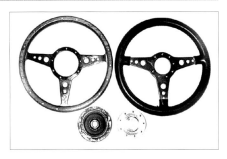

A pair of Mota-Lita 13in flat steering wheels, with their respective bosses below them – later, large boss wheel (wood rim) on the left, early and obsolete small boss wheel (leather rim) on the right.

the steering. Do not confuse inputting steering commands with the car's response to them. Just because the driver can input a steering command quickly, does not mean the car will respond quickly, because steering response is a function of the wheels, tyres and suspension components. However, if the vehicle can respond quicker than you can input steering commands to it, because, for example, the steering wheel has an enormous diameter (like a bus wheel!), then there may be some merit in choosing a smaller diameter wheel.

Note that what's a good size steering wheel for one car might not be so good for another. One example of this would be swapping a steering wheel from a RWD vehicle to a FWD vehicle. The reason for this is that FWD vehicles usually have a quicker steering response than RWD vehicles. A quite different reason is that steering rack ratios also vary from car to car; more of which later.

Steering wheels vary from ten to sixteen inches, usually going up an inch at a time. Metric sizes tend to range from 260mm to 350mm. In both cases the smaller sizes are really only suited to racing cars. Typically, a good choice would be between 12in to 14in, or its nearest metric equivalent.

Another consideration when choosing a steering wheel is its 'dishing,' ie the difference in depth between the steering wheel centre and

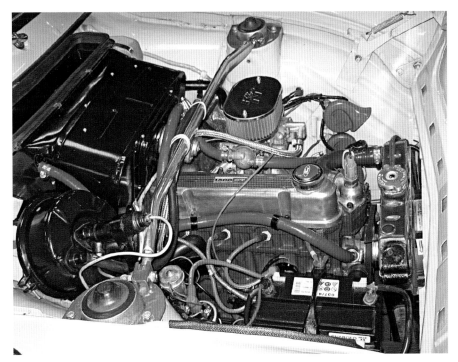

A strut brace fitted to a modified Ford Anglia.

the rim. The choice is usually between flat or dished, though sometimes a deep dish is available. On the face of it you might think it is simpler to move the seat nearer the wheel to adjust for arm reach. However, some models, makes, and not least individuals, have an arrangement which is less than comfortable for quick driving. If such circumstances apply to you and your classic car, set the driving position for the pedals and then choose a steering wheel to match the reach you require. Of course, if your car has an adjustable steering column then it really shouldn't matter.

Steering column

The steering column carries the steering inputs to the steering rack or box, and usually requires no modification. However, it's possible to have the steering column shortened, though the associated modifications require considerable thought before proceeding with the job.

Steering ratio, box & rack

The steering ratio is found by seeing how many turns and part turns of the steering wheel there are from lock-to-lock. To establish what the standard lock is on your car, turn the steering to full lock in one direction and then count the turns until it is on the full opposite lock. Note that a smaller diameter steering wheel does not change the steering ratio, but does change the amount your hands move to achieve it.

If your classic has a steering box there's nothing you can do to change its speed, though for some cars there are conversions to steering racks.

For those classics with steering

It's possible to replace the standard steering rack with a quick rack. (Courtesy Rally Design)

racks it's possible to replace a slow rack with a faster one. A fast rack is one that has a ratio of 2.5 lock-to-lock. Although some road cars do have slightly faster racks than that, the majority will be slower. Rally Design supplies exchange quick racks and conversion kits to convert a rack to a 2.5 ratio. Quaife does a quick rack for the MGC which is 2.9 turns lock-to-lock for left-hand and right-hand drive cars.

It's possible to lighten a steering rack on some cars (E-type Jaguars, for example) by gun boring the centre of the rack bar, and Kiley Clinton is one company that can do this.

Power-assisted steering racks

If you've fitted a small diameter steering wheel and a quick rack to your car you might have a steering action which is nice and fast, and is just what you

want. Alternatively, you might have left the steering standard but fitted wider wheels and tyres. It's possible, however, that a combination of any of these factors may have introduced the unpleasant side-effect of heavy steering. (It's worth checking the steering with the front of the car jacked up just to ensure the heavy steering isn't caused by unlubricated or worn out parts.) Another cause of heavy steering is under-inflated tyres. If everything is in order mechanically and the tyre pressures are okay, there are two solutions. The first is to spend some time working out with weights to strengthen your arms. The second is to find out whether you can fit a power-assisted steering rack. If another model or variant of your car has PAS it's worth investigating whether it can be fitted to your car. Your local dealer/parts outlet should be able to advise if this is possible.

Chapter 14
Rear suspension

INTRODUCTION

The main aspect of performance affected by the rear suspension is cornering speed. However, because of weight changes, which may be gains as well as losses, acceleration and deceleration are also affected. Depending on your car's drive configuration, there'll either be a little or a lot that can be done by way of improvement.

If the car is FWD, the rear suspension will consist of springs (which may be torsion bars), and dampers, acting on some form of stub axle with little scope for improvement. With a RWD car, there may be a live axle arrangement which will have scope for large improvements. Other RWD cars and 4WD cars will have a final drive unit and driveshafts incorporated as part of the overall rear suspension design, and these may offer some scope for improvement, but less than a live axle arrangement.

LIVE AXLE WITH LEAF SPRINGS

Of all the rear suspension designs the live axle and leaf spring has the

Top four options for improving live axle suspension (with leaf springs)

1. Renew all existing bushes (polyurethane recommended)
2. Fit anti-tramp bars
3. Fit a Panhard rod or Watts linkage
4. Convert suspension to four-link design with coil springs

greatest potential for improvement. It's also a design found on a whole range of classic cars which are likely to be developed for high-performance.

The reason that you can do so much to improve this setup is that it suffers from a couple of in-built detriments to good handling, and it's also heavy. The top four options table above can be used as a guide, and option three can also be used in conjunction with other RWD suspension systems.

ANTI-TRAMP BARS

When a car with a leaf sprung live axle and a sufficiently powerful engine does a full throttle standing start, one undesirable effect is that the axle will tramp or hop. The torque transmitted to the rear wheels causes the axle casing to

turn, twisting the springs into a shallow S shape. The springs then release the stored energy, twisting the axle in the reverse direction. This cycle is repeated until the torque loading is released from the springs as the car increases speed. As the car accelerates, the driver will feel as if the back axle is hopping up and

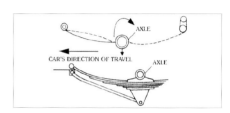

Rotational forces on the axle can twist or wind up the spring, resulting in axle tramp or hop. (Courtesy Dave Robinson/ Sharon Monroe)

An anti-tramp kit for the Ford Escort Mks I & II. (Courtesy Rally Design)

down (which is exactly what it is doing). Aside from being detrimental to good acceleration, axle tramp/hop can break the differential carrier. Tramp/hop can be controlled with nylatron bushes in the spring eyes on some cars, but the most effective solution (retaining leaf springs) is to fit anti-tramp bars, sometimes known as traction bars.

Anti-tramp bars are a pair of bars, one for the forward half of each leaf spring, that connect at one end to the car bodywork (nearest the front of the car) and to the centre of the spring at the other. The ant-tramp bar brackets can be mounted in conjunction with the leaf spring mountings, and are connected by a rigid bar or tube to form the complete assembly. Anti-tramp bars work by preventing the distortion of the leaf spring. If the bars can be designed so that the mounting brackets are not just mounted in conjunction with other brackets, but as part of them (a hybrid bracket), then the end product will be lighter. Purpose-built after-market kits are available for some cars. In other instances, you'll need to approach a local fabricator to have them made for you.

Fitting anti-tramp bars is not the best solution to solving axle tramp because they increase the overall weight. A far better and neater solution is to convert the rear axle to a four-link system with coil springs.

PANHARD RODS & WATTS LINKAGES

Leaf springs, when used in conjunction with a live axle, do more than just provide springing – they also locate the

axle, usually by U-bolts and nuts at the spring mid-length point. Each end of the spring is fixed to the car to locate the whole assembly. Although this mounting arrangement holds the axle in place, the compliance is such that the axle has some undesirable lateral movement. This will most likely be felt as a looseness or fishtailing action when driving through a series of bends. If the rubbers in the spring eyes are worn, the symptoms will be exaggerated. New rubber bushes, or perhaps polyurethane bushes with less compliance than rubber bushes, will eliminate the problem or reduce it to an acceptable level.

Dead axle FWD and non-live axle RWD cars may also suffer from inadequate sideways location, but, generally speaking, this can be addressed by fitting either a Panhard rod or a Watts linkage. A Panhard rod is a metal rod which connects the car's chassis to one end of the axle. By forming a rigid connection between the car and the axle, sideways movement is prevented. A Watts linkage performs

A live axle (RWD) with a Watts linkage for lateral stability on Ron Soave's racing Sprite 'White Trash II.' (Courtesy Ron Soave)

Brackets for a Panhard rod, in this case for the RWD Escort. (Courtesy Rally Design)

the same job, but has a rod fixed to each end of the axle, with a central pivot point at the centre of the axle. For non-live axle RWD cars and FWD with dead axles the arrangement is similar, but with one end of the pickup on a hard suspension mounting point rather than the live axle. For cars known to benefit from either item, an after-market kit will be available. In other instances you'll need to have something fabricated.

FOUR-LINK SUSPENSION CONVERSIONS

Because of the drawbacks of leaf springs, a conversion to four links and coil springs has considerable merit. This design works by using upper and lower axle locating links each side of the axle, thereby replacing the locating function of the leaf springs. Coil springs are then located on the axle at each side to provide springing, thereby replacing the second function of the leaf spring. Coil springs can also be used in conjunction with the shock absorber to form a single unit (coilover shocks). The disadvantage to converting to this configuration is that, in most cases you'll need to find a good workshop that can design and fabricate a system for you, unless you have a RWD Ford Escort for which conversion kits are available.

The following guidance will be useful if you're going to fabricate your own system. The first job will be to decide where the spring coils and shock absorbers need to be located. They will need to be as near the axle ends as possible, but without fouling on anything. They will generally need to merge into the wheelwell at some point, perhaps to the full extent of their height and, at the

A four-link kit for the RWD Escort, again from Rally Design. (Courtesy Rally Design)

top, they will intrude inside the car. The orientation of the coil and shock ideally needs to be vertical. However, if that causes problems, they can lean slightly from the vertical, either side-to-side, or front-to-back, in relation to the car. It will soon be apparent that where the top of the coilover shock needs to be located inside the car, if not fouling something, is in thin air. To provide a mounting for them a turret box will need to be fabricated. Even if no kit is available for your classic it's likely a turret box from the RWD Ford Escort kit could be adapted. Once all of this work has been completed you can experiment with springs, damper settings and ride heights. Although ride is a matter of personal taste it's recommend to start with a setting 10 per cent harder than the manufacturer's standard.

RIDE HEIGHT

You'll need to read the 'Ride Height' section in the 'Suspension – General' chapter before embarking on any modifications to ride height, and then decide how much you want to lower it. You'll also need to look at what sort of rear suspension your car has.

Leaf sprung rear ends are probably the easiest to lower, and the usual method is to insert a lowering block between the axle and the spring. The drawback to this method is it can either introduce or exacerbate axle-tramp/hop. An alternative is to change the springs altogether, for some designed to produce a lower ride height. If lowered ride height springs are not commercially available, the existing ones can be re-cambered to produce a reduced ride. A neater method is to reduce the height of the front spring shackle. This can be difficult to achieve, and may require fabrication of new, modified, front hanger brackets. Don't be tempted to try the same technique on the rear brackets because, although the lowering effect is the same, it changes the suspension geometry unfavourably.

Coil sprung rear suspension is easy to lower, merely requiring shorter springs. It's possible to cut springs shorter but not recommended. On some

A live axle car with leaf springs can be lowered via a lowering block set ...

... as shown here.

MacPherson struts (also known as Chapman struts) on rear suspension would require a different (modified) strut to allow lowering.

cars it's possible to lower the spring at the bottom mounting by using spacers

between the pan and the wishbone. An alternative is to use after-market shock absorbers (coilover-type) that have adjustable spring seats.

Torsion bar rear suspension is fiddly to lower but generally will involve no new parts/expense. Clean the end where you're going to make the adjustment and paint or mark a line for the standard position. Next, follow the workshop procedure for removing the suspension arm from the torsion bar, and, when you refit the arm, put the spline one tooth around from the original setting. Repeat this procedure until you get the desired reduction in ride height.

DAMPING – ALL TYPES OF SUSPENSION

The 'Suspension – General' chapter has guidance on damping (shock absorbers).

ANTI-ROLL BARS – ALL TYPES OF SUSPENSION

On some FWD cars, a rear anti-roll bar is fitted to reduce understeer by creating a degree of compensating oversteer. An existing anti-roll bar can be stiffened by using nylatron, polyurethane or solid aluminium mountings, or it can be replaced by a thicker bar. Spend some time and money minimising the front end understeer before considering fitting an anti-roll bar to the rear (or increasing the effect or size on a car that has one). If your classic has a live axle it's unlikely to require a rear anti-roll bar and, where one has already been fitted, it's usually there to balance an excessive amount of understeer by introducing some oversteer at the rear and should have its action increased.

REAR WHEEL ALIGNMENT

With a live axle car there's unlikely to be any scope for adjustment of rear wheel alignment. On some cars with independent rear suspension it's possible to make some adjustments to both camber and tracking at the rear, though this may not be a DIY proposition – see the general suspension section.

Chapter 15
Wheels & tyres

INTRODUCTION

For any classic car, the wheel and tyre combination is crucial to all aspects of the car's performance. Biggest is generally best, and the more rubber you can put on the road the better.

The limitations on how much rubber you can put down will vary from car to car, and, to an extent, the weight of the car and the power output of the engine will dictate a reasonable size range. However, it's easy to make a poor choice, or find that having made your purchase, it's not what you want after all. To avoid such errors, the table below suggests a logical order in which to make your decisions. The remainder of this chapter provides all the information you need to help you select wheels and tyres, as well as supplementary information on related issues.

ORDER OF DECISIONS FOR WHEEL & TYRE SELECTION

1. Overall diameter of tyre (note lower profile means smaller diameter)
2. Tyre profile
3. Tyre width
4. Actual tyre including speed rating
5. Wheel diameter to tie in with choices 1 and 2 (note if 2 becomes a higher value so does 1)
6. Stud pattern (Pitch Circle Diameter (PCD))
7. Wheel rim width, inset and offset (bearing in mind 3)
8. Style of wheel

TYRES

Given that the tyres should be chosen before the wheels it makes sense to look at the tyres first. Tyres are diverse in size and type, and each tyre comes complete with a bundle of useful but coded information on the side wall. The 'writing on the wall' illustration shows all the markings which may appear on a tyre sidewall, and covers both European and North American standards. The markings most likely to be of most interest are those indicating size, speed, and load rating. A typical designation might be 185/70HR14. The first number in our example is 185, and this

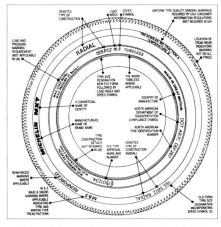

The writing on the wall. There's a lot of information on the side of a tyre. (Courtesy Michelin)

indicates the nominal width of the tyre in millimetres. The number 70 indicates the aspect ratio which is the percentage of nominal section height of nominal section width. The letter H indicates the speed rating. The letter R indicates the tyre is radial ply construction. Finally, the last two numbers indicate the wheel rim diameter the tyre is for.

TYRE SPEED RATING

Warning! Each and every type of tyre has a maximum safe running speed, and, if performance modifications have raised the top speed capability of your car, you must ensure the tyres are appropriately rated to be used at that higher speed, whether or not you intend to drive at your car's top speed. The table below provides you with all the information you need.

Symbol	MPH	KPH
L	75	120
M	81	130
N	87	140
P	93	150
Q	100	160
R	106	170
S	112	180
T	118	190
U	124	200
H	130	210
V	149	240
W	167	270
Y	186	300

OVERALL SIZE

When considering what size wheel and tyre to fit, there are a number of constraints and, therefore, a number of decisions which need to be made and planned for. The overriding constraint on overall diameter of the wheel and tyre combination is whether or not you're prepared to undertake bodywork modifications. Most widths can be accommodated, using spacers if necessary; more of which later. The restriction on overall diameter is dictated partly by what's available, the size of the car, and how little suspension travel you can live with. The important things to consider are practicality and cost.

TYRE OVERALL DIAMETER, PROFILE & WIDTH

The overriding constraint on overall diameter of the tyres is whether or not you want to undertake bodywork, braking, suspension, and perhaps gearing modifications, to allow the use of a larger overall diameter. Once you've decided on the tyre diameter, you must consider a tyre profile size. In other words, having decided on how physically big (tall) the tyre is, you must decide how much rubber you want between the tread surface of the tyre and that of the wheel rim. Note, the indicated tyre size is based on the wheel diameter, not the physical diameter of the tyre itself. The greater the amount of rubber between the tyre tread surface and the wheel rim (higher profile, higher number) the more comfortable the ride will be, but with correspondingly less driving response. The less rubber (lower

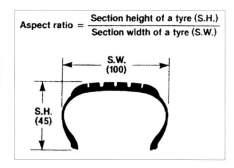

Aspect ratio measures section height to section width. (Courtesy Yokohama)

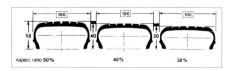

As illustrated, holding section width constant, section height will decrease as aspect ratio decreases. (Courtesy Yokohama)

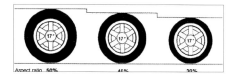

Another way of looking at this is that holding rim diameter constant, overall diameter will decrease as aspect ratio decreases. (Courtesy Yokohama)

profile, lower number) the sharper the response, but the harsher the ride. Depending on your choice of overall diameter and profile, you may or may not be able to change to a different profile in the future without running into clearance problems that can only be prevented by changing wheel diameter. For instance, if your car has 60 profile tyres, you can change to 50 profile tyres, with a resultant smaller rolling radius on the same wheel. However, if your car has 40 profile tyres, a change to tyres of 50 profile will increase the overall rolling radius unless you switch to a smaller wheel. Whatever your final choice, once it's made, bear in mind that it'll be expensive, or possibly very expensive, to change to something different.

As far as tyre width goes, widest is best, except for loose surfaces and snowy conditions. For road use, be realistic about the performance capability of the car, your own driving ability, the motoring laws of your country, and, not least, how much the extra width will cost. **Warning!** Another important consideration is that an increase in tyre width is likely to create clearance problems, and under no circumstances must the tyre contact any part of the car, be it bodywork, brake components or suspension components: it may also be illegal for the tyre to protrude beyond the bodywork. However, if you're prepared to undertake or pay for bodywork modifications, such as wheelarch flares, then most widths can be accommodated. In addition, clearance problems can be overcome by careful choice of wheel inset/offset, or wheel spacers.

TYRE SELECTION – COMPETITION USE

When choosing a tyre for competition use the first thing to check is what tyres are permitted within the regulations (in some instances there will be a single designated tyre). In other instances there may be freedom to choose a tyre

A high-performance Kumho Ecsta tyre on an Alpine Tiger.

but with restrictions for different classes. Tyres may also be treaded, slick, or grooved slick, and again choice may be restricted between classes.

For road tyres in UK motorsport, the MSA Blue Book has a list of tyres that can be used. Slick racing tyres can be either of radial or crossply construction, and not only does each have specific handling characteristics but each is suited to different lengths of racing and, in the UK at least, some races are of such a distance that the tyre type maybe crucial.

SCRUBBING & BUFFING COMPETITION TYRES

The term 'scrubbing' in relation to tyres used in competition refers to when new tyres are used on the car for two or three laps of a circuit at less than full racing speeds to bring them up to temperature before allowing them to cool. This heat cycle causes the tread compound to harden slightly, which makes the performance more consistent over a full race distance, although the absolute best lap time will be slightly slower.

'Buffing' is the name given to the process whereby a road tyre, usually new, is shaved down from a full height tread to approximately 4mm of tread, to prevent the tyre overheating on its shoulders. A buffed tyre will have greater tread stability, will last longer and perform better than a non-buffed tyre (except in the wet, when a fully-treaded tyre will perform better). For the

serious competitor it will be necessary to have a dry set of wheels and tyres and wet set, even when competing in a class stipulating road tyres, or even a specific road tyre.

TUBELESS TYRES & WIRE WHEELS

It's not generally recommended to use tubeless tyres with inner tubes. However, it's a necessity with all but the very latest wire-spoked wheels from MWS or Dayton, which are specifically designed to be used with tubeless tyres; more of which later.

When presenting a wire-spoked wheel to have a new tyre fitted it may be the case that the tyre fitter has no previous experience of fitting a tyre and tube to a wire-spoked wheel, and so may need to be advised of the peculiarities of fitting. After the tyre has been deflated and the tyre half removed from the wheel, taking care not

By moving the spoke wells inboard of the wheel flange, a suitable sealing compound can be used so that the wheel can be fitted with a tyre without an inner tube being required ...

... as shown here (the same wheel now with a Dunlop Sport tubeless tyre fitted to it).

to rip the inner tube, the tube must be carefully removed. Removal of the tyre from the rim can then be completed. It's recommended you fit new rim tape to the wheel at this point, or alternatively tank tape/gaffer tape – available from a motorsport retail outlet – can be used. The inner tube should be coated with plenty of French chalk and inflated to its natural shape. Next, with the tyre half fitted to the wheel, the inner tube should be placed inside the tyre. This ensures the tube is correctly positioned and in full contact with the tyre before completion of fitting the tyre to the wheel and inflation to working pressure.

Finally, tyre manufacturers advise that under NO circumstances should inner tubes be used in tyres with an aspect ratio of less than 65 per cent. The reason for this is that problems of air trapping and chafing can lead to premature failure of the tube, tyre, or both.

TYRE PRESSURES

Tyre pressure (which should always be checked cold) is just as important as tyre selection. Generally speaking, an increase in tyre pressure will improve the handling of the car. When the car will be used for regular fast driving, try inflating tyres to 10 per cent over the recommended pressures for normal driving. However, in some instances, better performance may be achieved by reducing pressure, but never by more than 2 or 3 pounds below the manufacturer's recommended setting. **Caution!** Whatever pressure setting you use, be extremely careful not to overdo it as the tyre may be damaged permanently. Over inflation causes excessive tension in the casing cords, which makes the tyre more vulnerable to impact damage. Over inflation by 20 per cent has been found to cause a 10 per cent reduction in tyre life (by wear). Under inflation allows excessive flexing and rapid overheating, leading eventually to casing break-up and failure. Under inflation by 10 per cent has been found to cause a 26 per cent reduction in tyre

To reduce understeer
Increase front tyre pressure
Decrease rear tyre pressure

life (by wear). There is, unfortunately, no golden rule for starting pressure for tyres, but a cold pressure of 20psi is a minimum. **Warning!** Always consult the tyre manufacturer for advice on optimal pressures. For guidance as to the effect of variation in tyre pressures on handling consult the accompanying table.

WHEEL WIDTH, DIAMETER & WEIGHT

Having made your choice of tyre, you now need to find a wheel that will suit it. There are a number of constraints and decisions which need to be made and planned for. Also, for any given tyre width there is a minimum and maximum rim size that will accommodate it. Wheel weight is very important – not just the part it plays in overall vehicle weight, or even unsprung weight, but because the wheel is accelerated twice, initially as it revolves, and then, as it moves forward as part of the car. Obviously the larger the wheel the more it will weigh. Wheels are generally made from steel, aluminium alloy, or magnesium alloy. 'Alloy wheels' is the general term for aluminium alloy wheels, and there's

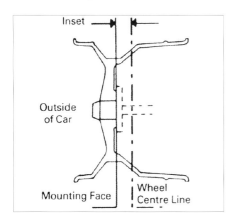

Inset is calculated by measuring in from the wheel mounting face to the wheel centre line. (Courtesy Alloy Wheels International Ltd)

To reduce oversteer
Increase rear tyre pressure
Decrease front tyre pressure

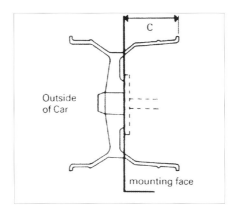

The C dimension is the measurement from the wheel mounting face to the edge of the inside rim. (Courtesy Alloy Wheels International Ltd)

a huge selection to choose from. Magnesium alloy wheels are the lightest, but most expensive.

WIRE-SPOKED WHEELS & SPINNERS

Wire-spoked wheels are available for many classic cars, sometimes as an alternative to bolt-on wheels. Traditionally, one drawback to using wire-spoked wheels was that you had to use an inner tube with them. In recent years that drawback has been removed, and Motor Wheel Service (MWS) and Dayton have wire wheels designed for use without an inner tube. At first it might not seem such a big deal to save the weight and hassle of the inner tube, but it opens up tyre choices with a lower profile than 65 per cent. However, for some cars a wire-spoked wheel designed to be used tubeless will be slightly wider and have a different rim profile and appearance to the standard OE fit wheel.

Bolt-on wire-spoked wheels are an alternative to knock-off wire wheels. By no means the performance option, because of their weight, they do stand out from the crowd, especially if

Here, the alloy wheel has been appropriately colour-coded to the car – a MkI Ford Cortina.

A polished four-spoke alloy wheel on a Ford Corsair.

A neat chromed steel wheel.

The Libre wheel on an MGB.

chromed, and they can usually be used tubeless (but check before purchasing).

For knock-off wire-spoked wheels there may be a choice of wheel spinner, though not all may have a manufacturer's name or logo on them.

The choice is: two-eared, hexagon, or three-eared spinner. Of these the hexagon is the lightest, while the three-eared is the heaviest. Note that the centre of any spinner can be carefully machined to reduce its weight.

WHEEL STUD OR BOLT PATTERN

Whatever wheels you choose, the stud or bolt pattern will have to be the same as that on the existing wheels, unless you're going to change the hubs (where possible) for ones with a different stud or bolt pattern. The technical name for stud or bolt pattern is Pitch Circle Diameter (PCD).

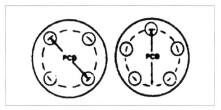

The Pitch Circle Diameter (PCD) is the diameter of the circle that passes through the centre of all the wheel studs or bolt holes. (Courtesy Alloy Wheels International Ltd)

WHEEL SPACERS, STUDS, BOLTS OR NUTS

Wheel spacers are often frowned upon as being a cause of premature wheel bearing failure, and certainly the use of a spacer will not extend bearing life. However, given that the use of spacers may allow higher cornering forces, all things being equal, higher loads are going to placed on the wheel bearings anyway.

The thickness of the spacer can vary enormously; usually between 10mm and 30mm. When using spacers, you must ensure that there's no tyre to wheelarch contact. Of course, if you're using a spacer to allow fitment of a wheel that doesn't have the right backface, then you should have allowed for the total clearance necessary anyway.

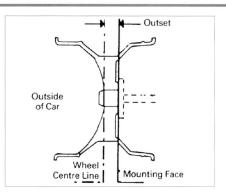

Outset is calculated by measuring out from the wheel mounting face to the wheel centre line. (Courtesy Alloy Wheels International Ltd)

The wheel lug gauge will tell you in an instant if the secondhand wheels you're considering have the right stud pattern; correctly known as the Pitch Circle Diameter (PCD). (Courtesy D J Eldman & Company)

Warning! Once you've decided on the spacer thickness, you must get longer studs (or bolts) to match. It's possible to get studs (or bolts) of a greater thickness than standard, to ensure the overall strength of the stud isn't compromised, but you may need to modify other wheel components, or even the wheels themselves, before using them.

Wheel nuts, other than locking types fitted for protection against theft, are usually replaced with non-standard items for aesthetic reasons, rather than performance considerations. However, for many types of alloy wheels you'll need to purchase special nuts to go with the wheels.

A typical wheel spacer, this one from Jamex, is used to increase the wheel track of the vehicle or create clearance for brake calipers, etc. (Courtesy Jamex)

Wolfrace slots on Frank Clarici's modified Sprite, as he lines up for autocross.

The original Minilite on a Big Healey, as used by the works rally cars.

Finally, if your vehicle has bolts to fix the wheels to the hubs, it's possible to convert to studs and nuts in some cases.

Chapter 16
Instruments & electrical components

INTRODUCTION

There are no significant performance improvements associated with instruments and electrical components. However, there are some electrical considerations associated with tuning, such as ensuring the engine will always start, or replacing a standard part with a lighter modified one. Instrumentation is important because a performance tuned engine needs to be monitored more accurately and more closely than a standard engine, and, under heavy loads, its operating temperatures (oil and coolant) can increase significantly quicker than they would on a standard engine. Other improvements and modifications in the chapter are self explanatory.

SPEEDOMETER MODIFICATIONS

If your car has been tuned to go much faster than standard you may have problems with speedometer accuracy at higher speeds. It may even be that the new maximum speed of the car is higher than the speedometer calibration.

Hybrid speedo from Speedograph Richfield for an MG midget. Originally an MGB speedo, it was chosen for its higher calibrated speed but standard appearance.

Also, any change in differential ratio from standard will definitely render the speedometer wildly inaccurate, reading on the slow side for higher gearing and on the fast side for lower gearing. A change in tyre profiles will have the same effect. In any event, with a tuned classic capable of highly illegal road speeds to match, it's preferable to know just how slow or fast your car is travelling. A speedometer can be checked for accuracy on the

The wheel and bodywork are marked to enable measuring of wheel revolutions in relation to speedometer cable revolutions.

rolling road and the results recorded. However, it's not practical to look at a set of corrected figures whenever you approach the legal speed limit.

If your car has a round speedometer that fits into an aperture in the dash, there's a range of circular after-market speedometers that are as good, possibly better, than many cheap original equipment units. Note though that if you have any direction indicator pilot lights in the unit, for example, they will need to be relocated. In addition, the calibration may be up to an optimistic 160mph! An alternative could be to use a speedo with a higher top speed from a car from the same manufacturer as your own (so as to match the style of the graduations and fit your car's speedometer aperture in the dash). One unusual example is the use of a 130mph Mini Cooper S in a Morris Minor. In a few instances, such as if your car has a particularly unusual speedometer – rectangular strip for example – your only option may be to build a custom dash.

Once you have a unit you're happy with, it'll need re-calibration to suit the gearing of the car, and possibly a hybrid cable. Speedograph Richfield Ltd can rebuild and recalibrate any unit with absolute accuracy. The following steps are required of you:

1. Disconnect the speedometer flexible drive at the instrument end.
2. Jack up one driving wheel and support the car with an axle stand. (Let Speedograph know if your car is fitted with a limited slip diff.)
3. Mark suspended driving wheel with a chalk line or masking tape.
4. Mark the wing of the driven wheel with a similar mark.
5. Make a small arrow from light cardboard and press it onto the end of the speedometer drive inner cable.
6. Revolve the driving wheel by hand, exactly twenty times, whilst an assistant counts the number of revolutions the inner cable makes to the nearest one eighth of a revolution.
7. Note the make and size of the tyre, and wheel revolution per mile figure if you have it.
8. Send the information from 6 and 7 to Speedograph along with the make (eg Smiths) and part number, giving a brief explanation of your requirements.

Alternatively, Speedograph can manufacture and supply a speedometer to suit any particular style or requirement. Another service offered is that of recalibrating a speedometer from kph to mph or vice versa. In addition, as a cable manufacturer, the company can reproduce a speedometer cable of any length for your gearbox/speedometer combination.

TACHOMETER (REV COUNTER)

If your classic doesn't have a tachometer and you want to fit one, you have a wide choice of face designs, colours, and calibration (0-7000rpm, 0-8000rpm, 0-9000rpm, 0-10,000rpm, etc). The diameter will usually be imperial four inch or metric 80mm or 100mm, with the latter working out at a fraction under four inches and being a straight swap for the imperial four inch. You'll need to consider where it will fit in the existing dashboard, which may entail a complete redesign. For cars with metal, fabric-covered metal, or veneered wood dashboards, incorporating a tachometer can be undertaken as part of an overall dash design. Alternatively, for an 80mm (3.15 inch) tachometer, LMA makes a suitable self contained pod in black or chrome, and at least one manufacturer has a combined tachometer and pod unit. The pod can then be mounted appropriately in the car, such as on top of the dashboard or fascia.

If you're after the ultimate in after-

Stack tachometers come in two sizes, can feature practically any face calibration you like, and also include a telltale (a shift light function). (Courtesy Stack)

market tachometers then take a look at the range from Stack. Not only are these highly accurate instruments, but there's a choice of calibrated display to suit your preference. The Stack unit comes complete with extremely comprehensive fitting and usage instructions. The two switches supplied with the kit control the tell-tale maximum display and the reset tell-tale facility. In addition, not only can you have a tachometer tell-tale, but also an action replay facility.

Stack tachometers come in two sizes, but such is the design of the larger size that it will fit the same size hole as the smaller unit (80mm/3.15 inch) or a 116mm hole. However, if your car has a four inch/100m aperture, you'll need to fabricate a blanking plate to make up the difference between the old and new sizes. You can use a flat sheet of aluminium and have a hole cut in it by a local car body repair shop if you don't have the necessary tools to do the job yourself. The plate can be pop riveted in place and painted to suit. However, before fitting the plate, consider whether it might be better fitted at an angle (eccentric) to the original hole so that it's easier to see.

The Stack tachometer has a block connector that fits into the unit at one end, and to respective wires at the other end. It may be necessary, therefore, to discard the old tachometer wiring and start afresh for the Stack unit. If this is the case, use correctly colour coded wiring from Vehicle Wiring Products Ltd. Note that the Stack unit is self illuminating and doesn't require the instrument light fittings used on most original or after-market tachometers.

If, however, you cannot afford a Stack tachometer, not even a secondhand one, then shop around and buy according to what you can afford. Be advised, though, that you get what you pay for, and budget tachometers are rarely totally accurate.

INTRODUCTION TO AUXILIARY GAUGES

Your classic may come with several

Smiths 90-degree sweep gauges in an AC Cobra.

A matched set of 270-degree Stack sweep gauges (left-to-right): fuel; coolant temperature; oil temperature; oil pressure.

auxiliary gauges, or just a fuel and temperature gauge. If you want to add additional gauges you'll have to decide whether to have those gauges mismatch the design of the originals, or replace the originals as part of an overall redesign. The simplest solution when it comes to installing additional auxiliary gauges is to fit a supplementary gauge pod at the centre, and directly underneath or above the main dash. Such a pod, or even a basic gauge mounting bracket, can contain anything from one to five additional gauges.

The first thing to decide when choosing new gauges is the amount of display. For any circular gauge the amount of display is measured in degrees of a circle, and the most common will be 90 degrees of display – where the needle sits to the left (at the bottom or top of the gauge) and moves to the right. On some gauges the gauge is split into two halves, with the top displaying coolant temperature across 180 degrees, for example, while the bottom displays oil pressure across 180 degrees, or vice versa. Lastly, and perhaps the best, are those with 270 degrees of display. These will provide the greatest movement of the indicator needle for any given change (three times as much as a 90 degree display).

The gauges will require a fitting aperture of 52mm (close enough to two inches such that a new 52mm gauge will fit snugly wherever an old two inch gauge was removed). The gauge action can be mechanical or electrical, or a mixture of both. Face colours can be white, black or cream, and indicator needles white, black or red. Stack produces one of the most comprehensive range of gauges (mechanical and electric), but all with the same matching face in 270 or 90 degrees of display. They're also available with a range of different scales and units, so you can, for example, choose between temperature (oil and coolant) gauges reading in either Fahrenheit or Centigrade. More recently, Stack has produced a range of gauges with programmable features. Controlled by buttons ('warn' and 'peak'), each one identified by a letter to the left ('W' for warn), and to the right ('P' for peak). Another extremely interesting feature is the use of different backlight colours to indicate low and high readings. On the water temp gauge it's possible to set the warning colour to red, and programme it as you see fit – for example 105°C. It's also possible to use the gauge to switch on or off an accessory, such as an electric fan, again at a programmed temperature.

A point to note about gauge sensing or sender units is if the gauge manufacturer does not have the right threaded (brass) fitting for your classic, Speedograph Richfield can almost certainly sell you an inexpensive adaptor, or even make a one-off for you.

Low oil pressure warning light

The low oil pressure warning light on your car is usually operated by an oil

Here, an adaptor has been fitted to the engine block to provide a location for the oil pressure gauge sensor for the low oil warning light (25psi switching), and oil pressure gauge fitting.

Whereas here, the oil pressure warning light sensor (25psi switching) has been taken from a tee fitted to the oil pressure gauge.

pressure switch (which may also operate the oil pressure gauge) in the engine block. Typically, the switch operates at roughly between 3.5lb or 7lb depending on the switch used. As a means of indicating some oil pressure has been achieved on starting the engine, this is fine, but useless if a sudden loss of engine oil pressure occurs at high engine speed as, with only 5lb or less of oil pressure, severe engine failure will be rapid. To provide earlier warning of low oil pressure, replace the standard switch with one that trips at a higher value; 20

or 22lb, for example. This higher rated, low pressure oil warning light switch is available from most suppliers of high-performance components.

Oil pressure gauge

Although the low oil pressure warning light provides an indication of low oil pressure, it's desirable to have a constant oil pressure reading available. An oil pressure reading can also be observed in relation to engine temperature, even as a guide to temperature in its own right, and, not least, pressure when cornering and braking. All of which can provide useful clues to possible other potential problems, such as oil surge. An oil pressure reading can also be observed and noted over a period of time, to give an indication of engine wear.

A gauge is relatively easy to fit – merely replace the standard fitting on the engine block (where the low oil pressure sensor fits), with a fitting that is of a tee design. Speedograph Richfield has a range of instrument accessories, one of which should do the job. An alternative is to fit a tee to the back of the oil pressure gauge, fit the low oil pressure to that, and then run the gauge pipe direct to the engine block.

Although the gauge will usually come complete with the requisite piping, it's possible to employ braided steel lines, such as those from Goodridge, with the attendant benefits (unlike plastic hose, they won't melt). Fitting is straightforward, though the feed pipe to the gauge may need to be bled of excessive air before the gauge will read properly. This can be done be cranking the engine on the starter motor, with the engine disabled so that it won't start (remove coil lead or plug leads), with the hose connection loose at the gauge end of the pipe. Tighten the hose and cease cranking the engine when oil spurts out!

Oil temperature gauge

Before choosing or fitting an oil temperature gauge you must decide what type you want and where to fit

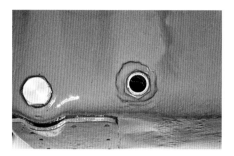

Note the position in the sump for the union into which the oil temperature gauge sensor fits.

the sensor. Gauge types can have a wax capillary sensor or an electrical sensor. The sensor may be mounted in the sump or in a suitable oil line. If your engine doesn't have an oil cooler there may not be a suitable oil line so bear this in mind. The gauge usually comes as part of a kit, though you may need a supplementary instrument pod to mount it in. The wax capillary type has the advantage in that you don't have to worry about electrical connections, but has the disadvantage in that capillary tubing can be broken relatively easy and, although repairable, the cost is almost equal to the price of a new unit.

Coolant temperature gauge

Since most if not all cars will have a coolant temperature gauge, it's likely you'll replace it to match new gauges you're installing. Note, though, that some gauges will require a sender unit to be purchased in addition to the gauge, others will use the existing sender unit; the Stack comes complete with a sender. It may also be necessary to purchase an adaptor for the radiator or cylinder head fitting-to-gauge sender. With a Stack coolant gauge it's possible, in conjunction with a relay, for not only the backlighting to change colour at a pre-set temperature reading, but for an electric fan to be switched on.

Coolant temperature warning light/buzzer

The car's standard coolant temperature

gauge will give a reasonable indication of coolant temperature. However, unless you keep a constant eye on the gauge, the first indication that a problem exists may be an embarrassing cloud of steam from a burst hose or radiator overflow. The solution is to fit a simple switch (from Kenlowe) which will activate a dashboard-mounted idiot light when the coolant temperature reaches a predetermined level. As an alternative, or in addition, a warning buzzer can also be wired to activate simultaneously with the light. If, however, you have a programmable Stack coolant temperature gauge, then the gauge is the light, and can be used to control the buzzer.

Voltmeter & ammeter

If your classic doesn't have a voltmeter or ammeter as standard, you may choose to fit one or both to your car. However, it's questionable how useful these are, since the same information can be readily obtained by using a multimeter on the car battery and electrical system. On that basis it's not recommended these are fitted other than for personal preference.

Shift light

If you've fitted a Stack tachometer it will have a built-in shift (gear change) light function. However, if you're using another make of tachometer, you can purchase a separate shift light. The Armteca shift light is called 'Speed Shift,' and incorporates a rev limiter and downshift function, as well as enabling full throttle gear changes to be made (it's not necessary to lift off the throttle) without over-revving the engine. The 'Speed Shift' is only recommended for use on competition cars, is easy to fit, and comes with full instructions.

HEADLIGHT UPGRADE

If you're doing any amount of night driving, you might wish to upgrade the lights on your classic. The most obvious and easy way to do this is by fitting spotlights. However, since any spotlights should only operate in conjunction with headlight main beams, you'll be no better off whatsoever when driving on dipped lights. The solution is to replace the existing tungsten bulb headlights with modern headlamp units that are purpose designed for halogen or xenon bulbs.

On the face of it, replacement of standard tungsten element headlamp bulbs with similar wattage halogen or xenon bulbs seems to represent no increase in power and hence light. However, a modern halogen bulb produces about 70 per cent more luminous flux (light) than a conventional tungsten bulb. While Xenon Plus bulbs produce a blue tinted light and are 30 per cent brighter than halogen bulbs of equivalent wattage, or twice as bright as tungsten bulbs.

Any classics using 7in (178mm) headlamp units, may be fitted with headlamp units with a separate bulb, or sealed beam headlamp units. For those fitted with old style pre-focus bulbs, it's necessary to replace not only the bulbs but the bulb harness connector block when converting to halogen or xenon bulbs. Hella Ltd can supply the units for right-hand drive cars under part number 1L6 002 395 -261 (less bulbs). For later cars with sealed beam lamp units it's not possible to convert them to halogen or xenon bulbs, and so the only solution is to purchase a complete headlamp unit and bulbs of your choice. If your car is fitted with headlamp units and a separate bulb, you still might want to consider using a later and more up-to-date design of headlamp and lens unit.

The choice of modern, purpose-designed-for-halogen, headlamp units is quite wide, and you need to decide whether or not you want the lights to bear a passing resemblance to the original units. Lucas H4 units come with either curved or flat glass. Another alternative is the Wipac Quad Optic unit. All of these units are available from Holden Vintage and Classic or Vehicle Wiring Products Ltd. A more recent and distinctive alternative is the

designed-for-halogen Lucas PL700 'tripod' replica, which combines a unique design with modern technology, and is ideal for the classic but without compromising on lighting performance.

Once you have your new headlamp units, or even if you are able to reuse your existing ones, it's well worth considering purchasing new lamp mounting units to go with them. The reason for this is that the lamp mounting units, correctly known as 'nests,' are often rusty to the extent that they're falling apart. An alternative to standard mounting units are the plastic items available from Vehicle Wiring Products. Not only is the plastic nest rust free, but it weighs half as much as a standard unit. The plastic nests are of a slightly different design to the metal ones, in that the lamp is held into the nest with clips and a screw rather than the inner metal semi bowl of the standard unit. A point to watch is that you fit the clips over the lamp mounts, otherwise the lamp will rattle. This point may not apply to all lamp units, though, only those with the open type of locating lug. The kit from Vehicle Wiring products comes complete with rubber seal, screws and clips. However, you may prefer to use large pop-rivets, you have the right type of rivets and rivet gun, as they are less fiddly.

If you're looking for even more light than the highest rated xenon bulbs can offer, you can use very high wattage halogen units (160/100 watts or higher) but check local legislation regarding the use of such bulbs before fitting them. Irrespective of type, any bulb that draws a current higher than the standard 60W will cause two problems that must be addressed. The first is that higher than standard wattage bulbs will increase the loading on switches, and so a relay must be used. The second is that the standard wiring is not designed for high wattage bulbs, and must therefore be replaced with wiring of a suitable rating for the higher current.

Depending on the wattage of the new bulbs, your car may need a relay

for both the main and dipped beam circuits (the safe limit for switching without a relay is typically 65 watts). A relay is an electrical switch, one that uses low current in one circuit to open another switch. It is the second switch that is designed to carry the higher current. The whole unit is about the size of a matchbox, with a screw hole or clip for fastening to the car, and a number of connector terminals (usually spade end type fittings) on the underside. Each relay must be wired through a fuse to the battery main feed or through the fuse box. To avoid a spaghetti-like wiring maze from the live terminal of the battery, it's recommended the relay(s) be wired through the fuse box. For those classic cars with a fuse box with a very limited number of outlets, it's preferable to fit a supplementary fuse box with a large number of outlets rather than use the existing fuse box and piggy-back-type connectors. Supplementary fuse boxes are available with four, six and eight outlets.

If you stick with the standard fuse box, make sure the main feed, via the relay for the headlamps, is not across a fuse, but on the 'feed' side. Then ensure that there's an in-line fuse, appropriately rated, in the wire to the relay.

To determine the correct rating for headlamp wires, divide the bulb wattage by the battery voltage to get an ampere rating. For instance, using 100 watt, 12 volt bulbs as an example, 100 is divided by 12 to get 8.34 amps, the nearest cable rating (erring on oversize for safety) is rated at 8.75 amps. If the standard cabling on your classic is rated at 8 amps, it can be seen that standard wiring is marginal for 100 watt bulbs. 160 watt bulbs will require 13.34 amps, with the nearest cable size rated at 17.5 amps. To determine the load rating for the relay – which will be required for bulbs over 100 watts – add the amps figure for each light (eg, for two 100 watt bulbs this will be 8.34 plus 8.34 – 16.68 amps). Having calculated the rating of the wiring required for the high wattage bulbs of your choice, you will next need to make a bulb harness connector block loom, and rewire your existing headlamp circuit from the relay to the headlamp connector block. In practice, this is not as bad as it sounds. This mini loom will consist of the connector block section and the run from the relay to it. Each part will comprise of three wires of the correct load rating (and colours). You'll need to purchase a pair of main bulb connectors to produce the new bulb connector section because old connector blocks are not re-useable. The wires are crimped to the special main bulb connector terminals, and then pushed into the main bulb connector. It's easiest at this point to thread the wires into the bowl unit via the grommet and exit hole. The remainder of the wiring runs are straightforward, but remember that the new runs are not copies of the older, lower wattage standard wiring because of the relay.

Where a bullet connector is of insufficient size for the cable (only a problem on the thickest cables), the bullet can be drilled out to a larger size. It's strongly recommended that all bullet connectors are both soldered and crimped. Bullets are available in either tinned brass or plain brass, and, while the plain brass solder better they're harder to crimp. At this point it's also worth replacing the snap connector blocks to be sure of a good electrical contact.

All the wiring you are likely to require (in the correct colour codes) as well as relays and bullet connectors, etc, can be obtained from specialists like Vehicle Wiring Products Ltd.

AUXILIARY LIGHTING

The two main forms of auxiliary lighting are driving lights (spot lights) and fog lights. For UK vehicles registered after 1971, driving lights can only legally be wired to work in conjunction with the headlight main beam, and fog lights should only work when the headlight dipped beam is on. There's also UK legislation on where the lights can be mounted. Driving lights have to be no

closer together than 35cm from their outside edge, and the light centre must be no higher than 106cm. Fog lights have to be no nearer than 40cm from the outermost edge of the car, and the top of the light must be no higher than 106cm. Note the information given in this section covers the UK only – legislation in your country may be different.

BATTERY

If your classic has a modified engine, you might want to fit an uprated battery to ensure that, even in the coldest weather, there's sufficient cranking power to start the engine. Alternatively, for a car used in motorsport only, you might want to fit a small, lightweight, sealed battery, in which case see the relevant section in Chapter 19. When choosing a battery, ensure the battery poles are both in the same position and of the same type as the existing battery. Also, before purchase, check that the battery will fit the battery tray/intended location.

WINDSCREEN WIPER MODIFICATIONS & TWO-SPEED WIPER CONVERSION

The windscreen wipers on many classic cars can be modified in a variety of ways to improve their performance, and in some instances the cost is quite negligible.

However, before rushing into wiper modifications, it's worth checking that the originals work as the manufacturer intended. To do this, remove the wiper motor cover and disconnect the drive

Wiper drive gear has degrees of sweep stamped on it: 120 degrees in this case.

cable from the wiper motor drive rod. Next, push and pull on the drive cable to operate the wipers manually. If there's a great deal of resistance it's most likely due to excessive friction in the wheelboxes, or damaged (kinked) drive cable or cable tube. To deal with each in turn, it's necessary to remove the drive cable and establish if the wheelbox shaft can be easily turned. If one or both of each respective wheelbox shafts is stiff or tight it will need to be removed and replaced.

With correctly functioning wheelboxes, the next area to look at for excessive friction is the control cable and control tube. If the control cable is kinked it will need to be replaced. However, irrespective of the condition of the control cable, it's possible for the control tube itself to be kinked, and need replacing. For some classics, replacement control tubes are only available as a single tube, which needs to be cut to the correct segment lengths and suitably flared. The bore of the tube is such that your local garage may not have a flaring tool large enough to do the job, in which case, try your local commercial vehicle garage. The flare shape itself is not critical, and is only required to hold the tube in position in the wheelbox.

A better alternative to using the original equipment steel tube is small bore copper central heating pipe, which can be purchased for a fraction of the price. It's recommended that 10mm (0.39in) bore pipe is used, which is larger than the steel tube being replaced. The advantage is not only in the reduced cost, but also that the copper pipe is softer than steel and easier to bend. The increase in bore also makes it much less sensitive to tight radius bends.

The next item to consider is how much of the windscreen is actually swept by the wiper blades. If the wiper wheelboxes, drive cable and tube were previously restrictive, you may already find that a greater area of the screen is now being swept than before.

Note that the size of the swept area is governed by the wiper drive cog or, more precisely, the position of the crank pin on the drive cog assembly itself. Note also that the wiper blades can park on either side of the car, and the drive cog needs modification if you want to change the park location. To remove the cog, put the motor face downwards and release the small circlip on the back of the drive cog shaft, along with the washer that sits underneath it. This will release the drive cog, the washer underneath it, and the drive crank assembly. If you find the wipers are not parking on the side intended or preferred, the drive cog can be removed and the metal faceplate of the cog integral with the drive crank can be separated from the nylon cog. Next, rotate the cog through 180 degrees before pressing it back together with the faceplate and crank assembly. Reassembly is a reversal of this simple process.

If your classic has a Lucas windscreen wiper motor it will most likely be either a shunt wound field type, in a body of rectangular cross-section (and fastened by three bolts), or of a permanent magnet design of cylindrical cross-section (fastened by a two-bolt clamp). The later permanent magnet type is the more reliable, and was initially single speed, but was later manufactured as a two-speed motor. For anyone wishing to convert their classic from single- to two-speed wipers, using the later permanent magnet type motor, it's possible to undertake a conversion using either a new (exchange) or secondhand motor. If your classic has the early rectangular cross-section motor and you want to convert to two-speed, you'll need to swap to a late type motor to the later type wiper wheel box and drive cable.

Note that if you purchase a new (exchange) motor (Lucas part number LRW110) it will not have the drive cog or crank fitted to it or any of the associated clips and fittings, so you'll need these parts from your old motor. The two-speed motor will need an additional otherwise it will not run at two speeds, so ensure the block connector has an extra wire to the spade terminal on the two-speed motor. Since it has a running current of only 3.1 amps, the new wire (preferably blue/green in colour) required for the second speed need only be of 1.01in (0.33mm) thickness, and can be taped to the existing wires for the wiper in the loom. However, to avoid problems getting everything to work as it should, it's preferable to remove the connector block and wiring runs (as long as is practical) from any BL/Austin Rover car that has a two-speed motor and splice this into your car's loom at an appropriate point. If you've mixed up the wires, re-attach them according to the following guide (noting that each pin on the connector block that attaches to the wiring loom has a number): Terminal (T) 1 black; T2 brown/green; T3 blue/green (only found on two-speed motors); T4 green; T5 red/green. Run the black wire to a suitable earth. Run the green wire into an ignition live in the car's main loom. The other connections will vary according to what classic car you have and will also require a three-way switch to complete the conversion.

STARTER MOTOR

Starter motors are of two specific types: inertia (Bendix), or pre-engaged. A standard inertia starter motor is adequate for a standard engine, but has a number of drawbacks. It can struggle to start a performance-tuned engine, especially one with a higher than standard compression ratio, and this is particularly the case if the car has not been used for a while or the engine is hot. Because the gear pinion is spinning at the moment of engagement it's drawn into the ring gear, over time both the flywheel ring gear and the starter gear pinion wear.

The alternative to the inertia starter is the pre-engaged starter motor which superseded the inertia motor on most if not all modern cars and some late classics. The pre-engaged starter

High-performance pre-engaged starter motor offers many benefits over standard Bendix or inertia types – this is an 'Edge' product from Cambridge Motosport.

motor's gear pinion engages with the flywheel from the opposite side to that of the inertia starter, and at the moment of engagement it's not rotating and so it doesn't damage the ring gear or its pinion gear. Cambridge Motorsport has a range (Edge) of competition pre-engaged starter motors for classic cars, and these are direct replacements for inertia motors. A typical unit produces in excess of twice as much cranking power of the standard inertia starter yet weighs in at the same weight (approx 10lb/4.5kg).

DYNAMO PULLEY

Older classic cars will be fitted with a dynamo and voltage regulator box, which, by design, is unsuited to high rpm. On very high revving, high-performance engines, the dynamo can 'over-speed,' which leads to its destruction. The solution is to reduce the dynamo rpm by replacing the standard dynamo pulley with a larger diameter one. There are a number of these large diameter pulleys available, in a variety of sizes, and some have a deeper 'V' section in order to prevent the belt jumping the pulley at very high rpm. It follows that if the dynamo is running at a reduced speed there'll be a corresponding reduction in charge available, and it may be necessary to adjust the voltage regulator box with the aid of a voltmeter to optimise the dynamo output given its reduced speed. However, even with higher wattage than standard headlamps, the dynamo output with a reduced speed pulley should be adequate for road use.

Finally, of the various Lucas dynamos manufactured the earlier C40 had an output of 22 amps, while the later C40L had the highest output of all at 25 amps, and is therefore better suited for use with an oversize pulley. Note, though, that a dynamo's output is always going to be much less than an alternator's.

CONVERSION FROM DYNAMO TO ALTERNATOR

Converting from dynamo to alternator charging is a fairly straightforward job, but a little more involved if your car is fitted with an FIA battery master switch. The use of any other type of switch risks damaging the alternator should the switch be thrown with the engine running (something which is not a problem with a dynamo). Your car also has to be negative earth polarity for it to work. The advantages of using an alternator are, firstly, that the alternator weighs much less than the dynamo, at typically 3.5kg compared to 5.25kg plus control box. Secondly, not only does the alternator have a higher output than the dynamo, it's produced across a wider range of speed, including quite low speeds, such as engine tick over. Unlike the dynamo which has an external voltage regulator (control box), on the alternator this is integral to the design and makes for a neater installation.

A feature of many DIY alternator conversions is that, for simplicity of wiring, the regulator box is retained in the wiring circuit, though it is no longer being used to regulate current but acts instead as a junction box. Note that a

dynamo produces DC current and an alternator produces AC current. AC current cannot be used to charge the battery, so it is converted to DC by rectifier diodes as it leaves the unit.

Moving to the parts required for the conversion, there are several choices: the most expensive is an alternator that looks near identical to a dynamo, to retain a period-correct look without compromise; a reconditioned unit of a type used on later models of your classic, which might typically be a Lucas ACR unit so looks reasonably period-correct; an alternator that looks like it can be made to fit, even if you have to make your own brackets, from a breaker's yard; and finally, a competition alternator.

The Lucas ACR series came with a variety of outputs, and was superseded in 1982 by the Lucas A133, and in 1985 by the A127 series. These later Lucas alternators are compatible with the ACR series by virtue of the same block connector. However, the A127 series weighs in at 4kg, which is 0.5kg heavier than the earlier ACR series, and they generally have less of a 'classic' appearance about them.

It's possible to fit practically any alternator from a modern car to a classic so long as you ensure correct pulley alignment, but in practice the larger ones often look out of place.

Standard, Mini Spares and Cambridge motorsport alternator pulleys.

When fitting an alternator you may find that the alternator adjustment bracket will allow only a negligible amount of movement before fouling on the front engine plate and engine mounting. If so, use the original dynamo-type adjusting bracket. The standard size alternator pulley will be okay even on highly-tuned cars (maximum safe alternator speed is 15,000rpm). The use of a larger pulley increases the cutting-in speed and maximum output speed, but does not reduce maximum output unless 6000 alternator rpm cannot be achieved. If you do want to fit a larger pulley than the standard 2.36 or 2.5in (60.0 or 63.5mm) pulley, the 3.93in (100mm) Mini Spares item will fit the ACR series of alternators as it does the dynamo, but

Lucas A127, Lucas ACR and Edge alternators.

for use with A127 series alternators you will need to drill the pulley shaft hole to this larger size because the pulley shaft is of a larger diameter. Fitting may require a spacer to correctly position the pulley from the fan. With the pulley and fan fitted to the alternator, and the assembly fitted to the engine, it's necessary to check that the pulley is correctly aligned to the crankshaft and water pump pulley (use washers or small spacers on the alternator mounting bracket). The cut-in speed with the Mini Spares pulley is likely to be around 3000rpm, but, as previously mentioned, this is not going to be a problem even with a road car, and the alternator will certainly produce a greater charge than a dynamo with the same pulley.

Bearing in mind that your car must be negative earth polarity, you'll need to refer to the workshop manual wiring diagram for the colour codes for the wiring. The wiring runs will vary according to whether or not you retain the voltage regulator box or removed it completely. Note that if you do retain the voltage regulator box, it's only being used as junction box rather than regulating the voltage supply. The ignition warning light wire will generally run directly to a terminal on the alternator. The supply feed from the alternator will generally run direct to the solenoid or battery depending on the make and model of car, and, in some instances, type of starter motor. If you're in any doubt about your ability to undertake this work, consult an auto electrician.

Once you have the alternator fitted, wired up, and the engine running, you may need to adjust the engine idle speed, especially if it is a race-tuned unit using a long duration cam. The reason for this is that when any electrical item is switched on (eg a Kenlowe electric fan), it draws a current which the alternator responds to. On a race-tuned engine which is not making a lot of power at idling speeds, this extra-ancillary power demand can make the

difference between the engine idling and stalling. The overall power demand of an alternator is slightly higher than that of a dynamo, drawing some 1.8 to 2.5bhp on full output compared to 1.5bhp of the dynamo.

COMPETITION/ PERFORMANCE USE ALTERNATOR

Cambridge Motorsport has developed a range of a lightweight, high-output alternators suitable for motorsport applications or performance road car use. Brand named 'Edge', these alternators can withstand the heat and vibration of racing applications much better than the standard Lucas ACR units. The CM550 is the smallest unit in the range, and has a cut in at 1000 alternator rpm and generates 45 amps at 3000 alternator rpm. Perhaps most importantly of all, it weighs in at only 2.9g. (A typical Lucas ACR alternator weighs 3.05kg, and a dynamo weighs 5.25kg plus control box). The 'Edge' alternators come with a 60mm steel pulley as standard, but a 115mm aluminium pulley is recommended as part of the purchase as the steel pulley is difficult to remove. Note that the pulley has a deep inset, and neither the Mini Spares or Longman large diameter pulleys are suitable for use with Edge alternators.

AUXILIARY POWER SOCKET

An auxiliary power socket, most likely an Anderson, is there to aid starting by the addition of auxiliary power. This is because the single biggest draw of power made from the battery is from the starter motor when cranking the engine. Also, the higher cranking speed often required to start a race engine can leave a standard battery struggling to provide maximum power for as long as required, even when in first class condition. The basic solution is to simply fit a bigger more powerful battery. However, given the fundamental criteria of keeping the car's weight on or as near minimum

class weight limits as possible, fitting a bigger battery is the last thing anyone wants to do. In fact, often as not the battery fitted is already smaller than the original equipment battery. The solution is to have an external battery, preferably on a portable trolley or with suitable carrying straps, that can be safely but temporarily connected to the on-car battery or the car's power circuits (eg, just the starter motor circuit), to provide more than adequate cranking power to start even a hot and bothered race car engine, no matter what its size (or compression ratio). The advantage of this approach is that the race car battery can be kept at a minimum weight without incurring starting problems (short of stalling on the grid or following a spin or shunt).

Connecting that auxiliary battery to the car's battery or power circuit (eg, the starter) could be achieved with a set of jump leads and the tried and trusty crocodile clips. Often as not, though, neither the crocodile clips or the operator is that reliable, and a flash of sparks gives the visual warning that either a clip has come loose and shorted the power, perhaps as the engine moves under cranking, or the clips have been fitted the wrong way around. There is a neater solution – the Anderson connector system.

The Anderson Jack Plug system has been around for many years, and whether the connectors are red or grey in colour they do the same job. Note that different colour connectors, eg, the red and grey, are NOT compatible, even if rated to carry the same power. Power rating matters, and the larger 175 amp connectors are 175 amp, while the smaller ones are 50 amp rating.

The stereotype surrounding the Anderson Jack Plug system is that they only come in red or grey. A glance at the 'Multipole connector series' on Anderson's website (www. andersonpower.com) will reveal the 50 amp and 175 amp connectors (as well as a 120 amp and 350 amp items) in a range of colours, including orange,

Anderson plug assembly.

Making the connection to the Anderson plug (here fitted to the battery clamp because it's a road car). For a racing car, the socket would be placed such that a connection could be made with the bodywork fitted – a necessity for race re-starts on the grid.

yellow, blue, black and green. You'll also find that Anderson doesn't call its connectors jack plugs, but rather two-pole power connectors with single-piece housings. As well as a pair of connectors, you might also want a handle to fit to the connector that'll be on the auxiliary battery to make life easier on disconnecting it, and perhaps a waterproof boot (all too rare) to prevent water and dirt getting into the connector. Not least, you might also want to get a waterproof sleeve for the same reason.

You'll need some red and black battery cabling to connect your auxiliary battery to one of the Anderson connectors. Likewise, you'll need to connect the other connector, either to the battery or an alternative power circuit like the starter motor, and here you'll need some suitable terminal contacts and protective rubber boots to go over the top.

The connectors can be crimped, but they're big, and unless you have a heavy-duty crimper you're unlikely to succeed, so soldering is the recommended option. Of course, it's as easy to melt the cable as solder the connections, so you might want to buy a ready-made lead from a supplier like Powervamp. However, before cutting the car leads and soldering terminal contacts, you need to find a suitable position to site the on-car connector. There are two basic options to choose from: one is to site the connector as near as possible to the on-car battery or power circuit using as short a cable run as is practical, while allowing for accessibility and rigid mounting. The second is to mount the connector on the car, perhaps even via a purpose-built aperture in the bodywork, so that the connector leading from the auxiliary power source can be plugged in with the minimum of fuss and without disturbing any body panels, but ignoring cable run length which might be considerable. Obviously, there's a multitude of variations on these two choices, and in part the siting of the battery will be key – eg: the battery may be in what was the passenger footwell, the boot, or under the bonnet.

Finally, with the connectors soldered and fitted, the on-car connector rigidly mounted, with cables secured in position as required, and the auxiliary battery charged, all that remains is a test to ensure that your work has been undertaken successfully.

Chapter 17

Aerodynamic devices & bodywork

INTRODUCTION

Aerodynamic devices and improvements to the car's bodywork will affect one, perhaps two, aspects of performance. An aerodynamic device should reduce drag, and thereby increase straight line top speed, or, in some cases, might produce downforce such that cornering speeds are increased. The problem, however, is that these two desirable effects are usually mutually exclusive (though a modification that reduces air going under the car might reduce drag and lift, the latter having a similar effect to increasing downforce). Classic cars are generally far less aerodynamically efficient than modern cars, especially older saloons or non-sporting classics. Consequently, there's a great deal of scope for improvement. The reality for a classic road car is that it's all too easy to make the car go slower, and this should be borne in mind, and for any modification it's first useful to consider why the bodywork is being modified in the first place.

When a car's bodywork is being modified it may be for practical

On some cars, such as this Datsun 240Z, (or the MGB), it's possible to fit a Perspex headlight cover improving aerodynamics and protecting the light unit.

purposes (flaring wheelarches or facilitating an engine swap), or aesthetic reasons (fitting a body kit to make the car stand out from the crowd). It may be

that the aerodynamic device (a wing or spoiler) is fitted in the vague hope that somehow the performance of the car will be improved. It is this latter point that we will tackle first.

There are two basic facts about air that must be understood before considering what effects aerodynamic devices have on a car. Fact number one is that air has a weight that, though small, is measurable. Fact number two is that air, although it cannot be seen in the way that water can, is fluid. The movement of a car through air causes the air to weigh upon the car, or perhaps more helpfully, apply pressure to the car. Secondly, a car passing through air requires power to do so.

From the first chapter of the book it's clear that a reduction in drag will increase the straight line speed of the car, and improving the way the car moves through the air can raise cornering speeds. It's dangerous, and not too helpful at this point, to jump to the examples of Formula One cars, rally cars, and touring cars, and assume that what's good for them must be good for the road. However, motorsport is very different from road use. In Formula One, for example, it's often not so much straight line speed that wins races but rather, cornering speeds. In rallying it's grip that's important in achieving high speeds on loose surfaces. In touring cars, like Formula One, it will be the cornering speed that is more important than straight line speed. The exception from racing examples is Le Mans, where the two mile plus Mulsanne straight is of prime importance.

However, in all racing the aerodynamic performance can be tailored to suit the type of race, circuit, and conditions. A final point to consider is that race tracks are very smooth surfaces, without the bumps, potholes and so forth found on the public highway.

The key to understanding what aerodynamic devices are useful for the road is in the relationship between drag and downforce; the less drag a car has, the higher its straight line top speed will be. For cornering, the limitation on the speed attainable will be down to the amount of grip available. If pressure, or more helpfully, downforce, can be applied to the tyres, more grip is achieved. An aerodynamic device can produce the required pressure but at the expense of increasing drag. In racing, drag and downforce are balanced to produce the best package. Drag is usually split into separate categories, namely: 'form drag,' 'lift drag,' 'interference drag,' and 'service drag.' Form drag is the drag due to the basic shape of the car. Lift drag is created by air that passes underneath the car and creates undesirable lift. Interference drag, also known as 'skin drag' is due to mirrors, trim, and the surface of the car itself. Service drag is due to the passage of air through the car for cooling and ventilation purposes.

So much for the bare basics, now it's time to take a look at what bits can do what. You should bear in mind, however, that we are looking purely at the theory here (a poorly designed

For some cars modified front sections are available, like this race bred Sebring front for the MGB ...

product will achieve little or nothing, and many manufacturers of after-market parts do not test their products in a wind tunnel).

AIR DAMS & SPOILERS
An air dam is generally considered to be an additional bodywork panel (vertical or sloping) fitted to the front of a car, with the objective of improving aerodynamic performance by reducing the flow of air under the car. An air dam is sometimes called a front spoiler, as the job of the front spoiler is likewise to reduce the flow of air under the car. However, a spoiler with a particularly vertical design is more likely to be called an air dam, and a spoiler which is particularly short but with a curved lip at the bottom is more likely to be called a front, or chin, spoiler.

A decent front spoiler, or perhaps a deeper front spoiler, can improve

... while for others it's possible to fit a spoiler.

A vent towards the rear of the wing will both reduce under-bonnet heat and improve the aerodynamic efficiency of the car, as seen on Ian McDonald's Warwick GT350 and which was a period modification on a similar Warwick that raced at Sebring.

the coefficient of drag of your car. Depending on how good or bad the car is, speed improvements of 2-6mph might be seen when a spoiler is fitted. At high cornering speeds a good front spoiler might also reduce front end lift, and provide increased traction for the steered wheels, and also the driven wheels on FWD.

You may be able to find a suitable spoiler from a sporting version of your classic, or perhaps a period after-market accessory, such as something from Richard Grant (eg, Marina, Capri, BMW 2002, etc). For some classics, such as the MG, it may be possible to fit a spoiler designed after the model ceased production. However, for some classics, it's likely that nothing will be available, and you'll need to fabricate from scratch, using sheet aluminium or fibreglass.

The spoiler can be fitted by basic pop riveting or nuts and bolts, perhaps with large load-bearing washers if the spoiler is made of fibreglass. A neater alternative would be to use self-ejecting Dzuz fasteners. The Dzuz is mounted in the panel, while an S-shaped 'spring' is mounted on the car into which the Dzuz fastens. For a particularly neat appearance, the Dzuz can be painted the same colour as the spoiler. While Dzuz take a little longer to fit, there is a large time-saving whenever the spoiler

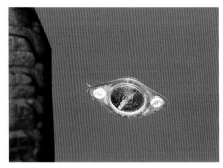

Dzuz fastener retaining the side section of an air dam.

The Dzuz fasteners come in a range of lengths as seen here with the spring, which is the same size for any fastner size.

Boot lid spoiler as standard on the Avenger Tiger.

The Sierra Cosworth had a double hatchback-mounted spoiler as standard.

needs to be removed – such as to allow clearance for a trolley jack.

Rear spoiler

A rear spoiler works by changing the way the air separates at the rear of the car, and thereby reduces drag. However, unlike the front spoiler, it's much easier to increase drag here than reduce it.

As far as increasing downforce goes many rear spoilers aren't going to make much difference on a road car except for the fastest cars. For example, Porsche pioneered rear spoilers starting with the 'duck' and moving onto the 'whale,' while Ford used spoilers to good effect on the XR4 Sierra and, more dramatically, on the Sierra Cosworth. The Hillman Avenger Tiger was probably the first production saloon car (albeit limited production) to have a boot lid-mounted spoiler, though it's not certain how functional it was.

As with the front spoiler, something from Richard Grant might be available. While fabrication from scratch might be considerably more difficult than for the front spoiler, and not a realistic proposition, it's likely any number of modern boot spoilers could be adapted to fit a classic.

BONNET LOUVRES

The idea behind the bonnet louvre is to allow hot air in the engine bay to escape. Louvres can be seen on the 1960s Jaguar E-Type, some Jensen Interceptors (six pack), and 1980s Sierra Cosworths and Escort Turbos; all cars with stunning performance. Austin-Healey used a louvred bonnet

Louvres can be GRP inserts (left), or punched into the metal itself (right), and can aid performance by reducing under-bonnet temperatures.

on its 100M model, and arguably set a precedent for having a louvred bonnet on a factory modified car. Louvred bonnets on a classic car clearly fit the bill as a functional, period-correct modification.

Bonnet louvres are simply angled slots that, on the Jaguar, Jensen and Healey, are punched into the metal (on the Fords they are moulded fibreglass panels). Either approach can be used on your classic car's bonnet or other panels.

If you want the punched metal look then Kool Louvre can punch your bonnet for you. The main restriction on the number, size and, most importantly, position of the louvres is the frame of the bonnet itself – the framework on the underside of the panel. All you need to do is take the bonnet to Kool Louvre, or a similar specialist, and it'll do the rest. Note, however, that the panel will require repainting afterwards.

If you want fibreglass louvres in your car's bonnet, you'll need to first purchase some inserts, and then either do the job yourself or find a reputable body shop that will neatly cut the bonnet to insert them. The louvres can be fastened by pop-rivets, but, if the fit is tight, you should be able to fibreglass them in.

ENGINE OR CARBURATION SWAP BODYWORK MODIFICATIONS

Sometimes a modification will require

A tidy relief let into the bulkhead to accommodate the distributor on an overhead cam engine.

that the bodywork be modified to accommodate it – something more sophisticated than the use of a large hammer. This short section provides an insight into why that may be the case, so you can plan before committing to an engine swap.

One of the key differences between some classics engines and most modern engines is that the classic engine may have pushrods and rockers, while modern engines are nearly always of an overhead camshaft design. Both designs are very likely to have the distributor driven by the crankshaft, though the very latest engine designs are more likely to have crankshaft-triggered electronic ignition. However, while the pushrod and rocker engine has the distributor placed low down and on one side of the engine, the overhead cam engine may well have the distributor driven off the back of the camshaft (or one camshaft for a twin-cam), at the top and rear of the engine. So, when it comes to what seems a straightforward engine swap, everything fits reasonably well except for the distributor at the top and rear of the engine. The solution is to cut a relief into the bulkhead, allowing enough room to remove the distributor from the engine if required.

When swapping from a downdraught or SU carb(s) to sidedraught carbs, such as the Weber DCOE, there may be a lack of space for air horns or filter, because of the depth of the sidedraught carb compared to the original equipment. For most cars that don't have MacPherson strut front suspension it's possible to modify the inner wing to create the extra room required.

ROLL BARS & ROLL CAGES

For a soft top classic (including classics with removable hard tops) it's worth fitting a roll-over bar; either a trimmed roll bar for everyday use, or a certified Roll Over Protection System (ROPS) roll bar for motorsport (whether

A roll hoop (this one is chromed), seen here on an Allard, or a roll bar, is strongly recommended for open top cars.

or not the car requires one by the regulations). If you want to fit a full roll cage to the bodyshell, either for safety or to increase torsional stiffness, the performance benefit will be in cornering, where suspension geometry changes due to flex will be alleviated. The downside is that a full cage is heavy and expensive. A lighter but stronger cage made from T45 tubing (or US equivalents) is lighter than cold drawn steel (CDS), but has a price to match. Safety Devices can supply and fit, or even design, a cage for any car, and is an acknowledged expert. While roll bars

are supplied painted matt black, there's no reason why they can't be painted to match the body colour of the car, or even a contrasting colour.

WHEELARCHES

If you've fitted wider wheels and tyres, or altered the track of your classic car, or any combination of these, you may find that the edge of the tyre protrudes past the bodywork of the car. It's a legal requirement in the UK that the tyre edge cannot protrude past the wing (fender) edge, so you'll need to fit a wheelarch extension kit or modify the arch flare. Looking at the extension kit first, there's a wide range of wheelarch kits on the market, most of which are fibreglass or aluminium. Fitting may be by pop rivet or self tapping screw. Before fitting, you need to consider the wheel travel, and whether you need to cut back the standard arch before fitting the kit, in order to allow for sufficient wheel travel without fouling.

An alternative to fitting an extension kit is to flare the existing arches. This can be achieved by cutting the arch rim at short intervals, peeling

A full, welded-in roll cage with door bars, painted to match the body colour of this highly modified MkII Escort from Den Motorsport. Note the FIA roll bar padding above the driver's door.

A set of arches for the Ford Escort. These can be fitted to standard wings.

On this Ford MkIII Cortina, the larger rear wheels and tyres are accommodated by a shortened width rear axle, and the inner wheel well being cut back.

Wider than standard wheels and tyres will require bespoke arches, or the arch widened to blend in with the original design.

the arch up and then welding the cuts back together. The arch will need to be finished with body filler to get a smooth finish. The obvious disadvantage to this method is that it can be expensive, and requires the paintwork to be resprayed.

WINDSCREEN

Windscreens will be either toughened (tempered), or laminated glass. While, ultimately, the toughened windscreen is harder to break than a laminated windscreen, when it does break it shatters, or crazes, into many small pieces, whereas the laminated screen will remain intact. You may find a toughened screen is no longer available for your classic, but a laminated screen is. Recently, it's become possible to have as small a production run of just a single windscreen for virtually any classic car, at a comparable price to that of a car still in production, and with the option of having a tint or darker sun strip on the screen. For other classics, like the Morris Minor, the Morris Minor Centre (Birmingham) will even have a choice of screens in stock. For some motorsports disciplines in the UK, a laminated windscreen is mandatory, with no age-related exemption.

WINDOWS

One weight-saving option is to have the side, including quarterlight, or rear windows of your car, including hard tops, replaced with polycarbonate or Perspex (with polycarbonate being recommended as it's less likely to splinter than Perspex, and is available in a range of tints). The only downside to using polycarbonate or Perspex in door glass is that they are easily scratched, and a conventional winding up and down action in the door will quickly render them opaque and thus next to useless. The alternative is to either never wind them up and down, or install them with sliders. In the UK, Airedale Race Components can supply the relevant products.

FULL BODY & FRONT BODY CONVERSIONS

For many classic cars there's a range of after-market fibreglass full body or front body conversion kits available – used original items or new produced on the same mould. For other classics it was the manufacturer, sometimes in collaboration with a specialist company, who produced a car with non-standard bodywork as part of a special model range, such as the Tickford Capri, Droop Snoot Firenza, and Avenger Tiger. Not least, for some classics it was possible to create what amounted to a completely different car, like the Hurricane, or Bond, while many kit cars were based on popular classics.

A number of companies, including Fibresports, produce these parts, so if you have a rare fibreglass front body it could be remade again. For some classics it's possible to obtain replacement or conversion parts made in aluminium rather than steel.

Chapter 18
Development & testing

INTRODUCTION

Development and testing should be undertaken to ensure the parts fitted to your car are working as they should (safely), and affecting all four aspects of performance. Engine testing and development will mostly centre on carburation and ignition changes and take place on the dynamometer. Dynamometer tuning ensures the parts fitted to your car are set up and calibrated to achieve the optimum power figure. Failure to get this right can result in expensive repairs and disappointment.

Suspension development will be mostly undertaken following first hand experience. Here, we'll explain how that testing takes place and what happens.

DYNAMOMETER TUNING

There are two distinct types of dynamometer, or 'dyno': the engine dyno, and the chassis dyno. The first is an engine test-bed dyno (not generally available to the public) where the engine is run independently of the car and power readings are taken direct from the flywheel. The second type (covered

A 1956 Triumph-engined Peerless on the rollers at Peter Burgess' workshop, ready for testing. (Courtesy Peter Burgess)

An alternative to the chassis dyno or rolling road is the flywheel dyno, shown here with a Porsche flat-six engine under test. (Courtesy Rothsport Racing)

here) is where the engine remains in the car and power readings are taken from the driven wheels, via a pair of rollers. Because chassis dyno runs are taken from rollers, this type of dyno is often known as 'the rollers' or 'rolling road.' The chassis dyno is the type of dyno you are most likely to encounter. Most chassis dynos are fixed facilities found at a garage since the rollers are set into the floor. A more recent alternative to fixed venue rolling roads is the portable rolling road.

What the dyno can do

The dyno is the best place to discover the power output and power curve of your car's engine, brake horsepower, and torque output figures, as measured at the driven wheels. You can also calibrate the speedometer and tachometer, while at the same time learning what exhaust emissions the engine is producing.

Primarily, though, you'll be running your car on the dyno to tune the engine for maximum horsepower by obtaining and applying optimum ignition and carburation settings under real-world running conditions. A point to note is that while power figures produced from the driven wheels can be converted to a hypothetical figure at the flywheel, the method done to produce the calculation isn't necessarily accurate, and more than one type of calculation method exists. Likewise, even the power figures produced at the wheels cannot realistically be compared to power figures seen with other vehicles on a different dyno. This is because calibration of dynos can vary, and even consistent use of the same dyno can produce variations in power figures due to atmospheric changes, and so on. Therefore, the dyno should not be used to produce a set of figures to boast about in the paddock or bar, but rather as an instrument with which to get the very best results from your engine. Not least, a good dyno operator can tell you if there is anything wrong with the engine.

Chassis dyno session

When choosing a chassis dyno don't simply pick the nearest. Instead, ask around for recommendations. Next, ensure that the operator of the dynos you're considering is familiar with your type of car, especially the carburettors fitted to the engine. If your vehicle is 4WD, you'll have a more limited choice of dynos because not all dynos have the two sets of rollers required. Some dyno installations are more modern than others, and produce a print out of the vehicle's performance, but what really counts is the ability of the dyno operator.

Preparing for the session

Make sure your car's engine is in good running order. Change the sparkplugs,

Sometimes the rolling road comes to you, or at least a classic car show or race meeting, and here is an **MG RV8** at Silverstone Live.

oil and filter, ignition points (where fitted), and the air filter. Note that as far as setting up the ignition system and fuelling calibrations, that's for the dyno operator to do. That said, it's useful if you know what the basic settings are, even after fitting modified parts, and, where possible, to know the sizes of carburettor jets and needles (where applicable). Lastly, take a pen and paper and a friend to record information about the session, such as oil pressure, coolant and oil running temperatures, and so on.

What happens at a chassis dyno session

The most important thing is to discuss with the dyno operator the specification of the engine, and any problems you're aware of, such as flat spots or hesitation at any point in the rev range. In turn, be prepared for the operator to ask about the sort of use the car is put to, such as road or track. Talking over, it's time for action.

The vehicle will be driven on to the rollers so that the driven wheels are in contact with them. The undriven wheels will be chocked and the vehicle strapped down using some tie downs. An emissions analyser will be connected to the exhaust system, and an electronic diagnostic system will be connected to the vehicle's ignition system. The engine will be started and the operator's ignition diagnostic will quickly show up any basic ignition problems, such as a bad lead or arcing distributor cap. If any faults are found at this point they will need rectification before any further progress can be made. At this point a visual check for oil and water leaks might be made.

Next, the first run will be undertaken. On this run the objective of the dyno operator is to establish a good ignition setting. The operator will do this by 'swinging' the distributor (having loosened the fastening first) while the vehicle is being driven on the rollers at an engine rpm that corresponds to the maximum advance the distributor produces, usually at about the mid range power point of the engine. Once

done, the first run is finished. When the rollers are stationary the dyno operator will tighten the distributor clamp and, using whatever ignition diagnostic he has wired up, either an oscilloscope or strobe (perhaps both) tell you what the static ignition timing figure is. This setting will be unique to your car's engine and tuning set up. If you're serious about ignition timing, it's possible to plot optimum readings right through the rev range, and this can be used to adjust the distributor's ignition curve to the ideal.

The second run is done to establish how well the engine is performing throughout the rev range. The operator will be watching the CO (exhaust) gas analysis to see if the air/fuel mixture is too rich or too weak at any point in the rev range. If the mixture is so weak that there's a risk of the pistons being damaged, even holed, the run will be terminated and the problem rectified. After this run is completed the operator will need to know the use to which the vehicle is put in order to set the mixture accordingly. For instance, a full race mixture is richer than a road use only mixture, though the final say is yours, guided, of course, by the dyno operator.

Once the mixture has been agreed, and in the case of a carburated engine, jets or needles changed, a full power run can be undertaken.

The full power run is pretty impressive (and possibly terrifying). Whatever your attitude to the full power run, it's the one that really matters. Depending on the sophistication of the dyno, a print out of the entire power output plotted against the engine rpm may or may not be produced. If one isn't, it's time to put your friend to good use and let him note each power figure at 500rpm increments, which can then be plotted on graph paper after the dyno session. During the full power run, more so than the previous runs, a close eye should be kept on engine coolant temperature, oil temperature (if there's a gauge) and oil pressure. If any of these give cause for concern at any time during the proceedings the engine should be switched off immediately. If you're the person driving the car, then this is your responsibility. Note that, despite the presence of a large cooling fan in the dyno bay, most vehicles will run slightly on the hot side. If the dyno run does highlight a problem in this area, guidance on how to resolve the problem is given in the relevant chapters of this book.

When the dyno session is complete, and there may have been more than one full power run depending on how things went, the operator may ask you to take the vehicle for a short drive. This is an interesting and revealing moment, because you'll feel the benefit of the dyno tune in the smoothness of the power delivery and the increased power liberated by the calibration changes.

The bill for the use of the dyno session is usually based on an hourly rate plus the cost of any parts. Although the bottom line on the bill may be quite high, and this is what puts people off dyno sessions, it's a modest cost given the gains in engine power achieved and the data gathered. If the dyno session has highlighted an engine problem, and the session had to be prematurely terminated, you've at least saved yourself an expensive engine failure.

The first dyno session should most definitely not be seen as the last or only session required. As further development and modification of the engine are undertaken, further visits to the dyno should be made. Where finances prohibit this for any length of time, a sad fact of life, keep a record of the work done and effects produced for future reference. The dyno session is the 'icing on the cake' of your tuning project, so enjoy it.

ROAD DEVELOPMENT

This will be difficult to do unless you have access to a private road, test or race track or airfield. Either way, one essential tool is the G Tech performance meter. This will measure horsepower, acceleration times, and G-force. It can be used to find out what effect changes to gearing and traction have on acceleration times, as well as comparing how much

grip one tyre has compared to another (by reference to lateral G). It's relatively simple to use, and, though reasonably expensive, not prohibitively so. It's a useful instrument but no substitute for dyno testing; rather a supplement to it.

SUSPENSION DEVELOPMENT

A key part of suspension development is to keep a record of the changes made to your car's suspension, and note any improvements. However, it's possible that some modifications, particularly if taken to the extreme, can worsen handling. Road or track testing is only part of the solution in establishing what works and what doesn't, and needs to supplemented with accurate data.

Five things should be accurately measured as part of suspension development: vehicle weight; front suspension tracking; ride height; front wheel camber; and spring poundage.

Vehicle weight can be measured on a commercial weighbridge, but, since they round up or down, sometimes to within 20kg, it's important to establish the rounding factor before use. A weighbridge at a racing circuit will be particularly accurate, and can generally be used subject to getting permission. Furthermore, a set of corner weight scales can be used. As their name suggests, these provide a weight per corner reading, measured at the wheel, as well as a total weight. Ensure consistency in the vehicle's condition – always weigh with the same amount of fuel in it, for example.

Vehicle ride height should be

measured to the bottom of the sill, with the car parked on a level surface.

To measure front wheel camber, it's necessary to use a camber gauge, and to take the measurement on a level surface. There are a number of different types of camber gauge available, and some are more expensive than others, though the Dunlop gauge isn't prohibitively so.

New springs should work at their advertised rate, but if you're buying secondhand you'll either have to rely on the seller's memory or have them tested. Coil spring testers for front springs are expensive, but many race preparation companies will have a tester and, for a small fee, may test your springs. However, when it comes to the leaf springs for the rear of any classic car, a leaf spring tester has to be found. However, to the author's knowledge, the only leaf spring tester in the UK, if not in Europe, is the Intercomp tester he purchased from the USA. Early work has revealed some interesting characteristics (as yet undocumented), that he plans to share with a spring manufacturer or parts specialist to develop better springs than are currently available, and which will be sold with accurate spring poundage data across the range of travel.

The Dunlop camber gauge in use.

The G Tech Performance meter – stick it on your car windscreen and plug it into your cigarette lighter socket.

The author's Intercomp leaf spring testing gauge being used to test a Sprite/Midget semi-elliptic rear leaf spring.

Chapter 19
Preparation for motorsport

INTRODUCTION

It's not possible to give totally comprehensive instructions for preparing your classic car for competition, as the safety regulations vary for different types of motorsport and different series. The regulations you'll need to refer to will be available from the sport or series governing body in your country.

PREPARATION FOR MOTORSPORT

This chapter aims to point you in the right direction with regard to basic safety preparation and modifications to your classic car which, even if not mandatory for your motorsports discipline or class, are, nonetheless, worth undertaking. Of course, you don't have to be competing in your car to undertake the modifications in this chapter, as they'll make your car safer, even if it's only ever used on the road.

COMPETITION SEATS

There are a number of reasons for changing the seat, even though it may not be necessary for the regulations,

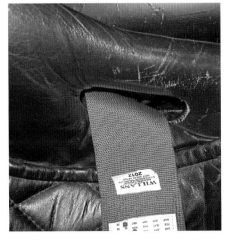

The Corbeau Sprint seat has the all-important harness slots, shown here with a Willans harness.

and the first is to have a seat that supports the head and neck, reducing the likelihood of whiplash injury in the event of an accident. The second is to reduce the weight of the car by replacing the standard seat with something lighter. After that you might be looking for a seat that provides better lateral support, and,

last but not least, if you have fitted or plan to fit a racing harness you may need a seat with suitable slots, especially a crotch slot.

Often the cheapest upgrade is to fit a seat from a later or higher specification model of your car, one that incorporated a headrest or was of a high-back design, for example. However, in most cases, any production car seat will weigh more than double a typical competition or after-market sports seat.

If you decide then to fit a competition or after-market sports seat the first selection criteria is to find one that will fit. The seat-well on some classics, especially those with a pronounced tunnel for the propshaft, is relatively narrow compared to modern cars. You'll also need to watch the width of the shoulder area of the seat which can come very close to the B-post, especially if the seat is positioned to the rear of the seat-well. A competition seat, whose construction will generally be a fibreglass shell trimmed with cloth, will weigh approximately 5kg, though it's possible to get even lighter carbon fibre versions. You'll also need to consider whether or not you'll be using the seat in conjunction with a racing harness, and, if so, to ensure it has suitable harness slots. Not least, it may be necessary to have a seat that meets a current FIA homologation standard – a point to watch if competing internationally.

Having purchased your seat, you need to fit it. For most if not all seats, a universal seat runner kit is available. There are two distinct types: the seat slider set, which may or may not be used in conjunction with a universal subframe or tilt kit, and the side mounting kit, which is generally lighter and made from either steel or aluminium alloy. With the former you retain the option or being able to move the seat fore and aft, whereas with the later the seat is fixed in a single position and can only be repositioned by undoing the seat-to-bracket fasteners, moving the position and then refastening. The advantage of a side-mounting seat kit is that it is very easy to raise the seat, albeit to a fixed height. Whatever seat and mounting kit you use it's almost a certainty that your car will need fresh mounting points drilled to accommodate it, and the seat should be fitted with ⅜in (8mm) bolts.

SEATBELTS & HARNESSES

There are differences between seatbelts and harnesses, and the requirements for the different disciplines within motorsport vary, as does the original equipment (OE) fitting in classic cars. The OE fit will either be nonexistent, a two mounting-point lap strap, or the more recent lap and diagonal shoulder seatbelt which has three mounting points. In motorsport generally, the lap and shoulder seatbelt needs to be replaced by what's known as a full harness, racing harness, or racing seatbelts, of which there are several types, brands and variations.

A harness will be either four- or six-point, and will usually have a central release mechanism, known as a release box (rather than a release mechanism), to one side. The harness will have a

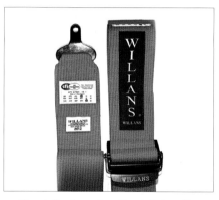

Check the homologation label on the harness to establish what standards it meets (eg: FIA or SFI) and how old it is. This Willans harness meets both FIA and SFI standards.

The six-point harness is superior to the four-point harness. This one is by Willans.

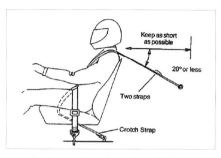

Optimum strap layout for Willans Silverstone LD V6 belt set. (Courtesy Willans)

Willans mounting ring and reinforcing plate, with belt clipped in and locked, and with an aircraft cowling pin for added security.

strap over each shoulder, and a strap on each side of the seat, at the lap, making four straps that meet at your waistline. A six-point system is similar, but has an additional strap that comes up between your legs, and which might comprise two belts on a common clip-in point on a 'T' or 'I' shape. The widths of the straps is important. While most harnesses used to have 2in (50mm) straps all round, FIA homologated harnesses now have 3in (75mm) shoulder straps (except for certain harnesses specifically used for a Hand and Neck restraint device (HANS), while lap and crotch straps can remain at 2in or be 3in).

In the USA, harnesses may meet the SFI rather than the (higher) FIA standard, and will be readily identified as such. Some harnesses meet both.

A key advantage of a four- or six-point harness over a three-point lap and diagonal shoulder seatbelt is that in the event of the car rolling over, either upside down or onto its side, the harness prevents the driver sliding vertically from the seating position. A three-point won't prevent vertical movement, raising the possibility of head injury.

The MSA regulations for the UK vary between hillclimb and sprint cars, racing cars and rally cars. Looking first at the hillclimb and sprint cars, for road going classes it's possible to stay with the factory-fit, three-point lap and diagonal shoulder seatbelt. For modified classes, a four- or six-point harness will be required, and this can have 2in belts and not be FIA homologated (at least at the time of going to press, but like all things subject to change). Race and rally cars need four- or six-point harnesses that are FIA homologated, typically with 3in shoulder and lap straps. There are, however, age-related exemptions, though it's hard to imagine why anyone would want to exercise them in preference to personal safety.

Having decided what harness you need or want, there are a few other things you might want to consider, and Willans has a very comprehensive order form that can be used if you're not buying off-the-shelf. Options include lighter than standard buckles, which also look neater than the standard items, adjustment pull up or pull down, release box fitted to the belt of your choice, snap hook fixing or bolt fixing, etc.

Also, don't forget to investigate a set of wrist restraints compatible with the harness (mandatory for some race series – 'run what you brung' drag racing, for example) as an additional safety measure, particularly for open classics.

Before buying a harness, check your car's seat is suitable for use with one, in that it has suitable apertures in the shoulder, sides and crotch section for the straps and buckles to fit over or through. Also ensure the seat apertures don't have any sharp edges that will chafe the harness. Similarly, check that the seat mounting brackets – particularly if external to the seat – won't chafe the harness. Remember these points because once you have the harness fitted and adjusted for the driver, they'll need checking regularly.

To fit the harness it's necessary to decide where the eyelet anchor bolts for the snap hooks will be (eyelet and snap hook fastening is recommended). Generally, these will be on the floor and the rear bulkhead. A point to watch about drilling the mounts on the floor is to ensure you don't drill through any rigid brake or fuel lines, both of which may be very close to the optimum mounting points for the harness straps. All of these areas (assuming your car is

structurally sound) should be sufficiently strong to be load-bearing in the event of an accident, but you may wish to add (by welding) small reinforcing plates for extra strength. Make sure you follow the belt manufacturer's instructions, in particular with regard to positioning the eye bolts, but also the care and use of the harness. When clipping in the harness be sure to check the orientation of the eyebolt and eye so there's no scope for accidental back releasing of the strap. As an additional safety measure it's recommended that you use the purpose-designed hole in most clips to fit what looks like a thick metal nappy pin, but is, in fact, an aircraft cowling pin, which, despite its origin, is readily available from many performance parts outlets. It's particularly important that the angle of the shoulder straps is as close to horizontal as possible, and no greater than 45 degrees from horizontal when you're sitting in the seat and strapped in. The reason for this is that, in the event of an accident, as your body mass is restrained by the shoulder straps, the straps will try to close the angle between the mounting point and your shoulder in a downward movement only resisted by, possibly, your seat, and certainly your shoulders.

Time at last to sit down and strap yourself in as tight as possible and check for any fouling of the straps. Next check you can reach everything (switches, circuit breaker (battery master isolator), fire extinguisher button or pull, etc). If you find you can't reach something, you'll need to re-position it so you can.

Finally, if the worst comes to the worst and the harness gets to do its job, it will have been shock loaded and will never perform to the same standard again, even though it may look okay. Cut the straps, discard it, and buy a new one.

CIRCUIT BREAKER (BATTERY MASTER ISOLATOR SWITCH)

A mandatory requirement for racing classics and some classes of sprint and hillclimb competition cars, is a clearly

FIA circuit breaker switch (top), and basic battery master switch (bottom).

External circuit breaker switch and plumbed-in fire extinguisher. There's zero scope for confusing which cable-operated pull handle is which, as both are fitted within their correct identifying safety stickers.

identified external circuit breaker – a switch that shuts off all electrical power on the car; everything, including the rear red warning light (rain light). Sometimes this switch is also known as the battery master isolator switch. Identification should be by a red spark on a white-edged blue triangle (12cm base) and, the on and off positions should be clearly marked. Conveniently, a suitable sticker is usually supplied with the circuit breaker on purchase.

There are a number of different circuit breakers available, including some period looking items, though those generally aren't compatible with alternator-equipped cars. It's recommended to use the one that takes a key – the Autolec – though a popular alternative is the pull switch, but this does have a couple of disadvantages. First, even though clearly marked, the pull for off circuit breaker is frequently identical to the pull for a plumbed in fire extinguisher (where fitted), so providing scope for mis-identification. Second, the pull cable is prone to corrosion and seizing, and can stick when being tested it, with the result that the handle snaps and cuts your fingers. On occasion a hybrid system, combining pull switch and key (the pull operating the key), or internal and external keys, can be used.

It's important to choose the correct circuit breaker for your car because a standard Autolec circuit breaker will isolate only the battery. So, if you car has either an alternator or dynamo charging circuit, the engine will almost certainly continue to run, and thus not comply with the regulation that the circuit breaker must cut all electrical power. If you car has a charging circuit, you'll need an Autolec FIA approved circuit breaker, which is recognisable by having four terminals for spade end type connectors central to its underside, in addition to the main power feeds.

Having purchased the appropriate circuit breaker for your requirements, it's relatively straightforward to fit. The UK motorsports regulation for circuit breaker position recommends (but is not mandatory) some siting points, one of which is adjacent the driver's side windscreen pillar. In practical terms this can be the top edge of the right-hand front wing, in the corner, adjacent to the scuttle panel. This location will not obscure your view, and does not require wiring to pass through the bulkhead. However, should your car be fitted with a one-piece front end, then you may have no alternative but to mount the switch on the bulkhead.

To fit the circuit breaker, drill the holes and bolt it in place (stainless steel bolts are recommended). Next, disconnect the earth lead at the battery (to prevent accidental shorts while working with the live leads), then remove the live lead at the battery. Two new leads (heavy duty battery type), are substituted for the single battery live lead, and you can make these y-ourself or ask an auto electrical specialist. One lead runs from the battery live terminal to the circuit breaker, and the other runs from the circuit breaker to the main battery feed point (usually the solenoid). To keep the leads tidy, use P-clips or large wiring clips. If you can get hold of suitably-sized connection covering boots, use them (solenoid type rubber boots fit), to keep moisture out and prevent accidental shorts against earthed component (eg steel bodywork). Finally, refit the earth lead.

An FIA approved circuit breaker needs extra wiring to function correctly. Of the four extra connectors on this type of circuit breaker, two are for the ignition, and two for the charging circuit (of particular importance for alternator-equipped cars, to protect the internal rectifier diodes from damage from a high voltage surge if the circuit breaker is opened whilst the engine is running). Incidentally, if your car's alternator is damaged in this fashion, the internal diode pack (Lucas part number UCB100 for 16, 17, and 18 ACR units), can be replaced for a fraction of the cost of an exchange or new alternator.

The Autolec circuit breaker contains fitting instructions and a simple wiring diagram. The alternator feeds to the solenoid don't all need to be wired through the 'W' terminal; what is required is that a single wire must run from the solenoid to the terminal. The other 'W' terminal is wired to earth via the resistor supplied with the circuit breaker. You can solder wires to each end of the resistor and then earth one, connecting the other to the circuit breaker. The ignition switch to coil wire can be cut at a convenient point and wired through the 'Z' terminals of the switch.

With the installation of the circuit breaker complete, you'll need to test that it works correctly. To do this, start the engine, put some revs on, so the alternator (or dynamo) is charging, and get an assistant to throw the connection. If you've done the job correctly the engine will stop and the alternator (where fitted) won't be damaged. If the engine doesn't stop you'll need to go back to the wiring diagram and check your work until you find the problem.

FUEL TANK CAP & TANK BREATHER

On many classics the fuel tank cap is ventilated to the atmosphere so that, as the fuel in the tank is consumed by the engine, it is replaced by air. However, should the car have an accident and finish up on its side or upside-down, fuel can drain out of the ventilation/breathing hole in the cap. Later classics (approx 1970 onwards) are more likely to have a cap which is of a locking design featuring a primitive one way valve so that, while air can be drawn in through the cap, any escape of fuel – should the car end up on its side or roof – is prevented. If you're not sure if the cap on your car is the valved type, check whether it has any kind of springing arrangement, or if the seal is of a basic flat design with a clearly visible breather hole – the former is most likely valved and the latter not. Since it's a regulation for most UK motorsport for the fuel system to prevent any escape of fuel, switch from a standard non-valved filler cap to a valved one.

If you particularly want to use the standard cap to present an outwardly original appearance, it's possible to seal the hole in the cap but fit a non-return valve to the tank filler pipe to ensure compliance with the regulations without compromising safety.

Where the standard fuel tank has been replaced with a purpose-designed racing fuel tank, the regulations are the same. However, because a separate breather pipe is built into the top of the tank, the cap may not have a breather at all. The breather pipe can be fitted with a purpose-designed non-return valve to ensure the car complies with the regulations, or it can be fitted with a long piece of tubing that doubles back on itself and ultimately finishes at a point lower than the fuel tank of the car so that, if the car finishes on its side or roof, no fuel can escape. However, there is the possibility that if the pipe is not sufficiently long fuel can surge out of this breather pipe under hard cornering, especially in an endurance race when the car will have a large fuel load. So, the use of a non-return valve is the recommended solution.

OIL CATCH TANK & ENGINE BREATHER SYSTEMS

The regulations for UK motorsport state that no engine oil breathing pipe can be vented to the atmosphere. What is acceptable, though, is for the pipes to vent into a catch tank (there are different sizes for different branches of motorsport and engine size). An alternative is for a breather pipe to form part of what is called a 'closed breather system,' so that the breather pipe is fed into the induction

A one-litre capacity oil catch tank, with sight gauge and weld bung threaded fittings on an engine breather tank (manufactured to a very high standard by AH Fabrications to the author's design).

... and here it is fitting neatly between the radiator expansion tank (fitted with a competition 16lb lever release Stant cap) and the fuel pressure regulator. The breather pipes are from: the rocker cover; engine block; and timing gear case, and all are plumbed with Goodridge threaded fittings and 120- and 90-degree tube/ swept fitting.

system where any oil is consumed and burnt by the engine. However, since burning oil is detrimental to engine performance, using a re-circulating breather system is not recommended.

While it's possible to buy a one of a number of standard pattern oil catch tanks, it's only slightly more expensive to have one made to your exact specification. AH Fabrications, for example, is capable of this type of work, and will talk through your design to agree finer details. Further information is contained in the section on engine breathing in chapter 7.

FLAMEPROOF BULKHEADS

The idea of having a flameproof bulkhead on a classic car used for motorsport is that in the event of an accident the driver's cockpit/passenger compartment amounts to a safety cell where no liquid or flame can penetrate quickly, if at all.

Most classic cars won't have this safety cell because of the area between the boot and rear seats which is unlikely to be solid metal. On many classic sports cars without rear seats the division between the boot and the cockpit might be a simple vinyl trimmed cardboard divider. It's necessary then to seal the area with several small aluminium plates,

Carpet and trim removal will reveal rear inner wing access apertures, which should be plated over for competition to ensure integrity of the bulkhead from the engine bay and the potential passage of flame and fluids. The trim can be re-fitted later if the class regulations require it.

Heater ducting to interior neatly blocked off to ensure integrity of the bulkhead from the engine bay and the potential passage of flame and fluids.

or a single large one, screwed or pop riveted in place, and sealed around the edges with a mastic sealer.

If the heater air outlet is from inside the engine bay it needs to be blanked off. Once again, a suitable plate can be made from aluminium or steel. Note that once it's fitted you won't be able to use the heater for demisting.

HANDHELD FIRE EXTINGUISHER

For UK motorsports most disciplines require fire extinguishers to be a plumbed in system. However, where permitted, or to supplement a plumbed-in fire extinguisher, a handheld unit can be fitted. With the demise of BCF/Halon extinguishants, the choice will be between foam, dry powder, CO2, or a gas generating system. However, neither CO2 or dry powder units meet the regulations, so the extinguishant is almost certain to be one of the branded foam or gas generating products, though the latter are expensive.

A good choice of handheld foam extinguisher is the 1.75L unit that comes complete with mounting bracket. The weight of the extinguisher and bracket is 6.25lb (2.83kg). When choosing the site for the extinguisher, consider driver/passenger ease of exit in an emergency. Note that a horizontal floor mounting is recommended (the footwell will be the lowest horizontal surface) as it helps keep the centre of gravity of the car low, unlike an upright mounting. When fitting the bracket, avoid drilling through fuel/brake lines, and exhaust pipe.

PLUMBED-IN FIRE EXTINGUISHER

Where the regulations require a plumbed-in fire extinguisher, check carefully what the exact requirement is so that your car's installation will meet or exceed it. The key considerations will be the size of the bottle, the number and position of discharge nozzles, and the number and type of triggering methods. As with the handheld extinguisher, a foam unit is most likely to meet motorsport regulations at the least cost.

You need to consider where you're going to site the extinguisher bottle beforehand, as there are wide variations in both bottle size and shape. The shape will always be cylindrical, but either short and fat (standard), or long and thin (slimline). Most bottles will be made from aluminium alloy, but cheaper steel items are heavier.

Lifeline AFFF plumbed-in system kit with cable pull operation and bottle polished for a classic period look.

Lifeline plumbed-in fire extinguisher just in front of the driver's seat. Note that triggering is by a manually-activated cable release.

Pull handle for plumbed-in fire extinguisher mounted in dash, with ignition off position indicated.

The regulations your competition car is required to comply with will stipulate the number and basic position of the nozzles for the fire extinguisher, and will typically be one for the engine bay and one for the cockpit/passenger compartment. It's suggested that the engine bay nozzle be placed adjacent to the carburettor(s) and manifolds. The installation of this nozzle will almost certainly require the bulkhead to be drilled, and a piping bulkhead fitting to be used. Care must be taken that both the hole and the pipework do not foul anything.

The operation of the fire extinguisher is rarely stipulated in the regulations, so the choice will be yours: electrical operation or mechanical (cable) operation. Electrically-operated installations tend to be more expensive than cable-operated systems, aren't necessarily more reliable, and are more often fired by mistake (in the author's experience). The electrical supply is by a small, dry-cell battery, which can be tested from a switch on the inboard triggering unit.

There will be a requirement for an external triggering point which will require wiring up to the triggering unit. The location of the external triggering point is recommended to be just below the windscreen on the scuttle panel on the driver's side. Not least, the external triggering point is required to be visually identifiable, and a suitable sticker is usually supplied with the kit or can be purchased separately. Location and identification for a mechanical (cable) triggering method is the same as for electrical triggering, but care must be taken to avoid kinking the cable and also to lightly oil the cable before fitting it.

As well as the external trigger whether electrical or mechanical it's usual but not always mandatory to have an internal trigger as well.

WINDSCREEN

MSA regulations for windscreens vary between racing cars and hillclimb and sprint cars in UK motorsport. Toughened (tempered) windscreens are only legal in hillclimbing and sprinting. In racing, the windscreen, if glass, must be laminated glass. Note that while a plastic (Perspex or polycarbonate) windscreen may be used, the car must still have a windscreen wiper. Further information on windscreens is contained in the bodywork chapter.

ROLL BARS, ROLL CAGES, ROLL BAR PADDING

For all competition and sports cars, it's recommended that a roll bar be fitted. Where a roll bar is fitted to meet a regulation for competing in motorsport (note some branches of motorsport don't require a roll bar, or, for older cars, there may be an age related exemption), it must meet the standards required, so check before purchasing. Roll bars may be for the rear of the car only, or for front and rear with door bars as well to form a complete roll cage, sometimes known

as a roll over protection system (ROPS). Some rear bars may have a diagonal bracing bar, which may be either fixed or removable. It's possible to fabricate a roll bar or roll cage system, but for a bar or cage used in motorsport it's recommended you purchase a purpose-designed item from a manufacturer, such as Safety Devices.

For any car with a roll bar it's a requirement that roll bar padding is used as well. While foam padding similar to pipe lagging appears adequate, it provides no real protection other than perhaps from scratching or scraping of a helmet. The solution is to use purpose-designed FIA homologated padding from Safety Devices, which is designed to absorb energy from an impact.

SHELL PREPARATION

It's a good idea to strengthen the bodyshell by welding the seams. In the

UK, Safety Devices can completely race prepare a shell to your specification. For instance, not only can it weld in the rollcage, but also flare the arches and weld all the bodywork seams, the latter to strengthen the shell.

BODYWORK FASTENINGS

For some classes of motorsport it's a requirement to have supplementary fastenings on the bonnet. Sometimes these fastenings are described as security clips in regulations, and come in a range of types, including traditional leather straps and buckles. The objective is to ensure that the bonnet, or even a single-piece front, cannot break loose if the primary fastening fails, or one catch or mechanism fails.

Other hinged panels, such as the doors, are generally required to have positive fastenings, which can

FIA homologated roll bar padding from Safety Devices.

1967 Speedwell Sprite owned by Tom Colby. Note the headrest pad incorporated in the roll bar. (Courtesy Tom Colby, Speedwell Engineering)

Secondary bonnet fastenings, in the form of rubber fastenings, have been used on this 1972 Porsche 911ST ...

... while a leather strap has been used on this MGB.

be interpreted as a standard catch and release mechanism, though it's recommended to have supplementary fastenings fitted as good practice.

BATTERY

For cars used in motorsport it may be desirable to re-locate the battery from the engine bay to the boot, or, in order to keep cable runs shorter, to the passenger footwell, whether to better balance the weight in the car or simply move the weight lower in the car. Note, however, that in UK motorsport it's a general requirement that no wet battery can be contained within the cockpit of the car, unless it's in a sealed battery box. Unfortunately, there is no definition of what a 'wet' battery is, so while any battery containing liquid acid is clearly wet, it's debatable whether a sealed

The dry cell battery doesn't need a battery box, even when installed in the cockpit of the car (for UK motorsport).

gel battery is wet or not. Clearly, the purpose of the regulation is to prevent the spillage of battery acid, whether due to the battery case being broken or simply being inverted. A sealed gel battery cannot leak liquid acid, and, while perhaps meeting the spirit of the

regulation, does not necessarily meet the letter of the regulation. It's recommended then that, if moved to the cockpit of the car, the battery is encased in a suitable battery box, usually fibreglass though a lighter carbon fibre box is recommended.

The alternative to wet or gel batteries is the dry battery, which can be safely fitted inside the car without a battery box, and can be mounted in any position. Dry cell batteries are available from DMS Varley (Red top), or Powervamp (Hawker Odyssey).

BATTERY EARTH LEAD

It's a requirement in UK motorsport for the earth lead to be readily identifiable, so if this is not the case make it so. The regulation can be interpreted to mean the earth lead from the battery rather than all leads, though in the event the car is inverted it would clearly be an aid to the marshals if other earth leads (for example, from the clutch slave cylinder to the body) were also marked. The easiest way to achieve this is by wrapping insulating sleeving or tape around the lead, yellow being the requisite colour.

RED WARNING LIGHT (FOG OR RAIN)

A requirement for racing in UK motorsport without any period (age) exemption is for a rear facing red warning light of 21 watts – generally called the rain light or fog light. For a classic car the light fitted can be a modern light unit, though lights with a suitable 'classic' appearance are available. The light can be mounted inside the car or outside the car, but always centrally, unless two lights are used, in which case they should be fitted to each side of the car.

On this Rae Davies Racing-prepared Volvo Amazon, a period-correct red glass 'beehive' light fitted with a 21W bulb gets the job done, and looks far better on a classic car than a modern LED or plastic fog light ever could. (Courtesy Nigel Thorne)

Chapter 20
Tools, fasteners & plumbing

TOOLS

If you intend to carry out any or most of the modifications and work detailed in this book you will need a reasonable set of tools to work with. If you're spending most of your available money on parts for your classic, there may not be a lot left over for tool purchases. However, using the right tools can prevent frustration and save you some money by making it easier to do some of the simpler jobs yourself.

Purchase quality tools, as they always work out cheaper in the long run. If possible, buy those that come with a lifetime guarantee. If your pocket doesn't run to buying sets of expensive tools, do purchase quality items that you know will get a lot of use. Remember that good quality secondhand tools (Snap-On, Britool), can also be an economical purchase, and eBay always has several pages of hand tools listed. Although it's nice to buy spanners and screwdrivers in sets, it's worthwhile purchasing single spanners, screwdrivers or sockets for a particular job or fastener. Note that what are often referred to as crosshead screws are often Posidrive rather than Phillips.

Many car accessory shops or motor factors will hire more expensive and infrequently used items, such as hub pullers and coil spring compressors. Always purchase or hire a hydraulic engine 'crane' for engine removal rather than use a cheap hoist. The cheaper hoists are slow to use and don't represent good value for money.

Here's the list of tools it's recommended you have. Although by no means exhaustive, nearly all of the tools will be required at one time or another:

Set of AF combination spanners standard length
Set of AF combination spanners short length, or a set of AF ring spanners and a set of AF open-ended spanners
Set of Whitworth combination spanners standard length
Set of Whitworth combination spanners short length, or a set of Whitworth ring spanners and a set of Whitworth open-ended spanners
Set of metric combination spanners
Set of metric combination spanners short length, or a set of metric ring spanners and a set of metric open-ended spanners
Sparkplug spanner
Brake adjuster spanner – flat type
Sump plug spanner
Set of Allen keys
Set of feeler gauges
Wire brush
Set of plain (slotted) head screwdrivers
Set of crosshead (Philips) screwdrivers
Set of Posidrive screwdrivers (not to be confused with Phillips)
Hacksaw (with coarse and fine blades)
Pliers
Combination pliers
Grease gun
Torque wrench
Half inch drive socket set AF or Whitworth or metric – largest set you can afford
Half inch drive breaker bar AF or Whitworth or metric in a 15in length minimum
Vise (Mole) grips
Impact driver
Set of cold chisels
Set of drifts
Dot punch

Pop riveter (riveting pliers)
Axle stands
Trolley jack
Ball joint splitter (screw thread type)
Crimping pliers (strippers/cutters)
Soldering iron
Circuit tester (12V)
Heavy hammer
Rubber mallet
Nylon face hammer
Oil filter wrench or socket
Stilsons (pipe wrench) in several sizes, eg
6in, 8in, 12in
Electric drill (with variable speed)
Strobe light or timing light and diagnostic
Jemmy (crow/wrecking bar)
Medium flat file
Small flat file
Round file
Easy out extractors (for broken studs)
Electrical extension lead
Brake pipe flaring tool – imperial or
metric as required
Nut and bolt/thread gauge
(Interdynamics from Speed Bleeder
products)
Tool box (to keep everything in).

WORKING ON YOUR CAR & USE OF TOOLS

The most important thing about working on your car is safety; after that, enjoying your work (the latter is harder to achieve if your classic has been neglected).

Although not always a sign of neglect, a frequent cause of trouble will be stubborn and seized fasteners. To ease their release, applying heat to the fastener with a blow lamp or welding torch is usually much more effective than the use of penetrating oil. If you have neither of these but can get the component to the household kitchen, stick it on the stove! Also, be sure to have a suitable replacement fastener before proceeding to destroy the old one. Another solution for stubborn fasteners is to consider Snap On's patented, specially-designed, open-ended design spanner with gripping teeth, which gives you more turning power and strength than any other design of open-end spanner. It's called Flank Drive Plus – not

These drawings illustrate the difference between Phillips (left) and Posidrive screwdriver tips. The Phillips screwdriver is the more common, yet, at least on many classic British cars, the majority, if not all, of the crosshead screws are of the Posidrive type – identified by the star type impression rather than just a simple cross. Use of the wrong screwdriver damages the tool and the screw to the point where both are useless. (Courtesy Snap-On)

A conventional spanner makes contact with the fastener on the corners, which can lead to rounding off. (Courtesy Snap-On)

The Snap-On Flank Drive Plus spanner's unique design ensures contact is away from the corner of the fastener: this feature produces up to 20 per cent greater turning force than a conventional spanner. (Courtesy Snap-On)

to be confused with Snap-On's normal flank drive system. Force is directed away from the weaker corners of the fastener and directed to the stronger flats. For stubborn fasteners this will make a genuine difference.

If you're using a tool in a difficult area, where retrieval is likely to be difficult – if not impossible – if you drop it, tie a length of string onto the tool, with the other end fastened around your wrist.

Finally, when working on components use a workbench and vice if possible, though many jobs can be done by improvising. A word of caution – improvisation does not mean taking a risk. If you need expert assistance, a local garage will often help for no charge at all or the price of a beer.

FASTENERS – GENERAL

All classic cars consist of a large number of moving and non-moving parts held together by a diverse selection of nuts, bolts, and screws, as well as clevis pins and circlips. As you might expect, this wide and diverse selection of items which we'll call 'fasteners' are often different on a classic car compared to a modern car, especially if the classic is British or American. The reason for this is that the British and Americans held out longest with the use of imperial fasteners before eventually following 'foreign' manufacturers and using metric items.

Nuts, bolts & set screws

The most common types of fasteners found on classic cars are, of course, nuts and bolts. Bolts are generally referred to as anything with a hexagonal-shaped top and a threaded portion, though, strictly speaking, if it has a thread right up to underneath the head it's a set screw (bolts must have a plain unthreaded portion under the head).

Everyone knows that nuts and bolts come in different sizes, but they can be classified in other ways too, as the accompanying table illustrates.

As you can see there are actually quite a few variables, and each needs to be considered in turn.

Thread types

Metric threads are defined by pitch, while imperial threads can be AF or Whitworth, and there are others too. For the most

Thread type	Imperial (of which there is more than one type) or metric
Thread pitch	Coarse or fine, but more accurately the angle of the thread
Head type	Hexagon, or 12 point, round (with internal hexagon)
Finish	Zinc coated, chrome, polished, black oxide, cadmium coated
Material type	Steel, stainless steel, aluminium, titanium, other special alloys (8740 chrome-moly)
Strength	British or American imperial rating – pounds per square inch (PSI) or tons rating – these last two expressed as tensile or shear. Metric ratings

part you'll find AF on older classics, Whitworth for anything prewar (British), and metric from anytime in the 1970s onwards (depending on whether the car is British or not), and pre-1970s if European. Britain adopted the AF thread during World War 2, so as to have a common standard with America. Watch out for modern performance tuning parts or European origin tuning parts fitted together with or designed to be fastened by metric fasteners, of which the best example is a Weber carb, whether on a Mini or Lotus.

Thread pitch

With AF nuts and bolts the thread is usually fine or coarse, or, more correctly, Unified Normal Fine (UNF) or Unified Normal Coarse (UNC). When you come to metric fasteners there are also fine and coarse threads, and these also have a secondary identifier, a percentage ratio, such as 1.00, 1.25 or 1.50. If that sounds confusing just consider that both fine and coarse metric threads can be 1.00 pitch! Generally, any thread in an iron or steel casting or component will be a fine thread, while it will most likely be a coarse thread if the material is aluminium. The reason for this is that a steel bolt will be stronger than aluminium, so, unlike steel bolts, the thread will strip out of the component before the bolt shears. The coarse thread in the aluminium provides a greater strength than a fine thread would.

It's possible to purchase a budget thread gauge set for metric and Whitworth threads, or a more expensive/ comprehensive set. An alternative

method of identifying threads is to match the unknown threaded bolt or screw against a known item; if the threads fully engage and mesh they are the same and identification is complete.

Bolt head type

Usually, bolt heads will be hexagonal, or occasionally double hex (12 corners). The 12-point head is only seen on special fasteners. Some bolts have a round head with an internal hexagon, known as internal wrenching. While often called Allen bolts or Allen screws, the correct term is Allen caps, and they can be imperial or metric. There are other internal wrenching heads on bolts and set screws, for example the Torx, commonly found on Fords.

Nut head type

Castellated nuts (in conjunction with split pins) are commonly used on classic cars – though mostly replaced these days by nylock nuts. Slotted nuts are often offered as a replacements for castellated nuts, and achieve pretty much the same effect (except for a concours judge). If you want or need to fit a castellated nut in a size that does not seem readily available, you should be able to get an aircraft AN nut in any UNF size.

Nuts & bolts with non-standard size heads

Occasionally, you may find that there's inadequate clearance for a regular hexagonal head nut or bolt. A useful alternative is an ARP nut or bolt with a 12-point head, but, more importantly, the wrenching part of the head will be

two sizes smaller than the standard hexagonal head, thereby providing clearance for a socket or spanner. For example, ARP's ⁵⁄₁₆in and ³⁄₈in bolts have a ³⁄₈in wrenching head rather than the ½in or ⁹⁄₁₆in head you'd find with a typical hexagonal head bolt. An alternative would be to use an Allen cap. Note that grades of socket head cap screws are usually higher than 'regular' bolts of the same size.

Finish

Nuts and bolts will usually be zinc coated to prevent rust, but, in some instances, chromed items are used. Apart from looking out of place, it doesn't matter too much if you interchange chrome and zinc coated fasteners. However, be sure that chrome plating really is chrome plating, and not stainless steel, for example, which, with the exception of special performance products, is NOT as strong as steel. Some aluminium nuts and bolts can be highly polished, and can be confused with chromed or stainless steel fasteners. Keep an eye out for black oxide finished nuts and bolts, because they're usually of a higher strength rating than zinc-coated items. If the nuts and bolts are bright colours, then they're usually made from anodised aluminium alloy, and so have a relatively low strength.

Material

The material the fastener is made from, and any heat treatment it has received, are critical for fastener life, as well as your own and that of others. If a fastener isn't strong enough for the use to which you're putting it, it may fail in service. Fastener failure can occur inside the engine, leaving you with an expensive repair bill, or it can occur elsewhere on the car, such as part of the suspension, leading to a potentially fatal accident. Part of the problem with selecting the correct fastener is that often there's no clear documentation as to what the original specification was. If you're replacing a nut or bolt on a production classic then ordering a replacement ought to guarantee the right strength of fastener, but doesn't always. Furthermore, once you get into a modified performance or classic race or rally car, it's likely something stronger than the original fastener will be required. Nut material usually follows that of the bolt or stud (except for nuts on exhaust manifolds which may be brass).

FASTENER STRENGTH & PERFORMANCE FASTENERS

Considering Imperial fasteners first, it's usual for the head of the bolt to have a letter on it, as well as perhaps the name of the manufacturer (GKN or Atlas, for example) or some other pattern or symbol. The letter is the most important, though, and in the majority of cases will be an 'S,' which equates to a yield stress of 85,120psi. The next most likely bolt rating is designated by the letter 'T,' indicating a yield stress of 92,840psi.

Don't forget to use high quality ARP fastenings in critical areas: they're cheaper than an engine failure caused by a fastener failing.

Stainless steel fasteners for less demanding situations ease the problem of corrosion.

Sometimes you'll see a letter 'R' on the bolt head – I don't have a precise rating for this, but it's lower than the S rating.

With metric fasteners you generally get much less information than with Imperial fasteners, often just having the strength rating in the form of a decimal number, of which the most common is 8.8 indicating a yield stress rating of 92,800psi, followed by 9.8, 10.9, and 12.9 (rated highest at 157,000). It can be difficult to find metric fasteners much higher rated than 8.8, except for metric Allen caps and ARP bolts.

If you have a non-standard application, or are concerned about the strength of a particular nut or bolt, it's often possible to source and fit something stronger (which might simply mean of a larger diameter). Generally, though, a bigger fastener isn't an option, and you'll have to source an aviation or motorsport spec fastener. There's a multitude of aviation bolt specifications, but the most readily available one is the AN range, available with or without drilled heads or shanks – but always cadmium coated, hence the dull yellow finish. For specialist motorsport fasteners, such as conrod and flywheel bolts, then the ARP range stocked by APT takes some beating. Like the AN fasteners, ARP stuff originates in the USA, and while available in the UK, it can be as cheap to order direct from the USA.

SIZING NUTS & BOLTS AND GAUGES

Nuts and bolts, whether Imperial or metric, are sized by the shank, or 'middle bit,' rather than by the head size. In fact, you can have varying head sizes for any given shank, which can be confusing. Imperial bolts are sized in fractions of an inch, whereas metric fasteners are sized in millimetres. Typical examples for Imperial and metric might be ⁵⁄₁₆in and 8mm, with the metric designated M8. If you're looking for a particular size bolt then the information on the head will indicate whether it's Imperial or metric, and you can measure it accordingly. Sizing nuts can be more difficult,

A nut and bolt sizing gauge is a valuable aid to sizing fasteners.

involving trial-fitting several bolts.

A nut and bolt gauge is a useful tool. For very little cost, NF Auto Development (www.nfauto.co.uk) has a simple plastic gauge that does the job, and, if you like using AN nuts and bolts, then Aircraft Spruce has an AN bolt specific gauge.

STUDS OR BOLTS

The stud is your friend when it comes to stripped threads because it can easily be replaced. Don't be tempted to replace it with a bolt if you don't have the correct replacement stud to hand, as the threaded end that secures the stud, usually in a casting such as an engine block, is much shorter than a typical bolt. The key advantage of a stud over a bolt is that the thread in the casting is almost never stripped if you use a stud, and it aids the alignment of whatever part you're fastening to it. With a bolt, if you cross-thread or strip the thread in the casting, you face the expense and trouble of sorting it out. You'll find that the studs used to fasten a cylinder head to an engine block have that matt black finish that is typical of heat treatment for strength, while manifold studs are plain steel or zinc coated. Since studs are often used to fasten aluminium components – such as thermostat housings – it's usual for electrolytic corrosion to take place over a number years, resulting in a lot of frustration when the aluminium component needs to be removed. The solution is to look to Advanced Performance Technology (APT) which has researched, and now markets, a wide range of advanced stainless steel studs that are manufactured by ARP. The range includes old favourites like the A-series engine, but also other MGs, and Triumphs, and not least pretty much any size you can ask for. The studs are of excellent quality and well designed, right down to the rounded bullet tip end to the stud that aids assembly. With a stud you have the freedom to use pretty much any nut you want, whether a 12-point specialist high-performance nut, or a conventional six-point nylock.

A stud with a difference is the one in a wheel hub, though you might find more recent classics, again not necessarily of UK origin, might have bolts instead. Of all the studs found on a car these are the ones most likely to break – usually through over enthusiastic tightening. Since the wheel nut isn't something you're going to want permanently fastened on, it's simply using the recommended torque, and regular re-torquing, that ensures they stay tight. The stud may be screwed into the wheel mounting hub, but on many British classics it's more usual to find that the stud is splined at one end, and it's this spline that prevents it from turning in the hub as the wheel is tightened. Broken studs will need to be tapped out using a suitable size drift and the new replacement inserted from the rear of the hub and gently tapped into position, though sometimes the hub might need to be removed to do this.

SLOTTED, PHILLIPS & POSIDRIVE SCREW HEADS

A screw can be fully threaded like a bolt, be imperial or metric, and is sized in an identical manner to bolts. Alternatively, it can have a coarse spiral thread for 'self tapping' into thin sheet metal. The head type is split between three broad types: slotted, Phillips, and Posidrive. The slot on any slotted screw head comes in a variety of sizes and presents few problems if the correct size screwdriver is used. When it comes to

the Phillips and Posidrive screw head there's a lot of confusion, not to mention damaged screw heads – the generic phrase 'crosshead screw' has a lot to answer for. First, the Phillips screw head is NOT the same as the Posidrive screw head. Second, each screw head requires its own specific screwdriver, which means that, including your slotted head screwdrivers, you have three full sets rather than two. Screws can be of a countersunk head design, so that, once fitted, they fit flush to any given surface; and occasionally you might come across a countersunk Allen screw.

Screw heads vary in size and thread diameter, with small, medium and large heads, so you need a minimum of three screwdrivers per set, and then different length versions as well. With what can amount to a large number of screwdrivers it's useful to have different colour handles for the different types; to avoid confusion and damaged screws. Damage is generally quick and terminal – in that the screw is useless after it's been removed, if it can be removed at all. Note that Posidrive screws tend to be more common than other types, and have star lines at the corners to aid recognition.

WASHERS & LOCK TABS

The most common types of washers are the plain and the spring. The plain washer is there to bear and spread the load of the bolt head, and comes in varying thicknesses and widths, including a useful extra wide width often known as a penny washer. The spring washer is supposed to be an aid to ensuring the nut or bolt doesn't come undone. I've never been convinced they really work, because they either cut and score the plain washer underneath them, or, if used without a plain washer which they frequently appear to be, they cut and score the component. It seems strange they are even used without a plain washer at all, but it appears to be the case, even from the factory. The other thing they do is go flat when the nut or bolt is tightened which raises the question of how springy they really are.

Controversial or not, I don't recommend them, bin them when I come across them, use alternative means of security, and don't have nuts and bolts work loose having not used them.

Lock tabs are used on several classic cars where there function is to prevent a bolt or nut from coming undone. However, a drawback with using them is that they are inclined to distort or compress under the loading of the nut or bolt. Instead, I recommend using either a liquid thread locking solution (Loctite), or bolts with drilled heads that can be lock wired. With some fasteners, such as ARP products, it's not necessary to use anything other than the company's own brand of thread lubricant.

LOCTITE, NYLOCK NUTS, LOCK WIRING

Nuts and bolts, or nuts and studs are held together by the wedging action of the engaged threads. However, it's possible for fasteners to work loose over time, resulting in expense or inconvenience. The most common solution to nuts working loose is the ineffective lock tab, while the effective modern solution is to use a threadlocking solution, of which the Loctite brand is perhaps the best known. There are different types of Loctite available, so make sure you buy the correct type for your application. For example, there is a specific compound for loctiting bolts screwed into aluminium alloy components.

With regard to nuts, it's the case that many classics were held together with plain nuts, since the nylock nut wasn't available at the time they were made, but it's simple to replace a plain

Loctite, bolt drilling jig, nut drilling jig, and locking wire.

nut with a nylock nut. It's a myth that nylock nuts can only be used once. Over time, however, the nylon will become less effective, at which point it should be replaced. Nylock nuts aren't much use where a lot of heat is present (this is also true, but to a lesser extent, with Loctite) – exhausts and turbochargers in particular require an alternative means of fastening. The traditional solution was to use a brass nut, though the threads are too weak where a very high fastening torque is required, and so the alternative is likely to be a castellated nut and split pin.

Bolts present a problem when secured into a casting because there's nothing to prevent them working loose (you cannot readily obtain a nylock bolt). The alternative to Loctite, and one well suited to classics, is to have the bolt head lock wired – usually to another bolt, but possibly to some other fixed point. With a few exceptions (MG Metro turbocharger, for example) the bolt head will not have a hole in the head for lock wiring. It's possible to drill a hole in a bolt head (difficult even with a drill press, and near impossible without). The solution is to purchase a drilling jig that positions the bolt head such that it can be readily drilled through its centre. An alternative is to buy aerospace bolts (AN or NAS), with the heads pre-drilled, though they're generally only available in UNF sizes. It's also possible to drill the corner of the bolt head or a nut, and again, you need a simple jig to do so. If you have a particularly hard bolt that's extremely difficult to drill –12 point ARP stainless steel, for example – you can have a hole drilled by a (costly) process called Electronic Discharge Machining (EDM).

HELICOIL

The solution to a stripped thread in a casting is to drill it out and re-tap the hole using the next size up. Occasionally, though, this isn't possible, the most common reason being the hole in question is the sparkplug hole. The solution is to have the hole drilled and tapped using specific sizes supplied in a helicoil kit, after which a thin spiral-wound section of metal is screwed into the oversize thread using a special tool. The tang is then snapped off to leave it permanently fitted. The design of the helicoil insert is such that it almost perfectly replicates the original thread size. While a helicoil kit isn't cheap, a good engineering machine shop ought to be able to undertake this work for you at a fraction of the cost of a replacement cylinder head, for example.

CLIPS

As well as nuts and bolts, there are a great many other fixtures and fittings to be found. Every classic will have wires and pipes (fuel, brake fluid, oil, coolant) that need to be secured. Many classics use a plain metal or plastic P-clip. However, these should be replaced with quality, rubber-lined P-clips, with the clip itself secured with a self tapping screw. The reason for the replacement is that the plain metal clips tend to rust, and, being all metal, are less than ideal for cabling. Aluminium rubber-lined P-clips provide a neat appearance, and the rubber insulation prevents chafing and corrosion damage. The plastic pipe clips are okay, but they can be a struggle to fit, and are easily broken.

Not so much a clip but usually doing a very similar job, is the ty-rap. While ty-raps are okay for emergency use, but care must be exercised with them, as, being plastic, they'll melt when exposed to heat. Worst of all, in use you're left with either an untidy long tail or, if clipped short, a sharp end to cut your hand or forearm when you least expect it. Car Builder Solutions has an alternative to the conventional ty-rap called a flattie cable tie; it's neater and doesn't have any sharp ends.

CIRCLIPS

While it may not be obvious at first glance, there are two types of circlip: internal and external. To fit and remove circlips without a proper tool is so awkward and frustrating it's recommended you buy a couple of pairs of circlip pliers. Why two pairs? Because you there are internal and external circlips, so you'll need a pair of pliers for each type, or, perhaps, a pair that converts from internal to external. Avoid the cheaper pairs because the metal end pieces are easily bent.

CLEVIS PINS

Clevis pins are an unusual type of fastener in they not only hold things together, but are also load bearing (forward and back or side-to-side). Clevis pins are used in linkages, such as those for brake and clutch master cylinders, and handbrake and clutch slave cylinders. They wear over time, with a resultant 'lost motion' introduced to the assembly, and so need to be checked and replaced regularly.

THREADED FITTINGS & BRAIDED HOSE

Although I'm sure that braided hose and threaded fittings need no introduction, I should mention that the fittings are available in gold and black (as well as the more common red and blue), and the hose can be a lightweight, but more expensive, alternative to the more usual stainless steel.

Threaded fittings and braided hose are more durable and reliable than rubber push-fit hose and Jubilee (or similar worm drive) hose clips. Of course, they're also more expensive. However, given the consequences of a failed hose, whether from simply working loose or bursting, the benefits of threaded fittings and braided hose outweigh the costs. There's one other big advantage that's rarely exploited, and that's the use of threaded blanking caps and plugs. A hose with threaded fittings, once removed, can be plugged with threaded

A couple of male/male adaptors – one is equal JIC, and the other unequal JIC.

Threaded plugs and caps, for 100 per cent dry sealing, as well as a couple of red plastic plugs for keeping out dirt (but not necessarily preventing fluid loss).

plugs for a 100 per cent dry containment of its contents, as well as to prevent dirt getting in. Not least, the component fitting end can be capped for a similar result. This not only prevents a lot of mess and wasted fluid, but prevents dirt ingress and contamination that could lead to damage.

Rather than buying a complete kit and getting stuck in, a better approach would be to do one fluid line at a time.

Adaptors
All braided hoses have female fittings at both ends. Each hose fitting end then requires a male fitting, and this is generally achieved using a male/male adaptor, with one end screwing into the component and the other into the hose. You'll need to be certain of the thread required for the adaptor, though the end screwing into the threaded hose fitting will nearly always be JIC, which is UNF with a cone on the end to aid seat-to-seat sealing. If the hose end isn't JIC it will be metric, though there isn't as wide a range of metric hose fittings as JIC. The component (female) thread can vary from metric (eg, non-British/American) such as Weber carburettors, to UNF, but include pipe threads: British Standard Pipe (Tapered) BSP (BSPT), or American National Pipe Tapered (Fuel or Fine) NPT (NPTF), the latter sometimes incorrectly called National Pipe Thread. For example, on oil pressure gauges, if a standard Smiths gauge, the thread will be BSP, but on a modern Stack gauge it will be NPTF. There's an extremely wide range of adaptors available, and it's always possible to find what you need. Admittedly, there may be the rare occasion when it's necessary to use

a female/female adaptor, followed by a male/male adaptor. You'll get used to using adaptors, whether equal or unequal and mixed or same thread. Aside from Aeroquip items from Think Automotive, and those from Goodridge, you could use AN (Air Corps/Navy or Air force/Navy in the USA) – one leading supplier's website incorrectly describes AN as Army/Navy – adaptors from aviation suppliers, such as Aircraft Spruce. If one side of the adaptor has a flat seat, it will need to be sealed with a copper or aluminium washer, O-ring, bonded or Dowty seal, or similar.

Weld bungs
On a typical race car it's usual to find that a lot of standard components have been replaced with aluminium ones (for example, fuel tank, radiator, or engine breather catch tank). Because these components will have been made from sheet aluminium, it's not possible to drill and tap them for an adaptor, but a male (sometimes female) fitting will need to be welded on. This weld-on fitting is generally known as a 'weld bung' and is like an adaptor sawn in half and situated wherever you desire on a component. Often, when buying a component such as fuel tank or engine breather tank, it's possible to choose push-fit or weld bungs for threaded fittings, the latter at no extra cost, and it's strongly recommended you use threaded fittings for reasons I'll make clear later. Of course, if you already have a component with a push-fit fitting, it's always possible to replace it with a weld bung later.

Hard or rigid line to flexible line
Some owners replace the rigid steel, copper or copper/nickel lines on their cars with very long runs of braided steel hose (for seemingly no obvious reason). While there's nothing wrong with that, it's not really necessary. What is important, though, if you're keeping your car's rigid lines, is that you use threaded fittings to connect to any braided hose.

You'll need to purchase a sleeve or

A hard/rigid line, with the sleeve and tube nut being used with an adaptor, joining to a threaded hose end and flexible line.

coupling, and a nut or coupling nut, in the same size as the hard or rigid pipe. Slide the nut onto the pipe, threaded end last, followed by the sleeve coupling, and then, using a flaring tool, put a female flare onto the pipe end. The flare on the pipe secures the sleeve, and the sleeve secures the nut so that a male adaptor can now be screwed into it. Your hard line is now ready to receive an adaptor, followed by the threaded fitting and braided flexible line.

Fittings or hose ends
The female threaded fittings are usually known as hose ends, or sometimes elbows if not straight, and are JIC (Joint Industry Council/Conference/Committee – also known as SAE 37 degree) threads for JIC fittings. The vast majority of hose fittings are designed for use with braided hose, typically stainless steel braided hose, but there are also some fittings which are female JIC at one end and barbed or swaged male end at the other, for use with push-fit hoses and jubilee or similar clips. Initially, it may seem pointless to use a threaded fitting with a barbed end for use with a rubber push-fit hose. If you're on a tight budget, though, you can buy your component, such as a fuel tank, with threaded weld bungs and use threaded fittings with barbed ends and rubber hose initially. Later, when funds permit you can upgrade to threaded fittings and braided hose without having to buy or modify the component. If you're using true hose fittings (not barbed or push-fit), it's recommended you have your hose supplier assemble and pressure test the hose for you. You could fit the hose to the fitting yourself, of course, but it's not particularly easy and can't

A 150-degree tube/swept fitting on the vacuum line to this brake servo.

A range of assembled (left) and disassembled fittings, with a weld bung (front left), and 90-degree fitting for push-fit rubber hose (front right).

Dash	JIC thread	BSP thread	NPTF thread	Comment
-3	⅜ x 24	⅛ x 28	⅛ x 27	Usual size for brake/clutch lines
-4	⁷⁄₁₆ x 20	¼ x 18	¼ x 18	
-6	⁹⁄₁₆ x 20	⅜ x 19	⅜ x 18	Usual size for fuel lines
-8	¾ x 16	½ x 14	½ x 14	Little used size except engine breather lines
-10	⅞ x 14	⅝ x 14	n/a	Typical hose size for oil cooler
-12	¹¹⁄₁₆ x 12	¾ x 14	¾ x 14	Large hose size for oil cooler

be tested other than waiting to see if it fails in use, due to incorrect assembly. Some hoses, such as brake hoses, are readily available from many classic car specialists, thus saving you the bother of working out the hose fittings and lengths yourself. Breather hoses or low pressure applications, such as fuel hoses, can provide the opportunity to try your hand at making hose lines while leaving hydraulic and high pressure hose lines to the professionals who can test the hose on a pressure testing rig. Full instructions, complete with illustrations, on how to assemble your hose lines, are contained in the catalogues/websites of the major manufacturers and suppliers if you do want to make your own.

Types of hose ends/fittings
Push-fit and fitted hose ends are available in the following formats: straight, 30 degrees, 45 degrees, 60 degrees, 90 degrees, 120 degrees, 150 degrees, 180 degrees, and banjo fitting. This wide selection is essential because braided hose can be damaged by turning it through an acute angle or bend. There's also the choice of swivel and non-swivel fittings, though the non-swivel fittings are less common and not recommended as they are more difficult to work with. Finally, there are crimped fittings, which can be found on both rubber and stainless steel braided hose. When fitted with braided steel hose these tend to be of the non-swivel design. The fittings will typically be the familiar red and blue anodised aluminium, though it's possible to have plain aluminium or black anodised fittings, as well as fittings made from stainless steel (typically brake hose fittings) or plated steel.

The dash size system
A confusing aspect of threaded fittings and braided hose is that the hose size doesn't obviously correspond to a thread size. However, you soon get a feel for hose sizes in relation to fittings, and will find that there are only three or four different sizes you'll use. The accompanying table details the most common sizes, along with JIC, BSP and NPTF threads you'll most likely need for an adaptor (eg: JIC to NPTF, such as for a fuel pump or regulator).

BRAIDED HOSE
Although there are more expensive alternatives, it's recommended that you use stainless steel braided hose. Note, though, that each manufacturer will have its own specification, so if you're using Goodridge hose fittings you should use Goodridge hose, and if using Aeroquip hose you should use Aeroquip hose fittings, etc. The advantage of stainless steel hose is that in nearly every instance it provides a stronger, more resilient alternative to a rubber or reinforced rubber hose, and is ideal for critical applications such as oil and hydraulic lines. It also has the added bonus of looking like new for longer than other types of hose. The single downside to braided stainless steel hose is that it will chafe through anything it comes into contact with, especially aluminium components and wiring, so make sure it's neatly clamped in position.

HOSE & FITTINGS – MISCELLANEOUS
While that's covered the basics it's worth quickly considering a few other options and 'nice-to-haves' when working with threaded fittings and braided hose. For example, you might want to swap a push-fit oil cooler with one that has threaded fittings. You could fit 100 per cent dry break couplings on everything from clutch hydraulic lines to fuel lines depending on which gives you most trouble on an engine or gearbox change. To complete an engine breathing system correctly you could fit in-line breather valves. Your ultimate goal will be to have a modified classic car with fluid lines that give trouble-free years of service, adds to your enjoyment, and simply looks right.

What a finished engine bay can look like.

Appendix

Specialists & suppliers

A Frame Engineering – Unit 3 Higherford Mill, Gisburn Road, Barrowford, BB9 6JH, UK, Tel: 01282 690184, www.aframeengineering.co.uk

AH Fabrications – Unit 6H, Thorn Business Park, Rotherwas, Hereford, HR2 6JT, UK, Tel: 01432 354704, www.ahfabrications.com

Aircraft Spruce and Speciality Company, 201 W Trunslow Ave, Fullerton, CA 92632, USA, Tel: 800 861 3192, www.aircraftspruce.com

Airedale Race Components, Airedale House, Hall Lane, Brafferton, York, YO61 2NY, Tel: 01423 360456, www.raceplastics.com

Aldon Automotive Ltd, Breener Industrial Estate, Station Drive, Brierly Hill, DY5 3JZ, UK, Tel: 01384 572553, www.aldonauto.co.uk

AP Racing, Wheler Road, Seven Stars Industrial Estate, Coventry, CV3 4LB, UK, Tel: 01203 639595, www.apracing.com

APT, 595 Iowa Avenue, Unit C, Riverside, CA 92507, USA, Tel: 800 278 3278 but check, www.aptfast.com

Bastuck & Co GmbH, Gewerbegebiet Heeresstraße West, Im Bommersfeld 11, D-66822 Lebach, Germany, Tel: 0881-9 24 91-01, www.bastuck.de

BGH GearTech Ltd, Unit 8, Verralls Busness Center, Maidstone Road, Cranbrook, TN17 2AF, UK, Tel: 01580 714114, www.bghgeartech.co.uk

B&M Racing & Performance Products, 9142 Independence Avenue, Chatsworth, CA 91311, USA, Tel: 818 882 6422, www.bmracing.com

Broadsport, Broadacres, Wall Hill Road, Corley, Coventry, CV7 8AD, UK, Tel: 01676 541980, www.guybroad.co.uk

Peter Burgess, Unit1 Amber Buildings, Meadow Lane, Alfreton, DE55 7EZ, UK, Tel: 01733 520021, www.mgcars.org.uk/peterburgess/

Burlen Fuel Systems, Spitfire House, Castle Road, Salisbury, SP1 3SA, UK, Tel: 01722 412500, www.burlen.co.uk

Burton Power, 617-631 Eastern Avenue, ILFORD, IG2 6PN, UK, Tel: 020 8554 2281, www.burtonpower.com

Cambridge Motorsport Parts Ltd, Unit 5 Lacre Way, Letchworth Garden City, SG6 1NR, Tel 01462 684300, www.cambridgemotorsport.com

Camcoat Performance Coatings, 127 Hoyle Street, Bewsey Industrial Estate, Warrington, WA5 0LP, Tel: 01925 445688, www.camcoat.u-net.com

Canley Classics, Fillongly, CV7 8DT, UK, Tel: 01676 541360, www.canleyclassics.com

Car Builder Solutions, Redlands, Lindridge Lane, Staplehurst, TN12 0JJ, UK, Tel: 01580 891309, www.nfauto.co.uk
Cool Louvres, 51 Waterloo Road, Aldershot, GU12 4NU, UK, Tel: 01420 588080
Coventry Auto Components, Unit 4A, Binns Close, Torrington Avenue, COVENTRY, CV4 9TB, UK, Tel: 024 764 1217, www.xkparts.com
Dayton Wire Wheels, 115 Compark Rd, Dayton OH 45459, USA, Tel: 937 438 0100, www.daytonwirewheels.com
Dellow Automotive, 37 Daisy St, Revesby, Sydney, Australia 2212, Tel: Australia 2 774 4419, www.dellowconversions.com.au
Denis Welch Motorsport, Sudbury Road, Yoxall, Burton on Trent, Staffordshire, Tel: 01543 472214, www.bighealey.co.uk
D J Edman & Company, 69369 Wilson Lane, Boardman, Oregon 97818, USA, Tel: 541 481 3085, www.wheeltool.com
Edelbrock, 2700 California Street, Torrance, CA 90503, USA, Tel: 310 781 2222, www.edelbrock.com
Excel Precision (Wire Spark Erosion) Ltd, 34 Sabre Close, Green Farm, Quedgeley, Gloucester, GL2 4NZ, Tel: 01452 419743, www.excel-precision.co.uk
Farndon Engineering, Bayton Road, Coventry, CV7 9EJ, UK, Tel: 024 7636 6910, www.farndon.com
Fibresports, 34-36 Bowlers Croft, Cranes Industrial Estate, Basildon, Essex, SS14 3ED, Tel: 01268 527331, www.fibresports.co.uk
Gasket works USA, Tel: USA 626 358 1616, www.headgasket.com
Fuel System Enterprises, Glencoe Ltd
Glencoe House, Drake Avenue, Gresham Road, Staines, TW18 2AW, UK, Tel: 01784 493555, www.fuelsystem.co.uk
Goodridge (UK) Ltd, Exeter Airport, Exeter, Devon, EX5 2UP, Tel: 01392 369090, www.goodridge.net
Gunson, The Tool Connection Ltd, Kineton Road, Southam, Warwickshire, CV47 0DR, UK, Tel: 01926 815000, www.gunson.co.uk
Guy Croft Racing Engines, Unit 3B, Whisby Road, LINCOLN, LN6 3QT, Tel: 01522 705 222, www.guy-croft.com
Hardy Engineering, 268 Kingston Road, Leatherhead, KT22 7QA, UK, Tel: 01372 378927, www.hardyengineering.co.uk
Hawk Brake Pads – Wellman Friction, 6180 Cochran Road, Solon, OH 44139, USA, Tel: 001 440 528 4000, www.hawkperformance.com
Hi-Gear Engineering Ltd, 82 Chestnut Avenue, Mickleover, Derby, DE3 9FS, Tel: 01332 514503, www.hi-gearengineering.co.uk
Induction Technology Group Ltd, Unit B, Quinn Close, Seven Stars Industrial Estate, Whitley, Coventry, CV3 4LH, UK, Tel 024 7630 5386, www.itgairfilters.com
Janspeed Engineering Ltd, Castle Works, Castle Road, Salisbury, SP1 3RX, UK, Tel: 01722 321833, www.Janspeed.com
Jule Enterprises, RR#2, Rockwood, Ontario, N0B 2K0, Canada, Tel: Canada 905 854-3555, www.jule-enterprises.com
Kenlowe Ltd, Burchetts Green, Maidenhead, SL6 6QU, UK, Tel: 01628 823303, www.Kenlowe.com
Kent Performance Cams Ltd, Units 1-7 Military Road, Shorncliffe Industrial Estate, Folkestone, CT20 3UJ, Tel: 01303 248666, www.kentcams.com
Kiley Clinton Engineering Limited, 52 – 53 Birchall Street, Birmingham, B12 0RP, UK, Tel: 0121 772 8000, www.steering-racks.co.uk
Lifeline Fire & Safety Systems, Burnsall Road, Coventry, CV5 6BU, UK, Tel: 024 7671 2999, www.lifeline-fire.co.uk/
Lempert Wheels, Tel: 001 843 856 7542, www.lempertwheels.com
LMA Performance, Motorsport Engineering (Bedford) Ltd, Unit 16 Murdock Road, Bedford, MkIV1 7PD, UK, Tel: 01234 268213, www.lmaperformance.com
Magnecor Europe Ltd, Unit 12 Jubilee Business Park, Snarestone Road, Appleby Magna, DE12 7AJ, UK, Tel: 0870 444 8644, www.magnecor.co.uk
Maniflow, Mitchell Road, Churchfield Industrial Estate, Salisbury, SP2 7PY, UK, Tel: 01722 335378, www.maniflow.co.uk
MC Motorsport, www.mcmotorsport.co.uk
Midel Pty Ltd, 4 Frazer Street, Lakemba, NSW 2195, Australia, Tel: 61 2 9759 5598, www.sumidel.com
Milton, Tel : 01233 730959, E-mail : info@miltonrace.co.uk
Minilite – Tech-Del Ltd, Tech-Del Ltd, Beveley Road, Off Holyhead Road, Ketley, Telford, TF1 4DS, Tel: 01952 620215, www.minilitewheels.com
Morris Minor Centre (Birmingham) Ltd, 993 Wolverhampton Road, Oldbury, B69 4RJ, UK, Tel: 0121 544 5522, www.morrisminor.co.uk
Moto-Lita Ltd, Thruxton Racing Circuit, Nr. Andover, SP11 8PW, UK, Tel: 01264 772811, www.moto-lita.co.uk
Motorsport Auto (Datsun Z parts), 1139 West Collins Avenue, Orange, California 92867, USA, Tel: USA 800 633 6331, www.thezstore.com
Motor Wheel Service International Ltd, Units 1-4 Elder Way, Waterside Drive, Langley, SLOUGH, SL3 6EP, UK, Tel: 01753

549 360, www.mwsint.com

Nosimport / World Wide Auto Parts of Madison (Armstrong unit specialists), 2517 Seiferth Road, Madison, WI 53716, USA, Tel: USA 0800 362 1025, www.nosimport.com

O/D Spares, 10 Arches Business Centre, Mill Road, Rugby, CV21 1QW, UK, Tel: 01788 540666, www.odspares.com

Overdrive Repair Services, Unit 1, 50 Rother Valley Way, Holbrook Industrial Estate, Halfway, Sheffield, S20 3RW, UK, Tel: 0114 248 2632, www.overdrive-repairs.co.uk

Pace Products (Anglia) Ltd, Homefield Road, Haverhill, CB9 8QP, UK, Tel: 01440 760960, www.paceproducts.co.uk

Pertronix Performance Products, 440 East Arrow Highway, San Dimas, CA 91773, USA, Tel: USA 909-599-5955, www.pertronix.com

Pierce Manifolds Inc, 321 Kishimura Drive, Gilroy, CA 95020, USA, Tel: USA 408-842-6667, www.piercemanifolds.com

Pop Brown's, PO Box 2198, Harlow, CM17 0TZ, UK, Tel: 08456 588191, www.popbrowns.co.uk

Procharger Accessible Technologies Inc, 14801 W, 114th Terrace, Lenexa, KS 66215, USA, Tel: 913 338 2886, www.procharger.com

Quaife, Vestry Road, Otford, Sevenoaks, TN14 5EL, UK, Tel: 01732 741144, www.Quaife.co.uk

Rae Davis Racing, PO Box 202, Sunbury, London, TW16 6XX, UK, Tel: 020 8570 8858, www.raedavisracing.com

Rally Design, Unit 4, St Augustine's Business Park, Estuary Way, Swalecliffe, CT5 2QJ, UK, Tel: 01227 792792, www.rallydesign.co.uk

Reco-Prop, Unit 4, Newtown Trading Estate, Chase Street, Luton, LU1 3QZ, Tel: 01582 412110, www.reco-prop.com

Ron Davis Racing products (radiators), 7334 North 108th Avenue, Glendale Arizona 85307, USA, Tel: USA 623-877-5000, www.rondavisradiators.com

Rothsport Racing, 19870 SW 129th Ave, Tualatin, OR 97062, USA, Tel: USA 503 885 9626, www.rothsport.com

RWD Motorsport, Slack Laithe Farm, Hollin Hall, Trawden, Colne, Lancashire, BB8 8PX, England, Tel: 01282 863286, www.rwdmotorsport.com

Safety Devices International Ltd, 1 Enterprise Court, Studlands Park Avenue, Newmarket, Suffolk, CB8 7EP, Tel: 01638 560524, www.safetydevices.com

Serck Services Motorsport, Unit 9-11, Bullsbrook Road, Brook Industrial Estate, Hayes, UB4 OJZ, UK, Tel: 020 8813 7470, www.serckservicesmotorsport.co.uk

SNG Barratt Group Limited, Tel: 01746 760299, www.sngbarratt.com

Speed Bleeder Products Inc, 13130 Apakesha Rd, Newark, IL 60541, USA, Tel: USA 815 736 6296, www.speedbleeder.com

Speedograph Richfield, Rolleston Drive, Arnold, NOTTINGHAM, NG5 7JR, UK, Tel: 0115 926 4235, www.speedograph-richfield.com

Stack Ltd, 10 Wedgwood Road, Bicester, OX26 4UL, UK, Tel: 01869 240404, www.stackLtdcom

Stant Corporation, 1620 Columbia Avenue, Connersville, IN 47331-1696, USA, Tel: USA 800 822 3121, www.www.stant.com

Stockbridge Racing (Willans safety harness), Unit 7, New Mills Industrial Estate, Post Office Road, Inkpen, RG17 9PU, UK, Tel: 01488 669001, www.Willans.com

Tran-X, ASE Building, Brandon Road, Binley, Coventry, CV3 2AH, UK, Tel: 024 76 659061, www.tran-x.com

TWM Induction, 325D Rutherford St, Goleta, CA 93117, USA, Tel: 805 967 9478, www.twminduction.com

Vehicle Wiring Products Ltd, 9 Buxton Court, Manners Industrial Estate, Ilkeston, DE7 8EF, UK, Tel: 0115 9305454 , www.vehicle-wiring-products.eu

Vibra-Technics, Unit 14, Alexander Court, Fleming Road, Corby, NN17 4SW, UK, Tel: 01536 202789, www.vibra-technics.co.uk

Vick Autosports (Fiat and Alfa), 5200 Vesta Farley Road, Fort Worth, Texas 76119, USA, Tel: USA 817 572 7793, www.vickauto.com

Weslake, Tel: 0870 900 43 03, www.www.weslake.co.uk

Willans (see Stockbridge Racing),

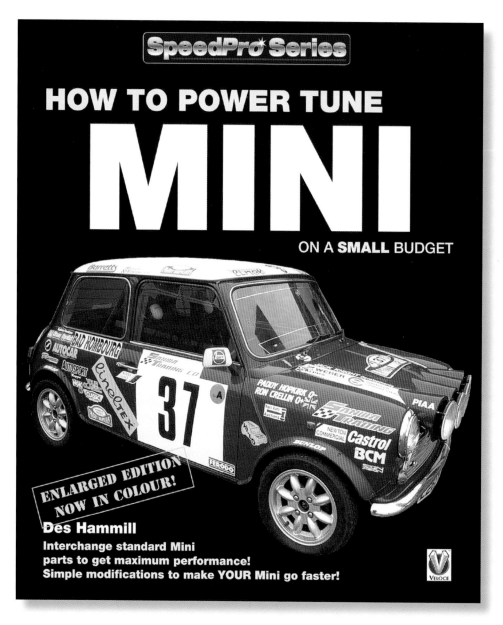

ISBN: 978-1-904788-84-3
Paperback • • £17.99* UK/$34.95* USA • 112 pages • pictures

For more info on Veloce titles, visit our website at www.veloce.co.uk
• email: info@veloce.co.uk • Tel: +44(0)1305 260068
* prices subject to change, p&p extra

ISBN: 978-1-84584-142-3
Paperback • 25x20.7cm • £24.99* UK/$49.95* USA • 176 pages •
400 pictures

For more info on Veloce titles, visit our website at www.veloce.co.uk
• email: info@veloce.co.uk • Tel: +44(0)1305 260068
* prices subject to change, p&p extra

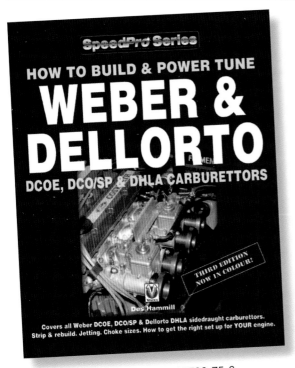
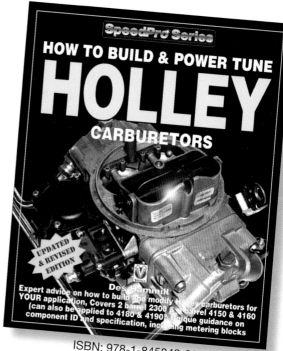
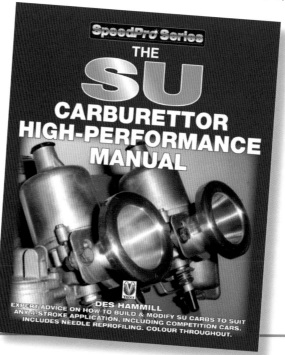

Index